RADICAL AND
WORKING CLASS POLITICS
A Study of Eastern Australia
1850-1910

RADICAL AND WORKING CLASS POLITICS

A Study of Eastern Australia, 1850–1910

Robin Gollan

FELLOW IN HISTORY
THE AUSTRALIAN NATIONAL UNIVERSITY

MELBOURNE UNIVERSITY PRESS
IN ASSOCIATION WITH
THE AUSTRALIAN NATIONAL UNIVERSITY

FIRST PUBLISHED 1960
PRINTED IN AUSTRALIA BY
MELBOURNE UNIVERSITY PRESS, PARKVILLE N.2, VICTORIA
REGISTERED IN AUSTRALIA FOR TRANSMISSION
BY POST AS A BOOK

LONDON AND NEW YORK: CAMBRIDGE UNIVERSITY PRESS

To my brother
WILLIAM GOLLAN

Preface

AUSTRALIANS of the late nineteenth and early twentieth century assumed that the history of Australia in the second half of the nineteenth century was a record of democratic political and social advance. By and large this picture was accepted by the historians, who, in the years before the second world war, laid the foundations of Australian historiography. But today it is becoming fashionable to question this idea. In part the questioning is the Australian version of English criticism of the whig interpretation of British history, based on the more detailed examination of the facts of the past in both countries than was possible for earlier historians. But also the criticism arises from the dissatisfaction of many contemporary historians with the ideas with which men of the nineteenth century identified themselves and of which most earlier historians approved. This book is written in the belief that the earlier historians were not so very wrong.

The obvious facts have never been disputed. In the 1850s the Australian colonies created what were for the time advanced democratic political institutions. In the 1890s political institutions were further liberalized and the first firm steps taken towards social and economic democracy. Social service legislation, an increasingly complex system of industrial controls, and a high general standard of living appeared to place Australia in the forefront of the worldwide movement towards social justice. A strong trade union movement, a Labour Party formed in 1891 and in office in Queensland in 1899, in the Commonwealth in 1904, and in power in the Commonwealth and New South Wales in 1910 were evidence of the political awakening of the working class.

Throughout the world the advance towards more democratic institutions, the growth of trade unions, the emergence of working-class political parties, were amongst the characteristic features of the politics of the second half of the nineteenth century. In this process, Australia appeared to be in advance of other countries, if not in theory at least in practice. Although a tiny community isolated from Europe by great distance, its political innovations were sufficiently impressive to attract the interest of people as diverse as Anthony Trollope, Sir Charles Dilke, Henry George, the Webbs, and Lenin.

This book is an attempt to follow from the middle of the nineteenth century to the eve of the first world war a persistent aspiration, varying in the form of its expression, under the influence of changing political and economic facts and the force of new ideas. The movements for democratic institutions, for the unlocking of the land, for the eight-hour day, for the 'recognition of unionism', and for the formation of the Labour Party, were different in the objectives sought. But there is a fundamental connection between them in that they all expressed the continuing search for a prescription which would make life more tolerable for the majority of the people. It is in this that any continuity this book may have will be found.

To record the names of those who have assisted with ideas, encouragement, and technical skills, in the making of this book, is too large an undertaking. I restrict myself to a general acknowledgment of the ready co-operation of the staffs of the Mitchell Library, the Australian National Library, the Public Library of Victoria, the Australian National University Library, the Library of the Royal Commonwealth Society and the British Library of Political and Economic Science. To the many people, who, with typewriter or pencil, have made publication possible, go my sincere thanks.

ROBIN GOLLAN

Australian National University
Canberra, 1959

Contents

	PREFACE	vii
	ABBREVIATIONS	xi
1	FREEDOM AND INDEPENDENCE FOR THE GOLDEN LANDS OF AUSTRALIA	1
2	INDEPENDENCE ON THE LAND	33
3	THE STRUGGLE FOR POWER, 1860-1880	50
4	TRADE UNIONS AND POLITICS, 1855-1880	69
5	TOWARDS TRADE-UNION POLITICS, 1880-1885	85
6	THE NEW UNIONISM, 1886-1890	99
7	NATIONALISM AND THE NEW RADICALISM, 1885-1890	110
8	THE FORMATION OF THE LABOUR PARTY	128
9	THE FOUNDATIONS OF THE WELFARE STATE	151
10	THE LABOUR PARTY FINDS A PROGRAMME	170
11	A NATIONAL PARTY AND A NATIONAL POLICY	193
	BIBLIOGRAPHY	215
	INDEX	223

Abbreviations

C.H.B.E.	Cambridge History of the British Empire
Hist. Studies	Historical Studies: Australia and New Zealand
I.T.U.C.	Intercolonial Trade Union Congress, Official Report
J.R.A.H.S.	Royal Australian Historical Society. Journal
N.S.W. V. & P. (L.C.)	New South Wales. Votes and Proceedings of the Legislative Council
N.S.W. V. & P. (L.A.)	New South Wales. Votes and Proceedings of the Legislative Assembly
Parl. Deb.	Parliamentary Debates
P.P.	Parliamentary Papers
Qld. V. & P. (L.A.)	Queensland. Votes and Proceedings of the Legislative Assembly
S.M.H.	Sydney Morning Herald
Vic. V. & P. (L.C.)	Victoria. Votes and Proceedings of the Legislative Council
Vic. V. & P. (L.A.)	Victoria. Votes and Proceedings of the Legislative Assembly

I

Freedom and Independence for the Golden Lands of Australia

The able and wealthy leaders of the old Australian legislatures wanted to transfer power from Downing Street to themselves: they succeeded in transferring it to their inferiors.[1]

In the second half of the nineteenth century Australia became a political democracy. The institutional basis was laid between 1850 and 1858, when the main points of the constitutional programme of English radicalism were put into effect in Australia. Manhood suffrage and the vote by ballot were adopted a generation before the third Reform Act completed a similar degree of democratic government in England.

The constitutions proclaimed in New South Wales and Victoria in 1855 were not the work of radicals. Initiated by consent of Sir John Pakington, Colonial Secretary in a conservative government, drafted by legislative councils in which conservatives predominated, they were given the force of law by a British parliament in which Palmerston led the Government and Lord John Russell was Colonial Secretary. Yet these constitutions were the framework within which in a few years an advanced democracy was established.

The explanation of this apparent anomaly lies ultimately in the quality of Australian opinion, itself the outcome less of the force of any commonly accepted radical political ideas than of a combination of unique political, social, and economic facts. Most Australians of the eighteen-fifties were radicals because circumstances made them so. Equally, Australian conservatives, if they were to pursue their own interests, however apprehensive they may have been of the consequences of their actions, had no alternative to 'sowing the seeds of a future democracy'.

Between 1850 and 1855 there was virtual unanimity of colonial opinion on one point—the need for self-government. On the nature of the government to be instituted there were wide differences. At the beginning of 1850 the whole of eastern Australia, comprising

[1] H. Merivale, *Lectures on Colonization and Colonies*, p. 644.

what are now New South Wales, Victoria, and Queensland, was still the colony of New South Wales, with the seat of government in Sydney. Government was carried on under the constitution conferred in 1842, which provided for a degree of representation in the colonial legislature. The Legislative Council consisted of thirty-six members, of whom twelve were nominated by the Crown and twenty-four elected, the franchise being limited to electors with property to the value of £200 and to £20 householders. Elective members of the Council were required to possess property worth £2,000 or an income of £100 per year. The executive was not responsible to the Council, its members being Crown appointees whose salaries were secured under the Constitution Act from legislative interference by the Council. Accepted in 1842 as an important advance on the unrepresentative system that preceded it, by 1850 the Constitution Act had become the object of widespread criticism. In Sydney the criticism amounted substantially to a demand for responsible government. Melbourne was more immediately concerned with the separation of the Port Phillip District (Victoria) from New South Wales, although there, too, the wish for responsible government had been voiced as early as 1840.

By an Act of 1850 the New South Wales constitution was amended in two ways. The property qualification of electors was halved and Victoria was separated from the parent colony, with a constitution similar to that of New South Wales. Separation satisfied the Victorians for a time, but the minor amendment of the New South Wales constitution gave little satisfaction in Sydney. Nevertheless, the 1850 Act did make it possible for the colonial legislatures, subject to the consent of the British government, to amend their own constitutions.

Between May 1851 and August 1852 the New South Wales Legislative Council, led by William Charles Wentworth, bombarded the home government with a remonstrance, a petition, an address, and a threat to refuse supply if approval were not promised for constitutional amendments that would permit responsible government. In September a draft constitution was presented to the Council by a select committee. In Victoria less definite action had been taken but moves were being made in the same direction. The appeals made by the New South Wales Council during 1851-2 increased in urgency and vehemence and culminated in the August address that insisted on a constitution similar to Canada; they referred significantly to the unredressed grievances that had led to the revolt of the American colonies; and they ended with a firm resolve to continue to assert rights of self-government. However, in December 1852, in one of the last acts of Earl Derby's conservative government, the Colonial Secretary, Sir John Pakington, dispatched to all the Australian colonies, except Western Australia, the government's decision to grant them self-government. A month later the Duke of Newcastle, who succeeded at the Colonial Office, confirmed the decision. The legislative councils then enacted constitutions which, after considerable delay, were amended and approved by an Enabling Act of the British parliament in 1855.[2]

The decision of the British government in 1852 to grant self-government was a result both of opinion in Britain and the pressure applied by the colonies. Broadly speaking, by 1850 in Britain liberal political assumptions were in the ascendant, although there was no general agreement on specific policies.[3] In its simplest, most extreme and general form, liberalism favoured complete independence for the colonies.[4] As expounded by the Manchester school, the liberal attitude was based on the assumption that the good of society would only be realized by the free competition of individuals and nations.

> Give to every man the right to buy in the cheapest and sell in the dearest market, urged the Cobdenite, and trade would automatically expand. The business career would be open to the talents. The good workman would command the full money's worth of his work, and his money would buy him food and clothing at the lowest rate in the world's market.[5]

This principle, applied nationally and internationally, it was believed, would remove the root causes of war. Trade would draw the nations together and, with the danger of war eliminated, expenditure on armaments could be reduced to a minimum, thus removing the greatest factor in government expenditure. Colonies could be given independence, with the ties of trade replacing the bonds of law. As Hobhouse puts it, 'personal freedom, colonial freedom, international freedom were parts of one whole. Non-intervention, peace, restriction of armaments, retrenchment of expenditure, reduction of taxation, were the connected series of practical consequences'.[6]

The emphasis of the colonial reformers, Edward Gibbon Wakefield, Charles Buller, Sir William Molesworth and others was differ-

---

[2] The South Australian and Tasmanian Acts were amended on the suggestion of the Colonial Office by the legislative councils of the respective colonies.
[3] C. A. Bodelsen, *Studies in Mid-Victorian Imperialism*, pp. 32 ff.
[4] This refers to colonies of settlement.   [5] L. T. Hobhouse, *Liberalism*, p. 79.
[6] Ibid., p. 81.

ent from that of the Manchester school, but the direction in which their views pressed colonial policies was the same. They were anxious to retain the integrity of the empire as a political, no less than an economic, entity. As the means to this end they advocated the extension of self-government in the colonies, with the retention of important powers over colonial affairs by the government and parliament of Britain. In this way, they believed, colonial aspirations would be satisfied and the imperial link safeguarded.

In the constitutional amendments of the forties and fifties the spirit, if not the letter, of the colonial reformers' plans was embodied in the new arrangements. Lord Durham's report, Lord Elgin's administration which conferred responsible government on Canada, and the Australian Constitution Acts were a sequence. Although, as the *Spectator* commented, 'the practice of the whole [Colonial] Office, as respects granting self-government to the colonies, has been resistance as long as possible, and then concession',[7] the concessions were made. In brief, liberalism in general and the colonial reformers in particular created the climate of opinion in which concessions could be made; administrators decided what concessions should be made; and Australian opinion decided when they must be made.

The pressure from the colonies which influenced the decision of the Colonial Office in 1852 had been building up since 1840. The Act of 1842 had provided, in the Legislative Council, a forum from which to address the British government. Responsibility of the executive to the legislature, complete control of the revenue, and control of the Crown lands had not been conceded. They were the essence of responsible self-government and, with changing emphasis from time to time, they were the objective of the Legislative Council and, under the leadership of the Council, of the people as a whole.

The Council elected under the 1842 Act was composed of the well-to-do: squatters, landowners, and merchants, with squatters predominating.[8] From both interest and opinion they were deeply committed to the achievement of responsible government. Until 1846 the squatting occupation of the Crown lands had only the conditional sanction of government. Licences, renewable annually at a fee of £10, gave squatters the right to depasture their flocks on an area of Crown land over which they had been able to establish effective occupation. The runs or the stations to which squatters

---

[7] 6 September 1851, cited in the *Empire*, 1 January 1852.
[8] C. H. Currey, 'The Legislative Council of N.S.W.', *Royal Australian Historical Society Journal*, vol. xxix.

laid claim under their licences were limited only, in the words of Sir George Gipps, 'by their own moderation, or by the pressure of other squatters on them'.[9]

Both the size and the number of runs possessed by individuals varied immensely: from the thirty or more runs and over a million acres of Benjamin Boyd and the eleven runs and half a million acres of W. C. Wentworth, to the single run of a few thousand acres of the smaller squatters.[10] But in all cases the squatters had no security of tenure. The financial difficulties experienced by many of them in the depression of the early forties, together with Governor Gipps's depasturing regulations of 1844, gave a vital urgency to the pastoralists' demand for security of tenure, and, more broadly, for responsible government to secure it. In this campaign the squatter leaders, notably Wentworth, became the effective leaders in the movement for self-government. Rising fears of the pastoralists' monopolistic pretensions did not become articulate until after 1847.

By an Act of 1846 and an Order-in-Council of March 1847, the British government acceded to the squatters' demands for security of tenure. They became entitled to leases of their runs. During the currency of the lease, the lessee alone could purchase the land, and at its expiry he had a pre-emptive right to purchase the whole or part. It gave the squatters immediate security and appeared to promise permanent possession. Although in practice the expectations raised by the Act were not entirely realized, as there proved to be immense difficulties both practical and political in its implementation, for the time being the squatters were satisfied. They, who had previously led the fight against imperial policy, and the New South Wales executive who administered it, now became privileged occupants whose interests were bound up with the executive. They lost interest in their previous allies and settled down to defend their privileges. On the other hand the urban middle and working classes, who had previously accepted the leadership of Wentworth, began to see in the squatters a frankenstein, raised in part by their support, about to digest what Gladstone referred to as 'the waste lands—the fund and treasure house of their future wealth'.[11] The political conflict between the pastoralists and the majority of the people, which was to be the most decisive factor in Australian politics in the nineteenth

---

[9] 'Report of the Commission appointed to enquire into the tenure of the waste lands of the Crown', Vic. V. & P. (L.C.), 1854-5, vol. iii.
[10] Recent unpublished work of K. Buckley and J. Kolsen (University of Sydney) indicates that Boyd may have had runs totalling 1,771,880 acres.
[11] Great Britain, Hansard (3rd ser.), cx. 1789.

century, had begun. It became not merely a struggle for possession of the land, but, quite as importantly, the social and economic basis of the political conflict on the nature of the constitution and the location of political power.

In the contest on the nature of the constitution, which was fought out in the council chambers, in the streets and halls, and on the goldfields, there were two fundamentally opposed conceptions of the nature of the good society and of good government. The issue was between political democracy and a society that reproduced the social and political institutions of England of the early nineteenth century. The debate was cast mainly in terms of political institutions, but in the mind of contestants it went beyond this, involving immediate economic interests and social aspirations. The radicals were for democratic political institutions and economic equality; the conservatives for limited democratic institutions, the guarantee of vested interests, and the evolution of a privileged class. The radicals won their political demands but merely cleared the way for the struggle that has gone on ever since for the realization of their social and economic aspirations.

Wentworth saw more clearly than his contemporaries, as Edmund Burke and Alexander Hamilton also had seen, at critical stages in the history of their countries, that democratic theory contains an implicit and ultimate threat to the institution of private property and the social organization based upon it. For Burke the preservation of the privileges of an aristocracy was the means of limiting the consequences. For Wentworth the problem was the creation of such a class. The raw materials were present, he considered, in the squatters, the 'shepherd kings', who, if confirmed in the possession of their broad acres and granted political privileges and distinctions, could become a class whose political influence would put a brake on democratic development. In the presence of the revolution, de Tocqueville said of France in 1848 that there remained but one privilege, 'the privilege of property', an institution that would be directly in question in all future political struggles. On the other hand, in Britain, except for a brief period in the forties, it was not until the very end of the century that property as an institution was seriously questioned. Contributing to this difference is the fact that much of the history of the English nineteenth century is the story of political differences between liberals and conservatives about other issues—in particular, political questions arising from the existence of an aristocracy and an established church.

Wentworth's proposal for a colonial aristocracy, which he was forced to discard under pressure in favour of a nominated legislative council, was thus in short term a measure intended to safeguard the immediate interests of the propertied class in general and the pastoralists in particular. In longer term, taken in conjunction with the expected conservative influence of the English connection and the difficulty of amending the constitution, it would encourage the growth of those elements of aristocracy which had been found in Britain to be a safeguard against what conservatives regarded as the excesses of democracy.

Wentworth's views appealed to pastoralists, to some government officials, and to those for whom the social aspects of a privileged class were attractive. In Victoria, however, society was too new for his notions to appear realizable, even to those who were just as concerned as he to establish a constitution with conservative safeguards. The select committee of the Legislative Council that proposed the draft constitution was satisfied 'that the social condition of this colony renders a close assimilation to certain British institutions impossible, and that an attempt to imitate them is likely not only to fail but to introduce the evils, without the advantages experienced from them in England'.[12] They referred in particular to the upper house, which they considered should be neither hereditary nor nominated, but elected by and from the men who 'hold a large stake in the land' and those who 'may reasonably be expected to possess education, intelligence and leisure to devote to public affairs'. In the event, the Victorian Legislative Council was found to be a more effective opponent of the radicals than the nominated chamber in New South Wales. In neither colony did the constitution stimulate the growth of an aristocracy holding its privileges with the consent of the majority. In both it became a chamber devoted to the defence of particular interests against the majority of the people.

Political radicalism was a product of the towns and the goldfields. The way of life of the back country fostered attitudes that were egalitarian, self-confident, independent, and socially radical.[13] But centralized government and the dispersion of population minimized the direct influence of these attitudes on politics until, in the eighties, railways, bush unionism, and a self-conscious nationalist literature gave the bushmen a voice that deeply influenced the

[12] 'Report of the Select Committee on a new Constitution for the Colony', Vic. *V. & P. (L.C.)* 1854-5, vol. iii.

[13] Compare: 'The backcountry, it would seem, had already developed the free and easy ways of a squatter world, shiftless, lubberly, independent, but animated by hostility towards the aristocratic Old Dominion, from which many of the settlers had come'. V. L. Parrington, *Main Currents in American Thought*, i. 139.

politics of that decade. The radicalism of the late forties and fifties was based on the alliance of the urban middle and working classes in opposition to the executive government (controlled in the last resort from Britain), and the political policies and social and economic pretensions of the squatters.

Until 1848, despite the vehemence with which self-government was demanded and the forthright denunciation of the unpopular acts of governors, as well as the expression from time to time of specific working-class grievances, there was nothing that could properly be called a radical movement. Trade unions in the forties were small and exclusive bodies of artisans formed to protect the interests of the trade and bore little evidence of the influence of the political unionism of the Age of Chartism. The closest approximation to working-class political organization was the Mutual Protection Association formed in 1843. Essentially defensive, it opposed policies that were considered contrary to the interests of workers, such as the renewal of transportation, the introduction of 'coolie' (Asian) labour, and the employment of convicts on public works. Its one positive policy was the advocacy of relief works for the unemployed. It had no political aims in the broader sense. In the discussions of the constitution of 1842 and the legislative council elections of 1843 there was some radical demagoguery in Sydney, but even the most radical spokesman, Henry McDermott, went no further than advocating the £10 franchise of the 1832 Reform Act.

In the 1848 election Robert Lowe, with the support of an active committee which included Henry Parkes and John Robertson, both later to be premiers of New South Wales, roused the middle and working classes of Sydney for an extension of the franchise and against 'coolie' or convict labour and the implementation of the 1847 Order-in-Council. Wentworth topped the poll, but Lowe was also elected despite the limited franchise. If the behaviour of the crowds at election meetings means anything, Lowe had the support of a large majority of the voteless. The activity aroused by the elections spilled over into the next year and initiated a movement that is essentially a part of the radical and democratic movement of the middle fifties.

The alliance of forces that grouped themselves round the Constitutional Association in 1849 was basically the same as that which won manhood suffrage in the fifties—with the exception of the miners, who after 1851 gave to the already existing movement added strength and urgency. The popular movement was led by urban middle-class men engaged in a contest for power with the pastoralists. In such a struggle they needed and obtained the support of the lower middle class and artisans. Like the liberals of 1832, they had no particular desire to enfranchise the masses. But unlike the English middle-class liberals, who having won the £10 franchise deserted their allies and supporters, the middle class in Australia, in the absence of either a substantial lower middle class or a pauperized proletariat, found themselves leading a movement that would accept nothing less than the full democratic programme. In 1849 the Constitutional Association was for extension of the franchise, but not manhood suffrage. The *People's Advocate* which supported it but went further, enthusiastically defended chartist principles—in particular, the demand for universal suffrage. A realistic critic remarked with truth that the city businessmen leaders of the franchise extension movement were merely aiming to further their own interests. 'I cannot but think,' wrote James Martin, 'that the "reduction" now proposed is sought for rather with a view to extend and consolidate the influence of that faction, than for the purpose of seeing justice done to those whose rights are thought to be unfairly and unconstitutionally withheld from them.'[14] What Martin could not see were the fundamental changes that would be caused by gold, or the fact that the 'city clique' would continue to need the support of the 'democracy'.

From 1850 to 1852, despite the growing opposition to the squatters, the unsatisfied demand for responsible government continued to provide a bond of unity between all classes. In the election of 1851, under the new electoral law, the radical John Dunmore Lang displaced Wentworth from the top of the poll. Wentworth continued to dominate the Council, but the tide of opinion in the community was running against him.

Inability to meet the property requirements for membership of the Council prevented Lang from taking his seat. Nevertheless, his popularity in Sydney and on the goldfields is evidence of the degree to which his opinions reflected the rising trend. Immediately after the 1851 election he made a triumphal progress through the Bathurst region. At the Turon he was presented with a bag of gold and an address which read in part: 'Your name will henceforth be associated with human progress, a watchword for liberty and will occupy a distinguished place in the history of your adopted country.'[15] The tribute was well merited, though modern historians have so far

[14] *People's Advocate*, 27 January 1849.
[15] A. D. Gilchrist, *John Dunmore Lang: An assembling of contemporary documents*, ii, 521.

failed to accord him his proper place in the history of Australian democracy.

In his tempestuous career of fifty-five years in Australia, from 1823 to 1878, Lang was the most influential of all radical publicists. A big man of prodigious energy, litigious to the point of pettiness, supremely confident of the rectitude of his own opinions, his life was a mixture of immense constructive labour, private quarrels, and public feuds. Whatever may be the final estimate of him as a man and a clergyman, there is no doubt that his opinions expressed the quality of radical political thought in the mid-century.

Lang's ideas were drawn from his own interpretations of the Bible, of the American revolution, and current English liberal and radical thought. His feelings were those of a Scot for whom 'the present reality of all that we owe to the victory of Bannockburn and to the memory of such men as Bruce, Randolph and Douglas' needed no proof. A romantic nationalist and a democrat, he transferred to the country of his adoption much of his feeling for the land of his birth. Of his ideal colonist he wrote:

> as he builds his house in the wilderness, and clears and cultivates the virgin soil; or as his sheep and cattle graze peacefully around him, while his children grow up, perhaps with only the faintest recollections of their native land, the colonist feels that a new object is gradually filling up the *vacuum* in his soul; . . . he finds that his affections are gradually and insensibly transferred to the land of his adoption.[16]

From 1837 he had been anticipating with marked approval the establishment of an Australian republic. In 1850 he announced that the time had arrived for the republican confederation of Australia. In the following year he saw in the diggers the instrument that would establish a free and independent Australia.[17] In 1852 he published his clarion call, *Freedom and Independence for the Golden Lands of Australia*.

Lang's argument for independence was not original.[18] The growth to colonial nationhood, he considered, was analogous to the maturing of a child who, on reaching adulthood, became independent. Australia, he believed, became adult in 1850. He rejected any alternative to full independence. Representation in the imperial parliament he regarded as impractical and wrong in principle. The majority of the members of the House of Commons were not interested in Australia,

---

[16] J. D. Lang, *Freedom and Independence for the Golden Lands of Australia*, p. 25. [17] Gilchrist, *John Dunmore Lang*, ii. 521.
[18] Bodelson, *Studies in Mid-Victorian Imperialism*, p. 13.

nor had they any right to govern it. Conversely, Australian representatives had no right to participate in the government of England. He called on the support of Benjamin Franklin, Jeremy Bentham,[19] the decisions of the American colonial legislatures, the New York Convention of 1765, and the Congress of Philadelphia of 1774. Similarly, Lang rejected the views of Wakefield and the advocates of municipal independence. He replied to their claim that the colonies should have full powers to deal with matters of local concern only, that it was impossible to draw a line of division between 'imperial' and 'subordinate' matters, for, in the words of Benjamin Franklin, 'such a line doth not exist'. Compromise was not included in Lang's vocabulary, and alternatives were as opposed as the Calvinist good and evil. Lang's argument was cogently advanced, but there is little doubt that in his own mind the most compelling argument was his deep conviction of the innate worth of national sentiment. 'It is the very soul of society, which animates and exalts the whole brotherhood of associated men,' he wrote.[20]

Lang was repelled by the idea of empire, and the claim that the empire could be governed from Downing Street he labelled political popery, a claim based on a blasphemous assumption—'an assumption of two of the incommunicable attributes of the Godhead—omniscience and infallibility'. The claim he considered to be the more ridiculous in the light of the people appointed by the imperial government to administer the government of New South Wales. Governor Darling he considered a military automaton, and Governor Gipps, while a man of ability and education, had but one idea, 'and, unfortunately for the colony, that idea was an egregiously wrong one'.[21] For Sir Charles Fitzroy he had nothing but loathing and contempt. The only reason that Lang could find for his appointment was that he came of the family of Grafton—a family, to quote Junius, 'on which nature seems to have entailed an hereditary baseness of disposition . . . the son has regularly improved upon the vices of his father, and has taken care to transmit them pure and undiminished into the bosom of his successor'.[22] Sir Charles, he considered, was a true representative of his family. Not impressed by the argument of *Pax Britannica*, he pointed to a public debt of eight

[19] 'Were I an American, I had rather not be represented at all, than represented thus. If tyranny must come, let it come without a mask. Oh, but *information*. True, it must be had; but to give information, must a man possess a vote?' J. Bentham, *Emancipate Your Colonies*, in J. Bowering (ed.), *The Works of Jeremy Bentham*, p. 408, cited Lang, *Freedom and Independence*, p. 64.
[20] Lang, *Freedom and Independence*, p. 75.
[21] J. D. Lang, *An Historical and Statistical Account of New South Wales*, p. 285.   [22] Cited, ibid., p. 352.

hundred million pounds 'incurred through her generally unjust and unnecessary wars'.²³ He considered that the only possibility of Australia's involvement in war for at least a century lay in the attachment to Britain—'and considering the warlike propensities of our worthy mother, and the character she has so long sustained of being the prize-fighter and pay-mistress of the world, our chance of peace under her wing is at best but very precarious'.²⁴ The panoply of empire with its aristocratic associations was posed in his mind in antithesis with a society of free and independent men. The virtues of the yeoman and sturdy artisan were contrasted with the decadence of aristocracy and its concomitant, depraved and debased pauperism.

The desirable future political structure of the country was as clear to him as the need for its immediate independence. The constitution would enshrine the principles of universal suffrage, equal electoral districts, bicameral legislatures, both assembly and senate being elective, short parliaments, no property qualifications for the members, and moderate payment for the representatives of the people. He favoured the ballot but considered it of less importance than in Britain because, 'since the era of the gold discoveries our working classes have nothing to fear from the corrupt influence of the employers of labour, and they have therefore no reason to conceal their votes'.²⁵ He was immediately concerned with independence for New South Wales, Victoria, South Australia, and Van Diemen's Land, but he foresaw a future in which eastern Australia would be divided into seven provinces federated under the name of the Seven United Provinces of Australia. The national legislature that he proposed for such a federation consisted of a house of representatives elected by equal electoral districts and a senate with equal representation of the provinces and elected by a joint meeting of the two provincial houses.

Lang's vision of the Australian future was of a petty bourgeois utopia. It would be a land inhabited by independent farmers, sturdy artisans, and respectable merchants and manufacturers. In such a society, he believed, democracy and protestantism would flourish. In it would be no place for either a privileged aristocracy or an impoverished proletariat. Its essential radicalism in the eighteen-fifties rested on the fact that it was directly opposed to both the

---

[23] Lang, *Freedom and Independence*, p. 102. [24] Ibid., p. 139.
[25] Ibid., p. 52. Compare: 'In Australia aristocratic influence cannot be said to exist but the ballot protects the voter against the occasional violence and dictation of democratic opinion.' S. Lane-Poole (ed.), *Thirty Years of Colonial Government: A selection of despatches and letters of Sir George Bowen*, p. 132.

immediate interests and long-term plans of the then economically and politically dominant class—the squatters; its popularity, on the fact that it was in line with much of contemporary English radical thought and because the utopia appeared to many people to be realizable in Australia.

Radical opinion in Britain owed most to Bentham and his disciples but also something to Paine, Spence, Ogilvie, Cobbett, and Owen. Bentham's doctrine appealed primarily to the middle class. It justified their claim for political power and it pointed the legislative path of attack on economic restrictions, social privilege, and the heritage of illogical and conflicting principles embodied in the law of the land. For the working class, Benthamism had something but not enough. Logically, it justified their claim for political rights, too, but the realities of developing industrialism pointed the need for something more to secure their greatest happiness. The answer accepted by many in the thirties, forties, and early fifties was the confused and often conflicting body of ideas known as chartism.

Although it is difficult to define the aims of chartism, because there were many, the nature of the movement is reasonably clear. It was a movement of the working class in revolt against the way of life that industrial capitalism imposed upon it. Although its most characteristic programme was the demand for political reform—the six points of the charter—it was also a movement for social reform. As one of the historians of chartism puts it, it was 'a movement whose immediate object was political reform and whose ultimate purpose was social regeneration'.[26] The political programme was the common element that linked together classes ranging from the lower middle class disappointed by the 1832 Reform, the skilled workers, the desperately impoverished 'fustian jackets' of the north, and the starving hand-loom operatives of Spitalfields. Till the failure of the 1839 petition, the movement kept within the bounds of the political programme. From then on it became increasingly concerned with social objectives. 'Universal suffrage means meat and drink and clothing,' said Bronterre O'Brien, 'good houses and good beds, and good substantial furniture for every man and woman and child who will do a fair day's work.'[27] In the vivid language that made him one of the great agitators of the movement, J. R. Stephens wrote, 'This question of universal suffrage is a knife and fork question, after all, a bread and cheese question, notwithstanding all

---

[26] M. Hovell, *The Chartist Movement*, p. 1.
[27] *Operative*, 17 March 1839, cited in M. Morris (ed.), *From Cobbett to the Chartists*, p. 144.

that has been said against it.'[28] Parliamentary reform was seen as the first step in solving 'the knife and fork question', but given political power there were differing recipes for providing the meat and drink.

Broadly, there were four lines of social policy. One emphasized the education and enlightenment of the working class to fit them for the possession of the political power that their numbers warranted. The second laid stress on trade unionism and the demand of 'a fair wage for a fair day's work'. The third, deriving from Owen and the practical co-operators, looked forward to the transformation of Britain into numbers of socialist or co-operative communities. Lastly, there was Feargus O'Connor's land plan for the co-operative acquisition of land and the settlement of workers on small holdings.[29]

Social reform was the objective, and the political charter the means to achieve it, but how to win the charter was the further problem on which there was deep division of opinion. Broadly, there was a division between the supporters of moral and physical force. The moral-force chartists believed that resort to force was both ethically unjustifiable and politically inexpedient.[30] Physical force was justified by its proponents by the force which they considered the state exercised against the mass of the people. The moral-force men, said Feargus O'Connor, 'have placed upon their banners a motto of which I highly approve, "Peace Law and Order", that is if peace procure the law, then I am for order; but if peace procure not the law, then I am for disorder'.[31] However, as with other aspects of the chartist movement, it is not possible to make any completely precise distinctions between the two trends of physical and moral force. The popularity of either waxed and waned with the fortunes of the movement. The Newport rising took place after the failure of the petition of 1839. Likewise the 'plug plot'—the general strike of August 1842, which was accompanied by widespread direct action, sometimes violent—followed closely on the presentation of the 1842 petition. Clear distinctions can be drawn between leaders who advocated or opposed violence; equally, the north and west with their desperate poverty were more inclined to violence than the artisans of London; but generally speaking it is clear that in the movement as a whole, united by the common objective of the charter but divided by differing social objectives and opposing opinions on

---

[28] *Northern Star*, 29 September 1838, cited M. Beer, *A History of British Socialism*, ii. 47.   [29] Beer, *A History of British Socialism*, i. 282.

[30] *Operative*, 16 December 1838, contains resolutions passed at a meeting of Scottish Chartists. Cited Morris, *From Cobbett to the Chartists*, p. 145.

[31] Ibid., p. 146.

how they could be achieved, the type of action taken was decided not by any theoretical differences but by what seemed most likely in the existing circumstances to bring success.

Minimizing the distinctions between the advocates of physical and moral force were the characteristic methods of the movement. The mass petitions, the immense meetings, the processions, the conventions that were implicitly or explicitly institutions laying claim to the powers of parliament—all, in the last resort, depended for their influence on the numbers involved or represented. At all times chartism was a movement depending on the force of numbers. From time to time it was precipitated by desperation or provocation to violence, in which the line dividing moral and physical force was further blurred.

The extensive migration into Australia in the forties and the flood of the fifties sprang from a Britain in which chartism was the mass protest of the working and lower middle classes against the intolerable conditions of early industrialism. Naturally, there was no chartist movement in Australia, for industrialization was still a thing of the future. But chartism had an influence. Some of the men who established trade unions had their political baptism in the chartist movement. The form of the mass protest meetings on the goldfields and in Melbourne was directly influenced by English experience. Manhood suffrage in Australia was in one sense the first victory for the People's Charter. These are all important facets of its influence, but if we are to discover the most profound and lasting influence, it will be by looking in another direction. In a brilliant summary Hovell says of the British movement: 'Political Chartism was a real though limited thing; social Chartism was a protest against what existed, not a reasoned policy to set up anything concrete in its place. Apart from machinery, Chartism was largely a passionate negation.'[32] In Australia it was a negation, too—a desire to prevent the re-creation of the old world relationships in the new.

The goldfields and the apparently limitless unoccupied land seemed for a time to provide opportunities for the establishment of entirely different human-economic relations from those prevailing in Britain. Gold was felt to be not merely the high road to wealth for the fortunate but the means of escape, even temporarily, from the oppressive bonds of wage labour. For the diggers in 1854 the worst possible future was to be forced to work for wages. There was little overstatement in the opinion of a witness before the goldfields commission who said, 'a man would rather work for himself for one

[32] Hovell, *The Chartist Movement*, p. 303.

pound a week than go to a master for six pounds a week'.[33] The same miner believed that companies should be excluded from the goldfields, otherwise 'there would be an introduction of the old European system of master and servant', in opposition to which he argued that 'the strong feeling appears to be in this country that the principle of self-labour should have a fair trial'. The implications for the future when the gold was exhausted were clear also. To the question whether he would apply the same principles to agriculture as to gold a miner replied, 'the more free homesteads we have with their own masters upon them the better—we want to protect ourselves against the introduction of such a system [as exists in Great Britain] here'.[34] Thus gold and land appeared to make possible a society in which men could achieve economic independence.

In Britain, chartist solutions to the problems of poverty and insecurity were most generally directed to mitigating the conditions of workers within the wages system. Only the socialists and the advocates of Feargus O'Connor's land scheme sought an alternative to it. In Australia, although the best of the land was occupied by the squatters, their title to it was insecure. Their interests were protected, not by a tenure the beginnings of which were enshrouded in the darkness of history, but merely by occupation and still uncompleted legislative and administrative acts. Thus economic independence to be achieved by small-scale possession of the land was a perfectly natural aspiration. In the political circumstances it became more than an individual desire for real property. In fact it was the cement that bound together a radical political movement whose social policy was the opening of the land to the people and the continuation of individual and co-operative mining, and whose political programme was the adoption of democratic institutions. Nevertheless, many skilled workers, after the first gold fever had subsided, saw in trade unionism, functioning in a favourable labour market, the means of achieving their own best interests. As in Britain, it was believed that these social policies could only be implemented if political power were in the hands of those who hoped to benefit from them.

In Sydney the leaders in the demand for a democratic parliament included many of the leading businessmen of the city. But in their contest with the squatter-dominated Council they needed and obtained the support of the working and lower middle classes. In

[33] 'Report of the Commission appointed to enquire into the conditions of the Gold-fields of Victoria', Minutes of Evidence, Vic. *V. & P. (L.C.)*, 1854-5, ii. 200.
[34] Ibid., p. 30.

1853 the issue was the proposal, drafted by the select committee of the Legislative Council, for an hereditary upper house. Before the proposal became public, the *Empire* had begun to warn of the dangers in the existing Council drafting a constitution. When it was published, it was opposed by all the press with the exception of the *Sydney Morning Herald*. The New South Wales Constitution Committee was formed to organize opposition, and public meetings and demonstrations voiced popular disapproval. Public meetings laughed with Daniel Deniehy at the 'bunyip aristocracy', and the readers of the *Empire* with Charles Harpur, who canvassed the tests to be imposed on potential colonial lords. Having dismissed 'drunk as a lord' as too unselective, 'rich as a lord' as inapplicable, 'humped as a lord' as useless in a community in which there was little 'lordly physical degeneration', he selected noses.

> In short, it is a thumping great nose! a round, robustious broad-backed, elephantine, Wellingtonian, dodo-like upper mandible! Be this your test, Sir Charles. Pack our nominee chamber with noses of such amplitude and consequently of such roaring sternutational power, that one and twenty of them, well provided with Prince's mixture, might even discharge (if need were) on the anniversary of a coronation, or what not, a very satisfactory and right royal salute, to the public saving of much excellent gunpowder.[35]

Forced to drop the hereditary house, Wentworth and the select committee, and ultimately the Council, adhered to the nominee principle for the upper chamber of the new legislature.

It is notable that the city agitation extended to the goldfields. A week before a mass protest meeting against the select committee's proposals, held at Sydney's Circular Quay, a meeting three thousand strong assembled on the Ovens goldfields. As reported in the *Empire*,

> a dray formed the temporary platform, on which the Chairman and the speakers were placed. Over the platform was a crimson flag on which was inscribed, 'Taxation without representation is robbery'. Another flag which waved from a venerable gum tree bore the inscription of 'Representation for the miners', and on a third on which was written 'Unlock the lands', a pick and spade crossed were painted.[36]

At this meeting in Victoria there was almost equal reference to the governments of New South Wales and Victoria. The mobility of goldfields labour, a general hostility to government, and the simi-

[35] *Empire* (Sydney), 6 August 1853, letter to the editor.   [36] 31 August 1853.

larity of conditions gave the goldfields the same nationalizing function as the American western frontier. For the diggers, governments, whether in Sydney, Melbourne, or London, were cut from the same cloth.

In the fifties there was still no Australian nation. Another thirty years were to pass before the majority of the people felt that they belonged to the continent. But in the fifties a long step was taken towards that day. From the eighteen-twenties, many people, whether born in the colonies or migrants, were in process of becoming Australians. In particular, life in the bush was moulding attitudes and attachments that constituted the raw materials of Australian nationalism. But it was not until the fifties that the first crude formulations of a political nationalism were made. It is noteworthy that they were made in the contest on the political institutions to be adopted.

In the long-drawn fight for responsible government, Wentworth and the colonial whigs had formulated their arguments in terms of the rights of Englishmen. In the constitution debate it became clear that for Wentworth in New South Wales, and for his political counterparts in Victoria, the rights of Englishmen were whiggish rights. In his famous speech in 1853 Wentworth declaimed:

> What do people aspire to here, who having accumulated perhaps £50,000 or £100,000 do not care to pursue the drudgery of money-making any longer? I will tell the Council: they aspire to a speedy migration to other lands, seeing it is better to themselves and families to build up homes where the democratic and levelling principles so rapidly increasing here are scouted; and where there are high and honorable pursuits and distinctions to which the children of the prudent may aspire ... Who, with ample means, would ever return, if once he left these shores, or even identify himself with the soil, so long as selfishness, ignorance, and democracy hold sway?[37]

The same basic assumptions are explicit in the words of a Victorian squatter, William Forlonge. In an appeal to the Colonial Secretary he wrote,

> politically, the pastoral interests are of great importance to England; the squatters to a man, are actuated by feelings of the most devoted loyalty to our beloved Queen, of veneration for the constitution of Great Britain and attachment to the connection between the colony and the mother country; they are the only

[37] C. M. H. Clark (ed.), *Select Documents in Australian History 1851-1900*, p. 338.

class in the colony who can successfully resist the encroachments of an unscrupulous democracy, and the Crown can rely with confidence on their supporting the Government in the maintaining of order and the rights of property.[38]

For Wentworth and Forlonge both the existing institutions of England and the colonies' attachment to them represented an important barrier to democracy.

As against this view the radicals posed not only the arguments of English radicalism, but also the special justification to be found in Australia. Daniel Deniehy, Irish-Australian, conjured up a vision of the future:

> Let them, with prophetic eye, behold the troops of weary pilgrims from foreign despotism which would ere long be flocking to these shores in search of a more congenial home, and let them now give their most earnest and determined assurance that the domineering clique which made up the Wentworth party were not, and should never be, regarded as the representatives of the manliness, the spirit, and the intelligence of the freemen of New South Wales.[39]

The vision of Australia as a land that could be free of the myriad oppressions of the old world was one side of the picture. The other was the notion that the wealthy were potential émigrés but the poor were attached to the soil of Australia. Wentworth was the obvious target of Henry Parkes when he quoted Bentham as saying 'property it is continually said, is the only bond and pledge of attachment to country. Not it, indeed. Want of property is a much stronger one. He who has property can change the shape of it and carry it away with him to another country.'[40] These two elementary ideas of democratic nationalism flowered thirty years later as the core of a more mature national consciousness. In the fifties they were an important component of the current of opinion that demanded some democratic departures from existing English institutions.

By the end of 1853 in New South Wales and March 1854 in Victoria the legislative councils had adopted constitutions which were dispatched to Britain for enactment by the British parliament. The New South Wales Act went to the imperial parliament without the provision for a colonial peerage, but otherwise showed little evidence of the popular demands made upon the Council. The upper house was to be nominated by the Governor, the lower house franchise was limited to £10 householders, and, most important, con-

---

[38] Forlonge to Pakington, Vic. *V. & P. (L.C.)*, 1853-4, ii. 57.
[39] E. A. Martin (ed.), *The Life and Speeches of Daniel Henry Deniehy*, p. 56.
[40] *Empire*, 7 September 1853.

stitutional amendments were to be made only with the consent of two-thirds of both houses. The last and most important of these illiberal provisions was removed by the House of Commons, which once again, as John Bright wryly noted in 1850, showed 'a marvellous absence of prejudice when the objects were ten thousand miles away'.[41] Lowe, now a member of the House of Commons, had led the attack on the New South Wales measure and had won against Wentworth's opposition in the lobbies. This meant that the constitution as adopted in Britain was easier to amend under the pressure of the radical forces in New South Wales.

The Act passed by the Victorian Legislative Council differed from its New South Wales counterpart in a number of ways: the upper house was to be elected by a limited electorate; the property qualification for the Assembly franchise was lower; miners who held a twelve-months' licence were to be entitled to vote in Assembly elections. Unlike the New South Wales Act, it received only minor amendments from the House of Commons.

Both Acts, however, suffered a long delay between the dispatch to London and their passing by the imperial parliament. The New South Wales Constitution did not receive the Royal assent until July 1855, and was not proclaimed in New South Wales until November 1855, almost two years after the passing of the original New South Wales Act. The delay to the Victorian Act was approximately the same. Whether or not the delay was necessary, inevitable, or justifiable is less important than the simple fact that it occurred. For, during the interval, radical opinion and feeling—in part provoked by the delay—reached an intensity that ensured that early in the life of the new parliaments democratic amendments would be carried. What part did the population of the goldfields play in this?

A study of political discussion on the goldfields reveals no consistent interest in the principles to be written into the constitutions. On the other hand, as we have seen, in Sydney and to a lesser extent in Melbourne, the arrival of Pakington's dispatch was followed by intensive public discussion. This fact has been taken by some historians to mean that the miners' influence on politics, except as they touched the immediate concerns of the diggers, was negligible. Such a view ignores the intangible but real influence of the goldfields on the current of opinion in both Britain and Australia. Gold hastened Britain's concession of the principle of responsible government,[42]

---

[41] G. M. Trevelyan, *Life of John Bright*, p. 176.
[42] Pakington to Fitzroy, N.S.W. *V. & P. (L.C.)*, 1853, vol. i.

and the miners strengthened the radical trend in the colonies. From the moment that gold was discovered there was an acute awareness in the press, in the comments of politicians, and in the commentaries of visitors, that a new factor had entered Australian politics—a factor that could not be ignored in the future. The temper of the diggers was radical not only because of the political opinions that many of them had brought with them from the old world, but also because of the conditions in the new. Their attitudes were only occasionally reflected in political action, because the diggings were remote from the centres of political power and because the miner's was a hard life, whether digging for a fortune or only for bread. Nevertheless, the large concentrations of men on particular fields meant that when grievances galled too deeply, political demonstrations, impressive in their numbers, forced the grievances under the notice of governments.

Victoria was more deeply and directly influenced by gold than were the other colonies. But what happened there had both a short- and a long-term influence in the other colonies. In Victoria, gold had brought at least 35,000 people to the diggings by the end of 1852, and 65,000 by the first quarter of 1854. In the ten years after 1851 it multiplied the colony's population by ten. Faced by the problem of governing a community whose numbers swelled every day, and in areas that were a few short months before inhabited by sheep and their shepherds, the government appointed goldfields commissioners whose authority was supported by a police force recruited hurriedly from the most varied human material. To meet the cost of administration a licence fee of thirty shillings a month was levied. In December 1851 this was doubled. There was immediate widespread opposition that gave an earnest of what was to become the central grievance of the miners and that ultimately precipitated the revolt at Ballarat in 1854. In 1852 the diggers opposed an increase in the licence fee to such effect that the government withdrew the proclamation. A year later they were demanding a reduction of the fee and in 1854 were in revolt. The licence fee and its manner of collection became the monster grievance, but it became so largely because of the diggers' conception of their rights.[43]

The diggers wanted liberty, and what they meant by liberty was conditioned both by the radical political and social ideas of the country from which they came and by their experience in Australia.

[43] Eureka Centenary Supplement, *Historical Studies, Australia and New Zealand*, 1954. Also B. Kent, 'Agitations on the Victorian Gold-fields, 1851-54', ibid., vol. vi, no. xxiii. Together, these provide the best discussion in relatively small compass of the goldfields movement and the Eureka revolt.

Basically, they wished to be economically 'free': free from the restraints and controls exerted on them by the economic and social relations of the old world. They saw the possibility of freedom in the conditions that prevailed in the early days of the goldfields, with each man working with his own tools for himself. They opposed the introduction of legislation permitting companies to operate,[44] and many of them flatly opposed the introduction of machinery,[45] arguing that it would be impossible for the independent man to compete with highly capitalized concerns. But as the surface alluvial gold became scarce, the days of the individual miner were numbered. At Ballarat in 1854 most of the gold was already being won from shafts driven from 150 to 200 feet into the earth. The shafts were too much for one man to work, so usually they were operated by informal co-operatives of six or eight men. The diggers were prepared for co-operation but not for the introduction of companies.[46] Similarly, they demanded the opening up of the land, with the immediate aim of obtaining gardening plots, but with the ultimate aim of seeking on a farm the independence that they realized must sooner or later be lost on the diggings.[47] As the barrier between themselves and the achievement of this aim they saw the squatters, a Legislative Council dominated by the squatters, and behind it the imperial government from which many of them hoped to escape in the new country. In the uncomplicated new society they were able to see the objectives to which they aspired more clearly than they had in the complex stratified society of the old world. And they could also see, they believed, the road to their goal. To many of the diggers the government appeared as a projection of the state as they had known it in Europe—hateful, and, in a new country, incongruous.

> I came from old Europe, [wrote Raffaello Carboni] 16,000 miles across two oceans, and I thought it a respectable distance from the hated Austrian rule. Why, then, this monster meeting to-day, at the antipodes? We wrote petitions, signed memorials, made remonstrances by dozens; no go: we are compelled to *demand*, and must prepare for the consequences.... We must meet as in old Europe—old style—improved by far in the south—for the redress of grievances inflicted upon us, not by crowned heads, but

---

[44] 'Report of Gold-fields Commission'. Minutes of Evidence, Vic. *V. & P. (L.C.)*, 1854-5, ii. 18, 29, 30, 52, 64, 68, 129, 136, 161, 173.
[45] Ibid., pp. 1, 63, 70, 72, 161. [46] Ibid., pp. 2, 12, 18, 29, 30, 72.
[47] Ibid., pp. 1, 9, 18, 34, 135, 200, also 'Petition of Miners of Bendigo to La Trobe', enclosed with La Trobe to Newcastle, 12 September 1853, Great Britain, *P.P.* 1854, vol. xliv.

by blockheads, aristocratical incapables, who never did a day's work in their life.[48]

Gold-laced commissioners and red-coated troopers were interlopers where home was a tent, and shovel and dish the evidence of honest toil. Had the police and commissioners conducted themselves with restraint and sympathy they would have been unpopular enough, but behaving as they did—with arrogance and lack of understanding—they became not only separate from the mining community, but the object of its intense hostility. 'Lynch law' was a product of social conditions on the goldfields of California; a squatter parliament, a governor appointed in London, gold-laced commissioners and red-coats equipped with rifles and bayonets attempted to impose what was felt to be an alien law on the goldfields of Australia. The situation generated the same kind of local democratic protest that marked the revolt of the American west against the control from the east.

Many of the diggers were convinced democrats when they arrived in Australia; many more became democrats as a result of their experience there. In 1854 the desire for a democratic parliament was universal, miners and tradesmen agreeing on the principle of manhood suffrage.[49] Short parliaments and payment of members were almost as generally demanded as manhood suffrage. In 1853 and 1854, as an alternative to immediate enfranchisement, it was mooted either that a representative acceptable to the miners should be appointed to the legislature by the Governor, or that they should regard representatives of the goldmining towns, that is of men with the necessary property qualifications, as their representatives. Miner opinion rejected the first as unsatisfactory,[50] and but few were prepared for indirect representation. In reply to the statement that the shopkeepers would be influenced by the opinions of their digger customers, a miner pointed the moral of English experience:

> The same argument might be used in England [he said]. Why are not the shopkeepers influenced by the larger masses, and why do they not elect men agreeable to the working classes? I would

---

[48] Raffaello Carboni, *The Eureka Stockade*, pp. 44-5. The 1942 edition, with an introduction by H. V. Evatt, was the first reprint since its publication in Melbourne in 1855. The author participated in the Eureka revolt.
[49] 'Report of Gold-fields Commission', Minutes of Evidence, pp. 8, 28, 33, 48, 62, 191.
[50] La Trobe to Newcastle, 12 September 1853, Great Britain, *P.P.*, 1854, vol. xliv.

rather not be represented at all than be misrepresented by a man who might have the character of representing me.[51]

The majority of the miners stood firm in support of direct representation in a fully representative parliament, and many agreed with Stephen Cummins, who wanted 'the six points of what we used to call the Charter in England'.[52]

All the strains of political thought that made 1848 the year of revolutions were present on the goldfields. Chartism was present in the very words and slang of some of the leaders. Raffaello Carboni refers to Thomas Kennedy, whose 'merit consists in the possession of the chartist slang; hence his cleverness in spinning a yarn, never to the purpose, but blathered with long phrases and bubbling with cant'.[53] The discussions of the diggers are filled with the rival merits of physical and moral force. Carboni was impatient with chartism but bitter with the memories of Austrian oppression. The Irish were there too. They left some of their number dead on the Eureka stockade; and they bore on their shoulders all the wrongs that had been inflicted on their country, and in their hearts all the bitterness generated by two centuries of alien rule. The meeting on Bakery Hill, where ten thousand diggers supported the programme of the Ballarat Reform League, passed a resolution viewing 'with the bitterest indignation the daring calumny of his honour, the acting Chief-Justice, while on the bench, of the brave and struggling sufferers of Clare, Tipperary, Bristol and other districts in their endeavours to assert their legitimate rights'.[54] There were Germans, Americans, and even French. Indeed, the revolt at Eureka was attributed by some who opposed it to the influence of aliens. With that peculiar combination of ignorance of their own countrymen and a desire to condemn by attaching ideas which they oppose to an existing prejudice, the governing class in Victoria tried to establish that the bloodshed at Eureka could not have been due to the actions of Britishers, and therefore must have been the result of the agitation of foreigners. They failed in this attempt because it is apparent that the ideas that lay behind the revolt were shared by men of many nations drawn together with common aims and viewpoint, as diggers.[55]

Throughout 1853 and 1854 agitation against the licence fee developed strength and direction. The tax and its method of collec-

---

[51] 'Report of Gold-fields Commission', Minutes of Evidence, p. 38.
[52] Ibid., p. 37.   [53] *Eureka Stockade*, p. 24.
[54] Great Britain, *P.P.*, 1854-5, vol. xxxviii.
[55] 'Report of Gold-fields Commission', Minutes of Evidence, pp. 55, 85, 100, 237.

tion was the grievance, but the miners saw it as a part of a total situation to which they were opposed. In August 1853 meetings were held at Bendigo to protest against the licence fee, and the Governor reported that much violent language was used against the government. From these meetings issued a petition with five thousand signatures listing the miners' grievances. It referred to the squatter land monopoly, asked for the provision of facilities to enable diggers to purchase plots of land, prayed for a reduction of the licence fee to 10s. a month and for a discontinuance of the collection by the armed forces.[56] In Melbourne, meetings were held in support of the diggers' claim for a reduction in the licence tax and also to emphasize the danger of disaffection by the mining population if their reasonable claims for political and social rights were not heard. Although the miners had petitioned in due form praying the Governor to take action, their temper was anything but humble. In July, the Governor was reporting a protest meeting at Castlemaine against an act of wrongful seizure by the police, at which three men were appointed as 'people's commissioners'. At Bendigo shortly after the meeting which prepared the petition, on 20 August 1853, direct action was decided upon. The meeting agreed that a week later they should meet again and in concert offer to pay 10s. for their licences. At the meeting in the following week the decision was reaffirmed and it was further decided that anyone who paid the full fee of 30s. should be given twenty-four hours' notice to leave the diggings. Some diggers offered to pay the 10s. and had their offers refused by the authorities. In fact, the government was faced with full-scale revolt. All available military forces in the colony were drafted to Bendigo, leaving the sailors of a British warship to patrol the streets of Melbourne and to guard the Melbourne gaol. A regiment was dispatched from Van Diemen's Land to support the forces in Victoria, but at the same time the Governor decided to seek a compromise. He sought to meet the demand for representation by appointing a goldfields resident to the Legislative Council, but the diggers treated this with scorn—passing a resolution of no confidence in the appointee, at which he was compelled to resign. Although his opinion may have been an attempt to justify his own actions in pouring troops into Bendigo and then compromising, it was significant that the Governor wrote to the Colonial Secretary that unless something was done there would almost inevitably be bloodshed at Bendigo. He decided to compromise, and the Council met and reduced the fee to 40s. a quarter. The crisis was temporarily over, but

[56] Great Britain, *P.P.*, 1854, vol. xliv.

the larger issues of representation, the unavailability of land, and opposition to the instruments of state power were still there. In the neighbouring fields of Ballarat, however, these questions came to a head a little more than a year later in the battle for the Eureka stockade.

A revolt against established authority is not a simple social phenomenon. It is not simply the result of a political viewpoint, nor is it the result simply of specific grievances. Both these factors must be present, the one complementing the other to produce unanimity of action. Usually the grievances are universally felt, but felt most acutely by those who see them in terms of political assumptions that reject the right of authority to act in the way it does. The revolt at Eureka was a democratic protest against arbitrary government. On the part of some it was a positive action aiming to achieve the radical democratic programme; on the part of all it was a desperate revolt against the heavy hand of an irresponsible authority.

The grievance that was felt by all was the method of collecting the licence tax. At least once a month, and during 1854 more frequently, the police would pour on to the diggings, round up the miners, and demand to inspect their licences. Those who were not able to produce their licences immediately were arrested, treated to all kinds of indignity and petty cruelty, and fined, or if without the means to pay, imprisoned. The character of those raids is amply demonstrated by the accepted name of 'digger hunts'—hunts carried out with all the brutal sportiveness of the hunting field. Raffaello Carboni, himself one of the foxes, says that

> both in October and November, when the weather allowed it, the Camp [the police who were encamped behind a stockade on a hill] rode out for the hunt every alternate day. True, one day they would hunt their game on Gravel Pits; another day, they pounced on the foxes of the Eureka; and a third day on the Red Hill; but, though working on different leads, are we not all fellow-diggers?[57]

The royal commission that sat immediately after the revolt found that the conduct of the police—the 'traps' or 'Joes' as the diggers called them—'was trenching very closely on the limits of human endurance, although a course sanctioned by the letter of the regulations'.[58]

The bitterness caused by the conduct of the police was aggravated by the conviction that some of the administrators were corrupt, a conviction that was confirmed by the case of James Scobie, a miner.[59]

[57] *Eureka Stockade*, p. 20. [58] 'Report of Gold-fields Commission', p. xli.
[59] 'Report of Board appointed to enquire into late disturbance at Ballarat', Vic. *V. & P. (L.C.)*, 1854-5, vol. i.

He was found murdered near the Eureka Hotel and the evidence pointed to the licensee, James Bentley, as the murderer. Bentley was tried before a court whose president was suspected of being in his debt, and was acquitted. Resentment burst into riot, and ten thousand miners burnt his hotel to the ground, Bentley escaping to the protection of the police camp. The Governor, Sir Charles Hotham,[60] intervened and Bentley was re-arrested. But at the same time three miners, apparently selected at random, were put on trial for burning the hotel and sentenced to short terms of imprisonment. An immediate agitation was commenced for the release of the miners who were considered to be scapegoats selected by the corrupt police.

The incident of Bentley is important in two respects. On the one hand it confirmed the diggers' conviction that the administration was corrupt; on the other, the inability of the police to save the hotel gave the diggers confidence in their new power—'The entire diggings,' wrote Carboni, 'in a state of extreme excitement. The diggers are lords and masters of Ballaarat; and the prestige of the Camp is gone forever.'[61]

In November 1854, the Ballarat Reform League became the representative organization of the miners. The political viewpoint that had been expressed in protests and petitions, but which wanted the unanimous and active support of the diggers as a whole, seems to have gained that support from the acute sense of grievance over the licence tax and the manner in which it was collected, allied with the sense of power produced by the incidents described. In January of 1854 La Trobe had reported the organization of a 'Diggers' Congress' but was not impressed by its significance.[62] On 11 November, however, a meeting of ten thousand miners on Bakery Hill, Ballarat, adopted a radical democratic programme and decided on a course of action that would immediately lead either to important concessions by the government or to a state of civil war. Because it summed up both the political viewpoint of the miners and their specific grievances, the programme must be quoted at length:

[60] Strictly, Lieutenant-Governor Sir Charles Hotham. Between 1851 and 1861 the Governor of New South Wales was also entitled 'Governor-General of all Her Majesty's Australian possessions' and the officers administering the other colonies were called Lieutenant-Governors. This was a remnant of Earl Grey's defeated federation proposals. For purposes of simplicity, and because there was little essential difference between the function of the Lieutenant-Governor in Victoria and the Governor in New South Wales, I employ the title Governor throughout. For a full discussion of this matter, see: J. M. Ward, *Earl Grey and the Australian Colonies, 1846-1857*, pp. 227 ff. [61] *Eureka Stockade*, p. 27.
[62] La Trobe to Newcastle, 16 January 1854, Great Britain, *P.P.* 1854-5, vol. xxxviii.

That it is the inalienable right of every citizen to have a voice in the making of the laws he is called upon to obey. That taxation without representation is tyranny. . . . That it is the object of the League to place the power in the hands of responsible representatives of the people to frame wholesome laws and carry on an honest government. That it is not the wish of the League to effect an immediate separation of this Colony from the parent country, if equal laws and equal rights are dealt out to the whole free community; but that, if Queen Victoria continues to act upon the ill advice of dishonest ministers and insists upon indirectly dictating obnoxious laws for the colony, under the assumed authority of the Royal prerogative, the Reform League will endeavour to supersede such Royal prerogatives by asserting that of the people, which is the most royal of all prerogatives, as the people are the only legitimate source of all political power.

The meeting decided further to strive for the immediate achievement of a full and fair representation, manhood suffrage, no property qualifications for members of the Legislative Council, payment of members and short duration of parliaments.[63] On the question of the goldfields administration they demanded the abolition of the office of goldfields commissioner and the total abolition of the diggers' and storekeepers' licences. To achieve the demands it was decided to organize the Reform League by providing a tent for its headquarters and issuing membership cards.

The Reform League had been in existence before 11 November, but on that day it became an organization supported by the whole of the mining community in Ballarat. A number of leaders had emerged, of whom the most important were perhaps John Basson Humffray and George Black. Humffray was the secretary of the Reform League, and Black the editor of the *Diggers' Advocate*. Both were radical democrats, but neither of them, by temperament or conviction, were revolutionaries. As events moved rapidly towards violence, they were pushed aside by other men whose democratic convictions were not so deep, but whose resentment at direct oppression made them prepared to lead the diggers in revolt. Such a one was Peter Lalor, who emerged as a leader only when the mass of the miners had decided upon armed resistance to the tyrannous acts of the administration. He put himself at their head and around him gathered a group moved by motives similar to his own.

After the meeting on 11 November, the committee of the Reform League continued to meet. It prepared and dispatched a deputation to the Governor, Sir Charles Hotham, with a statement of the

[63] Ibid.

grievances and a *demand* that the miners imprisoned for burning the hotel be released. The Governor received the deputation but refused to consider a request couched in the form of a demand. The deputation pointed out that the terminology was that of the men they represented and that the men were no longer prepared to pray or petition; they now demanded. The matter of releasing the prisoners was set aside and the other grievances discussed, but to all of them the Governor was either unable or unwilling to give a favourable reply, though he pointed out that the constitutional issues raised could only be dealt with by the imperial parliament or by the colonial legislature under the constitution that was pending.[64]

The deputation reported back to a mass meeting on Bakery Hill on 29 November. Humffray advised them to leave the matter in the hands of the Governor, whom he claimed to be sympathetic yet powerless and in the hands of bad advisers. But by now the movement was out of the control of Humffray and Black. The men wanted action, and new leaders came forward. Peter Lalor, who spoke to a mass meeting for the first time, proposed a meeting of the Reform League for the following Sunday to elect a central committee. And then, on the motion of Vern, a German, came the decision to throw defiance in the teeth of the authorities by a public burning of licences.

On the following morning, with the myopic provocativeness that had characterized so many of their actions, the police, under the direction of the goldfields commissioner, rode out on a raid of the diggings, and 'by that act destroyed the remaining influence of the friends of moral force action among the diggers'.[65] A riot was precipitated, the Riot Act read, and shots fired. The diggers prepared to carry through their pledge of the previous evening. Arms were collected, squads formed and began drilling. Peter Lalor was elected 'Commander-in-Chief of the diggers under arms'. In the evening, under their flag, the Southern Cross—of which Carboni said 'there is no flag in old Europe half so beautiful'—Peter Lalor swore in the diggers. They swore, 'by the Southern Cross to stand truly by each other and fight to defend our Rights and Liberties'. Defensive works were begun and a rude stockade thrown up within which elected leaders attempted to establish some kind of military organization and prepare for what was still quite an indefinite course of action.

The spirit of the diggers was one of tremendous enthusiasm for

[64] Hotham to Grey, 30 December 1854. Ibid.
[65] W. B. Withers, *The History of Ballarat*, p. 66.

their act of defiance. Carboni wrote of the meeting on 29 November that 'no one who was not present at that monster meeting, or never saw any Chartist meeting in Copenhagen-fields, London, can possibly form an idea of the enthusiasm of the miners of Ballaarat'.[66] A delegate was sent to the neighbouring field of Creswick and from there came a squad of three hundred men, singing the 'Marseillaise' and making a forced march through the night over the hills and gullies. At their head, as they made their way through a thunderstorm, was Thomas Kennedy, who flourished a sword and declaimed chartist slogans.[67]

For two days a state of *de facto* civil war prevailed. The diggers sent out scouts and patrols and drilled behind their barricade. But their preparations lacked decision and direction. It is clear that there was no real revolutionary leadership preparing to overthrow the existing state power and establish the power of the diggers under arms. They had come together to defend themselves against the rough hand of authority, but because they were not prepared to take the initiative, the spirit of enthusiasm and defiance of 30 November was rapidly dissipated. When the police and military attacked the stockade in the early morning of 3 December, they found it but thinly defended. After a brief battle the stockade was taken and the revolt suppressed.

The news of the situation at Ballarat had the most profound effect on people in every part of the colony. At Bendigo it was decided, after hearing a delegate from Ballarat, to send a delegation, but the stockade was taken before it arrived.[68] In Melbourne, a meeting called by the Lord Mayor to express support for the government was taken over by the majority, who supported the diggers and carried resolutions in their favour. On 6 December, a monster meeting in Melbourne declared that the unconstitutional proceedings of the miners had been due to provocation, and condemned the whole policy of the government. Meanwhile, in Ballarat the military *coup* had not settled the issues in any way. It had merely changed its direction. On 6 December a mass meeting on Bakery Hill restated the miners' grievances, and John Humffray, who had opposed the resort to arms, re-established himself as leader of the agitation.

The immediate result of the revolt was the investigation by a royal commission whose recommendations went some way to satisfy the grievances of the miners. The miners' licence was abolished and replaced by a miners' right, which carried with it the right both to

[66] *Eureka Stockade*, p. 47.   [67] Withers, *History of Ballarat*, p. 67.
[68] G. Mackay, *The History of Bendigo*, p. 37.

dig for gold and to vote. The existing administration of the goldfields was abolished and the goldfields commissioners replaced by locally elected courts, of which the first was elected by a show of hands at a meeting on Bakery Hill in the middle of 1855.

The extent to which the goldfields agitation in general and the revolt at Eureka in particular influenced the larger issues is, however, likely to remain what it has been for a century—a matter on which historians will disagree. The basis of their disagreement will be less a question of fact than of opinion on the mechanism of social and political change. It has been correctly pointed out by some who minimize the significance of the goldfields movement that most of the purely political demands of the diggers had been conceded in principle almost a year before the revolt—the Act accompanying the constitution to Britain providing for a vote for the miners. Equally, it has been emphasized that a number of the demands made on Governor Hotham were not in his power to concede.[69] All this is perfectly true, but it is insufficient.

The fact is that between 1850 and 1856 a profound change occurred in public opinion. In 1850 the voices demanding manhood suffrage were almost unheard. In 1856, in the first parliament elected under the new constitution, manhood suffrage, although qualified by the property vote, was put into effect without opposition and without a division.[70] In the debates both inside and outside the legislature much was made of the idea that the relative prosperity of people in Australia, the high level of literacy, and the absence of distinct social classes made possible the concession of the vote to all. In the minds of many conservatives, the retention of the vote for property compensated for the concession. The ending of transportation and the elimination of the possibility of its re-introduction was a further factor. But it seems certain that however much importance attaches to these factors, the goldfields movement, in which from time to time there was a massive demonstration of democratic sentiment, played a quite decisive part because of its own weight and because of its influence on other sections of the community. By 1856 all members of the Victorian legislature were convinced either of the desirability of manhood suffrage or the inexpediency of opposing it. The resort to arms in 1854 was a significant event in the process that brought this about.

Of Shay's Rebellion, Thomas Jefferson wrote:

What country can preserve its liberties, if its rulers are not warned

[69] C. H. Currey, *The Irish at Eureka*, ch. ii.
[70] *Victorian Hansard*, 1856-7, i, 97-105, 166.

from time to time, that this people preserve the spirit of resistance? Let them take arms. The remedy is to set them right as to facts, pardon and pacify them. What signify a few lives lost in a century or two? The tree of liberty must be refreshed from time to time, with the blood of patriots and tyrants.[71]

For Peter Lalor the revolt was necessary. 'Neither anarchy, bloodshed, nor plunder,' he wrote, 'were the objects of those engaged in the late outbreak. Stern necessity alone forced us to do it.'[72] By and large, Australian democratic opinion in 1854 and since has been on the side of Jefferson and Lalor.

Manhood suffrage was a fact in Victoria in the life of the first parliament under the new constitution. This in itself was a most important step on the road to democratic government, but it did not *establish* either political or economic democracy. Plural voting and a property-qualified upper chamber limited the consequences of manhood suffrage for the lower house. Economic inequality and the monopolistic possession of the land placed keen weapons in the hands of the propertied class in general and the squatters in particular. In New South Wales the demand for the opening of the land to small-scale settlement was the main social component of the political movement which led to manhood suffrage, the ballot, and equal electoral districts in 1858. In both New South Wales and Victoria the 'solution of the land question' was the key which the majority of people believed would open the door to social justice and the realization of the ideal of economic independence. The majority were mistaken, at least in the short-term consequences, but in the political conflict about the land some democratic advances were made. More important in the long run, it decided that the language of Australian politics would from then on be the language of democracy.

[71] Cited J. Dewey, *The Living Thoughts of Thomas Jefferson,* p. 66.
[72] *Argus* (Melbourne), 10 April 1835.

2

Independence on the Land

The earth was the gift of God to all, not to a few. It was never intended that one portion of mankind should starve while another portion revelled in idleness and luxury.[1]

The sole object of a price is to prevent labourers from turning into landowners too soon: the price must be sufficient for that one purpose and no other.[2]

THE Land Acts adopted in New South Wales and Victoria in 1860-1 were the culmination of a political struggle between two opposed concepts of society. The alternatives were an aristocratic social organization founded on the large-scale possession of the land, and a society in which the radical ideal of equality of opportunity would become the 'idea in office'. The radical ideal triumphed, although the practical outcome of the new land laws did not fulfil the expectations of those who had fought for them. But in the political movement of which they were the result, democratic political principles, the first achievement of which was manhood suffrage in Victoria, were confirmed as the ruling ideas in Australian society during the second half of the nineteenth century.

In the previous chapter passing reference was made to the significance of the demand for 'the opening of the land'. Now it is necessary to look more closely at the situation that had developed by the mid eighteen-fifties. From the foundation of New South Wales until 1830, land was alienated from the Crown, in the main, by grant. In this way a little less than four million acres passed into the possession of individuals or companies.[3] From 1831 to 1838 land was sold at a minimum price of 5s. an acre, nearly a million and a half acres being alienated in this way.[4] In 1839 the minimum price was raised to 12s. an acre and in 1842, to £1. In the thirteen years before 1851 less than half a million acres were sold.

The adoption of the method of sale in 1831 and the price rises in

[1] *Land and Labour in Victoria by an Old Colonist.*
[2] E. G. Wakefield, *A View of the Art of Colonisation*, p. 347.
[3] S. H. Roberts, *Australian Land Settlement, 1788-1920*, p. 75.   [4] Ibid., p. 99.

1839 and 1842 were the result of the attempt to find a common-sense solution to the problems that pressed on the colonial office officials and of the 'sufficient price' theory of Edward Gibbon Wakefield. Colonial secretaries such as Goderich and Stanley were impressed by a practical problem—to shift part of what was conceived to be a surplus population from Britain to Australia. Their solution was the sale of Crown lands to men of property and the use of part of the proceeds to transfer population to the colony. Wakefield went a good deal further. He considered that the proceeds of land sales should be employed to transfer population, and also that a 'sufficient price' should be charged for land to prevent all but a minority acquiring it. This would ensure both landowners and a propertyless wage-earning class. He considered that some of the wage earners would ultimately acquire land of their own, but his immediate concern was to ensure not merely the transfer of men but also the employer-employee relationship of capitalism.

However, it was not mainly by the application of the empirical policies of the Colonial Office nor by the theories of Wakefield that the basis of capitalist institutions was laid in Australia. The policy and theory contributed by providing a propertyless class, but the barrier against their occupation of the land was raised by the occupation, at first illegal, of vast areas of Crown land by a relatively small number of men who, with their flocks and herds, took possession of it. They required neither the support of a theory nor the sanction of a government that was, at the time, powerless to remove them. Having occupied the land, the squatters fought to retain possession.

The 1846 Act and the Order-in-Council of the following year seemed to promise security of tenure, but practical difficulties stood in the way of the issue of leases. The land had to be surveyed, and the difficulty of having this carried out prevented the issue of leases before 1852, by which time, particularly in Victoria, the flood of people wanting land had begun to bank up before the wall erected by the squatter occupation. To the practical difficulties was added a growing political opposition.

The issue as it was fought turned on the interpretation of the Order-in-Council of 1847—what rights had been conferred on the squatters and what reserved to the government by these regulations? Under the regulations, the colony was divided into three regions: settled, intermediate, and unsettled. Squatters in possession of grazing licences were entitled to leases for one, eight or fourteen years according to the region, with pre-emptive rights of purchase. However, there was a proviso. Areas might be reserved for townships, for a number of other specified objects, and to meet 'the prospective wants of the community'. After the influx of miners made the community even less identifiable with the squatters than hitherto, Governor La Trobe sought to give a wide meaning to the proviso. In fact, he interpreted the wants of the community to be such that large areas should be reserved from the operation of the clauses permitting the issue of leases to the squatters. On the other hand the squatters, who saw in this interpretation the usurpation of their assumed rights, took up the position that the Order contained specific rights: they maintained that the government was obliged to issue the maximum leases provided in the regulations, and that in fact the government had from the date of issue of the regulations lost all power of sale of land to the public, independent of preemption conceded to the lessees.[5] They admitted the right to reserve land for the specific purpose enumerated in the proviso, but denied the validity of the broader interpretation La Trobe sought to give it.

In the middle of 1852 the squatter majority in the Legislative Council passed a resolution demanding an immediate issue of the leases. Meetings of squatters were held and resolutions passed, letters written to the Colonial Secretary, and a memorial drawn up and transmitted to the Queen.[6] The assumed rights and the supporting reasons were outlined in the resolutions adopted at a meeting held in September 1852 at the Prince of Wales Hotel, Melbourne. These stressed the squatters' conception of their rights under the Order-in-Council and of the overriding importance of the pastoral industry to the colony. The squatters had no doubt that the welfare of the pastoral industry was identified with their continued possession of their runs. They emphasized, further, their humble loyalty to the Crown, and underlined their own importance as a conservative class. William Forlonge, who claimed to be the largest stockholder and occupier of Crown lands in the Murray district, characterized any course of action other than the implementation of the regulations as interpreted by his class as 'an act of the most flagrant repudiation and confiscation of private property without parallel in the annals of political dishonesty'.[7]

Governor La Trobe, faced by the disagreement of his law officers on the interpretation of the regulations, and knowing that his

[5] La Trobe to Pakington, 3 September 1852, Vic. *V. & P. (L.C.)* 1854-5, vol. ii.
[6] Vic. *V. & P. (L.C.)*, 1853-4, vol. ii.
[7] Forlonge to Pakington, Vic. *V. & P. (L.C.)*, 1853-4, vol. ii.

acceding to the squatters' demands would probably result in the most violent protests, referred the whole question to the Colonial Secretary. A large public meeting in Melbourne appealed to the imperial government to amend the regulations and to the Governor not to grant the leases. The resolution stated that the Order-in-Council had been made in ignorance of the actual conditions and that the conditions had so altered in the intervening five years as to make them even less appropriate.[8] It was patently unjust, it was asserted, to hand over sixty million acres, including some of the best land in the country, to some eight hundred men. A petition to the Legislative Council from the goldminers of Bendigo praying for an immediate amendment of the land policy was supported by four thousand signatures.[9] Farmers and business men signed petitions couched in similar terms, and a minority in the Legislative Council carried on a running battle with the squatter majority. John Pascoe Fawkner, a large landowner and one of the first settlers in the colony, penned a long and violent letter studded with statistics and accusations against the squatters to the Colonial Secretary. He pointed out that up to June 1851 a total of 391,094 acres of land had been sold, of which more than half had been sold at an average price of above £3 an acre. He considered that landowners who had paid high prices for their land had a particular grievance against a policy that might give to the squatters vast areas of land at a nominal fee.[10] The petitions that flowed in from agricultural districts indicated that Fawkner was expressing the general viewpoint of farmers.[11] As against the squatters' protestations of loyalty to the Queen, Fawkner protested—'the land is not the property of the squatter, and all the men they employ serfs! If the Government of Great Britain does not interfere, and that quickly and effectually, I fear that anarchy and bloodshed may yet be the upshot.'[12]

At the end of 1853 the Duke of Newcastle gave his instructions. The instructions were general, and emphasized the spirit rather than the letter of the regulations. In effect they handed the problem back to be solved in the colony, where it was referred to a royal commission. In its report the commission surveyed the development of land policy, the interests involved, and made recommendations for the future. The recommendations were a triumph for those opposed to the squatters and seemed to promise that land policy in the future

[8] Vic. V. & P. (L.C.) 1853-4, vol. ii.   [9] Ibid.
[10] Fawkner to Pakington, Vic. V. & P. (L.C.), 1853-4, vol. ii.
[11] Ibid.; for example, 'Petitions from 566 landed proprietors, farmers, capitalists, merchants, tradesmen and others of Geelong, County of Grant'.
[12] Fawkner to Pakington, Vic. V. & P. (L.C.), 1853-4, vol. ii.

would be directed towards the welfare of the 'small man'. In summary they were as follows: that survey and sale of Crown lands should proceed continuously with reference to the requirements of all classes of purchasers; that the claims of the squatters should be rejected in their entirety; that leases should not be issued but that pastoralists be provided with licences, renewable from year to year; that rent paid by pastoralists should be proportioned to the grazing capacity of the runs and the division of the colony into the various regions to be done away with.[13] Only three members of the commission signed without reservations. Two of them considered that there was insufficient protection for existing property interests. Three considered that the method of computing the rent was too liberal, and one, William Forlonge, refused to sign and in a long and bitter statement threatened that the squatters would 'resist such proceedings by every legal and constitutional means within their reach'.[14] The licences were issued as recommended by the commission, but the future of the land policy was held over for attention by the new government under the new constitution.

In New South Wales there was much the same story,[15] the main difference being that some leases, a very small number, were issued there. By 1861, of approximately 3,000 runs only 148 were held under lease. Possibly more important was the fact that from 1854 onwards the clause of the 1846 Act, which permitted the issue of licences for fourteen or eight years, was implemented. In practice, these licences in most respects differed little from the leases that might have been issued.

With the inauguration of responsible government the colonial parliaments acquired full power to decide land policy in whatever way they thought fit. Public opinion was quite determined that in both New South Wales and Victoria legislation should be passed making access to the land possible for the small settler. In both colonies after 1855 'opening the land to the people' was the way in which radicals formulated their essential political-economic demand.

After 1855, the declining gold yield faced a swollen population with the dire need to find alternative employment for those whom the goldfields would no longer feed. From 1858, men began leaving the goldfields in large numbers, the population of the Victorian fields falling from 166,550 in 1858 to 70,794 in 1866. This displacement

[13] Ibid., 1854-5, vol. iii: 'Report of the Commission appointed to enquire into the Tenure of the Wastelands of the Crown', pp. 23-4.   [14] Ibid., p. 40.
[15] See D. W. A. Baker, 'The Origins of the Robertson Land Acts'.

occurred in a total population which grew from 463,135 in 1857 to 636,982 in 1866.[16] Economic independence was the social objective of the diggers on the goldfields. Vast areas of unoccupied land gave promise of a similar degree of independence on the land, if only the land could be acquired.

The attitude of those who hoped to benefit from land reform scarcely needs any explanation. It was an expression of simple self-interest, but it also had the sanction of prevailing liberal and radical assumptions. Equality of opportunity and personal independence were articles of faith which, in a new country, appeared to have more chance of realization than in the old world. However, the interests of the men who actually carried the reform in parliament were in general not directly involved in the opening of the land. In the main they were landowners and members of the urban middle class—business men, manufacturers, and members of the professions. Though they were less directly involved than the potential farmers, the classes from which they came were interested parties in the disposition of the land. Landowners were convinced, as John Pascoe Fawkner and the petitioning farmers had pointed out in 1852, that it was unfair to those who had paid for their land that the squatters should acquire immense areas merely by possession; this would tend to reduce the value of property as well as remove a possible source of government income. For the urban middle class, small-scale settlement for agricultural purposes appeared to be the way both to expand the home market and to increase the home production of foodstuffs. These motives were clearly not so compelling as those activating the men who hoped to become farmers. At their strongest, they were enough to make many middle-class people firm advocates of reform. At their weakest, they at least constituted no serious reason for opposing it.

However much the material incentives for middle and working classes may have differed, there was agreement at the level of political opinion. Both agreed on the virtue of equality of opportunity; and both opposed the social and economic pretensions of the squatters. They differed only in the urgency with which they demanded reform. Thus middle-class politicians legislated under pressure of the masses out of doors.

In Victoria, early in the session, the first parliament considered a series of resolutions embodying principles that might be applied.[17] These were followed by a Crown Lands Bill, which the Government

---

[16] Vic. *Year Book 1893*, 'Statistical Summary of Victoria from 1836 to 1892'.
[17] *Victorian Hansard*, i-ii. 120, 140, 149, 325, 376, 403, 480

claimed was based on the principles contained in the resolutions. After months of debate and delay, the Bill passed the Legislative Assembly in September 1857,[18] but was stood over by the Council.[19] It never became law. No one was satisfied with it. The squatters considered that it did not meet their claims for security or compensation; the radicals, that it was the first step to granting a monopoly of the greater part of Victoria to the squatters. Both ultimately accepted less than they demanded in 1857.

The radical opposition to the Bill was genuinely popular. Petitions from all corners of Victoria flooded the Assembly—forty of them, signed by more than 55,000 people.[20] The general plaint was twofold. The squatters were to be guaranteed only temporary possession of their runs (five years), but it was believed (probably correctly) that this would have led to permanent possession, thus excluding the potential small settler, the yeoman farmer. Typical of the petitions is the one from 'Householders, Landholders and Inhabitants of the Kyneton Boroughs', which stated in part: 'That in the opinion of this meeting the Crown Lands Bill, introduced by the present Government, will, if passed, be an act of spoliation calculated to injure the best interests of this Colony, and to prevent the settlement of an enterprising and hardy yeomanry on its broad and fertile lands.'[21] Secondly it was argued that the legislature was not completely representative since it had not been elected by manhood suffrage, although it had amended the electoral law to provide a vote for all adult males.

Petitions were one medium of public protest; letters to the press and public meetings were others. But the most effective in both expressing and moulding public opinion was the Victorian Convention, which assembled in Melbourne in July 1857. Its purpose was to work out a policy for the settlement of the land question and to demonstrate that popular opinion would not tolerate any settlement that did not make all the lands of the colony readily accessible to the man of small means. The convention, attended by upwards of ninety delegates, sat for three weeks. It adopted a radical programme of land and parliamentary reform.

The key points in the land policy were: free selection by any adult of an unspecified amount of any unalienated Crown land in the colony whether surveyed or not, subject to payment of ten per cent of the purchase money on taking possession, continued possession to be subject to substantial occupation; the cessation of all

[18] Ibid., pp. 766-1169.   [19] Ibid., p. 1222.
[20] Vic. *V. & P. (L.A.)*, 1856-7, vol. iii.   [21] Ibid.

exclusive occupation of unalienated Crown lands for pastoral purposes and the opening of such lands as common pasturage; a special tax on all privately owned uncultivated land.[22] The convention opposed assisted immigration because 'the system of immigration at the public expense is an integral part of the present land system—a land system constructed to create a country of masters and servants—and can have no place in a land system constructed for a free people'. Radical parliamentary reform was urged to make 'parliament itself the Convention of the people'. This would be secured, it was believed, by manhood suffrage without preliminary registration of voters; equal electoral districts, and short parliaments; and payment of members. The last was justified in the mind of the convention by the conviction that 'the history of the present Land Bill proves that it has been a very dear bargain for the people to have accepted for nothing the services of gentlemen who ultimately propose to pay themselves by confiscating the public lands to themselves and their friends'.

The convention was the left wing of the popular movement. A good deal of its policy was common to all who were opposed to the squatting occupation and advocated small-scale settlement for agricultural purposes. The policy common to most reformers was selection in small lots of any Crown lands, whether surveyed or unsurveyed, and whether claimed by squatters or not. Normally, reformers advocated sale at an upset price with a proportion of the total cost paid as a deposit and the balance in deferred payments. Effective occupation and some type of improvements were generally required. Where the convention went beyond the moderate reformers was in its views on common lands and the responsibilities associated with freehold title. In effect it argued that all land which was not under cultivation should be held in common, and that land which had been alienated for agricultural purposes and remained uncultivated should be subject to a special penal tax. These views are clearly seen in the succession of agrarian socialistic ideas which run through sophisticated thinking from Sir Thomas More to Thomas Spence, William Ogilvie and Thomas Paine, and through agrarian and working-class revolts from the sixteenth century to the chartists. More immediately, they reflected the contemporary United States policy in dealing with the western lands. The idea of the special tax on uncultivated land harked back to Spence and Paine, echoed Patrick Dove, and anticipated Henry George, whose single-tax theory became one of the important ideological influences

[22] *Resolutions, Proceedings and Documents of the Victorian Convention.*

on the infant political labour movement in the late eighties. In the fifties, these left-wing ideas, given particular point by the apparent availability of land, never obtained more than minority support. Their importance historically rests on the fact that they expressed, however inadequately, a questioning of the absolute right of private property. In effect, they asserted that the practice of agriculture alone should be the necessary condition of freehold possession.

With disagreement in parliament and the popular movement vociferously opposing it, the Land Bill was held over until a new parliament was elected in 1859. By then the slogan of the convention—free selection and free grass—had become the legitimate voice of the people. The Nicholson Ministry in 1859 introduced a measure that provided for selection after survey, with deferred payments. This did not meet the demands of the convention, which wanted the right of immediate selection, before survey, on any part of the Crown lands. Nor was it acceptable to the squatters, who were unprepared to concede any of their present possessions. Consequently it was unpopular with the masses and rejected by the Legislative Council. After three attempts to compromise with the Council, the Government resigned. In this crisis, since no other government could be found, popular feeling reached fever pitch. Mass meetings were held in the Eastern Market reserve and in the grounds of Parliament House. 'Graham Berry urged the masses to follow Garibaldi's example and Wilson Gray [the Irish leader of the convention] provided the catchword by demanding for each man "a vote, a rifle and a farm—the rifle to defend his property".'[23] Coming at the end of long years of agitation, the breakdown of parliament in its attempt to deal with the question was interpreted by many as evidence that it was unprepared to accede to the popular will. In August 1860 a crowd of people, after meeting in the Eastern Market reserve, invaded parliament in protest against the hold up in land legislation. The Riot Act was read and the crowd dispersed, but the popular demonstration broke the deadlock between the Houses. Compromises were made by both the Assembly and the Council, and before the end of 1860 the Land Bill had become law. It was only the first of a series of measures, all of which were intended to unlock the land for agricultural settlement. The first Act broke down immediately but was none the less important, as it marked the acceptance by both houses of the principle that means must be found of making the land available for agricultural settlement.

In New South Wales the agitation for land reform did not arouse

[23] Roberts, *Australian Land Settlement*, p. 236.

the same popular interest as in Victoria. Yet in all other respects it was similar. As in Victoria, the parliamentary leaders of the reform movement were liberal-minded landowners and city business men. The most notable was John Robertson, Minister for Lands and architect of the 1861 Land Act. He was a consistent liberal, a pupil and lifelong friend of John Dunmore Lang. He believed sincerely in the principles of equality of opportunity and democratic representation. In 1848 he supported Robert Lowe in his campaign against the squatters; in 1853 he welcomed the return of Lang from England to lead the opposition to Wentworth's Constitution Bill; in 1858 he was a member of the Cowper Ministry which introduced manhood suffrage and the ballot; and in 1864 he voted in a minority for the abolition of the Legislative Council. Contrary to a popular fiction he was not a squatter, but, like John Pascoe Fawkner, a wealthy landowner. As a landowner his economic interests, which were opposed to the wholesale alienation of the Crown lands by mere possession, reinforced his liberal principles. Robertson's Land Act was not adopted until 1861. In the meantime, although the agitation never assumed the same proportions as in Victoria, popular feelings ran hot.

The New South Wales equivalent of the Victorian Convention was the New South Wales Land League. Its formation was stimulated by the existence of the Victorian organization. Prodded by the *Empire,* public meetings were held in Wynyard Square, Sydney, towards the end of 1857. These meetings adopted a number of principles which they considered should guide parliament in reforming the land law. They also decided to form an organization—the Land League. After the first burst of enthusiasm, the activity of the league was diffused in inept political manoeuvres and support for electoral reform, then being considered by parliament. Basically working-class in composition and leadership, the league lacked effective direction. During 1859 there is evidence of renewed activity. Branches were formed in several suburbs and an aspiring politician named John Black was chosen as president. Under his guidance the league drew up a manifesto whose principles were directly comparable with those of the Victorian Convention.

The standpoint of the league is made clear in the manifesto.[24] The land monopoly of the squatters was seen as the fact that stood between the majority of the people and the possibility of economic independence. Eleven principles for land reform were enumerated, of which the most important were: free selection before survey; a

[24] Manifesto of the New South Wales Land League (Mitchell Library, Sydney).

price of £1 per acre with ten per cent deposit and deferred payment over ten years; common pasturage on all unalienated land within the settled districts; a land tax on all alienated land; and the reservation of areas for town sites.

As in Victoria, the principles of the land tax and commonage were not accepted as practical propositions by the legislators. But the other main points were incorporated in the Act of 1861. This Act was passed in the parliament elected by manhood suffrage in 1860. In the election campaign, the critical question for candidates, at least in Sydney, was their attitude to the proposed land law. In the minds of conservatives no less than liberals and radicals, the proposed land law was seen as the first social fruit of democratic representation. For many conservatives it appeared as the first instalment of legislation which would undermine the economic and social basis of stable society, of which the foundation, in their view, was the broad acres which would nurture an aristocratic and cultured class. For liberals and radicals it was a levelling measure which would create the possibility of a developed society based on 'the most stable of all classes', an independent yeomanry. They were both wrong. It was a political triumph for liberal and radical politics, but the economic consequences were quite different from those expected.

The reform of 1861 was contained in two Acts, the Crown Lands Alienation Act and the Crown Lands Occupation Act. The first of these provided for selection of Crown lands, its most important clauses being numbers 13, 16, and 18. Clause 13 provided that any person could select any block of Crown land, whether leased or not, of an area between 40 and 320 acres at a price of £1 per acre. One-quarter of the purchase money was to be paid immediately and the balance as deferred payments. Certain areas were excepted from selection, the most important being town and suburban lands and lands which had been 'improved'. By improvement was meant the construction of buildings, dams and so on. Clause 16 provided for selection before survey—simply that a selector could occupy any area of unoccupied land and then apply for a survey to be made. If it were not surveyed within a year, he could give up the property and have his deposit refunded or could have it surveyed privately but at government expense. Clause 18 provided for the granting of permanent title to the selector's land. The balance of the purchase money had to be paid in three years and bona fide residence, as well as improvement to the value of £1 an acre, proved. One further qualification needs to be noted, namely that as an alternative to completing the payment within three years, payment could be postponed indefinitely by paying interest of five per cent on the amount outstanding.

The Crown Lands Occupation Act defined the method of granting leases of Crown land. Leases could be issued for one year in the settled districts and five years in the rest of the colony. The annual rent was to be £2 an acre in the settled districts and was to be based on the carrying capacity of the run for other areas. A further important clause in regard to leases was contained in the Alienation Act. A system of pre-leases was established under which any person selecting under the Act was entitled to a lease of Crown land adjoining the selection of an area three times as great as the land selected. Thus a person selecting 320 acres could claim the adjoining 960 acres of Crown land under pre-lease, a form of tenure that took precedence over other types of lease.

The essential fact that emerges from the study of this legislation is that the same land was offered to two different sets of people: to the squatters under lease, to selectors under conditional purchase and pre-lease. To the reformers this appeared to be a rational solution. In effect, they said, the pastoralists may have the land until it is required by the farmers. But the *Sydney Morning Herald*, which had consistently opposed the reform, came much closer than the reformers to describing the outcome. In a sub-leader it said:

> It is the reproach of Mr Robertson's bills, that . . . they will tend to create a feud between the two classes of settlers. He pits the two deliberately against one another. He says to the squatter, 'if you can hold your ground against these free selectors, by hook or by crook, do so'. He says to the free selectors, 'if you can screw the squatter off the run, it is your interest to do so, and you have every opportunity'. Under such circumstances it seems almost certain that there must be incessant strife until the contest is ended either by the squatter succumbing and taking his departure; or by his purchasing the whole of the run or its commanding positions.[25]

The Acts failed to establish a substantial yeomanry. The Morris-Ranken committee of inquiry, which reported in 1883, found that from the beginning of 1862 to the end of 1882, no less than 170,242 applications for selections under the Act were made, but that only from 18,000 to 20,000 homesteads had been established.[26] It is clear that, apart from the minority who obtained and held their selections, the greatest number of selections were made either by squatters or

---

[25] *S.M.H.*, 22 March 1861.
[26] N.S.W. *V. & P. (L.A.)*, 1883, vol. ii: 'Report of Inquiry into the State of the Public Lands and the Operation of the Land Laws'.

their agents, by selectors who were unable to establish themselves, or by men who used their conditional purchases to blackmail others into re-purchasing their selections. The squatters obtained by far the greater part of the land alienated. By 1886 more than half of the land alienated from the Crown had passed into the freehold possession of 552 men, who in that year held freehold titles to over eighteen million acres.[27] Titles to the rest of the land alienated were in the hands of 44,380 people of whom a little less than half had properties of from fifteen to two hundred acres, and the rest larger areas.

This result had been achieved by various means, 'dummying' and 'peacocking' being the favourite methods by which pastoralists used the terms of the Acts to acquire large areas under freehold title.[28] Sale of selected land by auction continued after 1861. Particularly in the seventies, millions of acres were sold in this way, in the main to squatters, for they alone could obtain the money to buy it.[29] Important also was the process of consolidation by which a relatively small holder with available capital bought up a number of selections. Although it is not possible to follow the process of consolidation from 1861, the evidence for the period between 1878 and 1886 is significant. In these eight years, the number of men with holdings of over 10,000 acres increased by eighty-six per cent, whilst the numbers with smaller holdings increased at a much lower rate.[30] The total picture was summed up by the New South Wales Statistician who wrote: 'settlement in New South Wales has hitherto tended towards the concentration into comparatively few hands of the lands alienated to a large number of individual selectors'.[31]

The reasons why this occurred have not yet been adequately investigated, but certain things are clear. Given that the squatters, or some of them, were prepared to misuse the terms of the Acts, their strategic position was far superior to that of potential settlers. They occupied their runs, they had various improvements which could not be selected, and capital was more readily available to

[27] T. A. Coghlan, *Wealth and Progress of New South Wales, 1886*, p. 201.
[28] 'Dummies' were nominal selectors, acting on behalf of someone else, living on a selection to fulfil the residence conditions of the Land Act. 'Peacocking', or 'picking the eyes', referred to the selection of vantage points so placed as to render the intervening land useless.
[29] See Roberts, *Australian Land Settlement*, pp. 227 ff.; also 'Report of Inquiry into the State of the Public Lands'.
[30] Holdings of less than 15 acres increased by 39 per cent; 15-100 acres by 47 per cent; 400-1000 acres by 48 per cent; 1000-2000 acres by 68 per cent; 2000-10,000 acres by 64 per cent. Coghlan, *Wealth and Progress of New South Wales 1887-8*, p. 204.
[31] Coghlan, *Wealth and Progress of New South Wales, 1892*, p. 273.

them. Then there was the fact that the greater part of the land available for selection was more suitable for grazing than for agriculture, at any rate for agriculture at the existing level of technique. On the other hand, there were many factors which stood between the selector and the possibility of establishing a successful farm. Lack of capital was certainly one of the more important. The minimum capital required varied from place to place and from season to season, but in all cases it was greatly in excess of the down payment on the land required by the Act. The land available for selection was by and large in the lower rainfall belt—land which was later extensively farmed by techniques not then existing and on areas greater than those provided for in the Act. It is notable in this respect that the two areas in which the 1883 committee of inquiry found successful settlement were the coastal districts of Bega and of the Richmond and Clarence rivers. They are both districts containing large areas of rich soil and abundant water, eminently suitable for agriculture and dairying as well as for pastoral purposes. For both, sea transport was available to overcome the problem of reaching the market with reasonable economy. A further important fact that needs to be taken into account in explaining the large number of selections which failed to produce permanent settlement was that many selections were not made for the purpose of settlement. 'Peacocking' was used by some selectors to blackmail squatters. To protect their interests squatters were forced to buy, often at very high prices, land selected for the sole purpose of forcing them to do so.

Here, we are less concerned either with the economic causes or results of the failure of the land selection legislation to establish a large class of prosperous small farmers than with the political consequences of the legislation. In the lack of capital, unsuitability of the land for easy agricultural development, problems of transport, the contingencies of climate, the suitability of the land for grazing purposes, and the favourable market for wool, are to be found the basic economic causes for the relative failure of agricultural settlement. Politically, the main consequence of the legislation is summed up in the conclusion of the 1883 committee of inquiry. It commented, 'the most noteworthy matter that has come to light and the most ominous for the future well being of the colony, is the class contest for the possession of its lands which has covered five-sixths of its surface'. In this contest forgery, blackmail, false swearing, bribery, intimidation and violence were the weapons in common use. Before the passage of the 1861 Acts, land reform was a political question in which the opinions and interests of the people of the city were deeply involved. After 1861, the land became the prize in a struggle that took place on the land itself, in the lands offices, and in the parliamentary lobbies. Although it coloured politics at the parliamentary level—was a constant factor in the formation and dissolution of parliamentary factions[32]—its main lasting effect was on the outlook of the people of the countryside.

In a recent work it is argued compellingly that the distinctive national ethos which burst forth in the late eighties and nineties had developed even before the gold-rushes as the response of the bush worker to the natural and social environment to the west of the dividing range.[33] Broadly, this region was what was known to the selection Acts as the intermediate territory. From 1861 the most important fact in this social environment was the conflict between pastoralists and selectors, a conflict more acute there than in any other part of the colony.[34] When, as the result of a conjunction of circumstances, the workers and selectors of this region began in the eighties to play a more active part in politics, the reality of this struggle was basic to the determination of their outlook.

In Victoria the selection Acts were eventually more effective; nevertheless, until 1869 the process was very similar to that in the older colony, with the squatters securing their title to significant areas of their runs. Under the Land Act of 1860 (the Nicholson Act) and the Acts of 1862 (the Duffy Act) and 1865 (the Grant Act), various provisions were made for agricultural settlement. The first Acts were passed only after acrimonious struggle between the Assembly and the Council, but still loopholes were found by means of which many pastoralists acquired freehold title to important parts of their stations. 'Dummying' and 'peacocking' appear to have been as common as in New South Wales, and until 1869 no effective methods were found to prevent them.[35] For example, under the Duffy Act of 1862 more than 900,000 acres were obtained by one hundred people. This failure was reflected in the continued popular agitation against the squatters and in the sequence of amendments to the Acts. Means were ultimately found of achieving the desired end by making occupation precede alienation, with a selector proving

[32] See A. W. Martin, 'Political Groupings in New South Wales, 1872-1889'.
[33] Russel Ward, *The Australian Legend*.
[34] 'This Territorial Division is the largest, the richest, and the most important of the three. Within its limits the great difficulties connected with land legislation have arisen and here the problem now before the country must be solved'. 'Report of Inquiry into the State of the Public Lands', p. 13.
[35] Roberts, *Australian Land Settlement*, pp. 239 ff.

his intention to make permanent settlement by three years' residence. Means of countering 'dummying' were found between 1865 and 1869 by vesting discretionary powers in the hands of the Minister, who was given powers to decide the bona fides of the intending settler. This experience was put to good effect in further legislation and regulations framed by Grant in 1869. This Act was the most successful of all land Acts of the period.

The measure of the relative success of the Victorian legislation is to be seen in the figures. By 1867, nearly twenty-three thousand people held areas of land up to five hundred acres.[36] Some of these holdings changed hands and were concentrated into large farms and pastoral properties, but, as compared with New South Wales, the policy of settling farmers on small agricultural holdings was successful. This fact is underlined by the figures of land under cultivation in the two colonies.

In 1860-1 the area under crop in Victoria amounted to less than half a million acres, but by 1880-1 it had increased to almost two million acres.[37] As well as being a total increase of a million and a half acres, this represented a great increase in the area under crop per inhabitant. In 1872-3 there were 1·33 acres per person being cultivated, but ten years later this had been increased to 2·27 acres per person. In the following decade a further slight increase took place.[38] In New South Wales, on the other hand, as late as 1876 there was less than three-quarters of an acre of land per person under cultivation. Eleven years later it had risen to only a little less than one acre per head of the population.[39] That is to say, as expressed in the amount of cultivation actually engaged in as a result of small-scale settlement policies, the policy as carried out in Victoria was much more successful than in New South Wales.

The story of land legislation in Queensland is no less complicated than in the other colonies. Its details need not concern us here, as at least the early legislation was much less the product of popular movements than in either New South Wales or Victoria. Early legislation aimed at two things: agricultural settlement of coastal and near coastal areas (in effect the kind of settlement that had taken place in the older colonies before 1860); and the granting of substantial security of tenure to the squatters. Broadly, the outcome of the legislation was to secure squatting tenure, both leasehold and

[36] Vic. *V. & P. (L.A.)*, 1868, vol. iii: 'Agricultural and Livestock Statistics of Victoria for the year ending 31st March 1867'.
[37] Vic. *Year Book 1882-83*, 'Agricultural Statistics'.
[38] Vic. *Year Book 1892*, ii. 252.
[39] Coghlan, *Wealth and Progress of New South Wales*, 1887, p. 205.

freehold, more completely than in any other colony; to establish some medium-sized grazing farms; and to foster small-scale agriculture in a few favourable areas. Of course, natural environment and difficulties of transport were even stronger determinants than in the other colonies in establishing the dominance of the pastoral industry.

The attempt to establish an independent yeomanry was one of the characteristic liberal and radical socio-economic policies of the third quarter of the nineteenth century. With the exception of Victoria, where it was partly successful, it failed to bring about the results its protagonists expected of it. Clearly this result was due in part to the inadequacy of laws that were based on the principle of equality of opportunity but failed to take into account the fact that opportunities were not equal. In the competition for the land, the squatters occupied the positions of vantage from which they successfully defended the greater part of the property they occupied.

Politically, the results did not so decisively favour the squatters. In short term the squatters were unable to defend their interests with the traditional sanctions employed by conservatives. Pressure groups in parliament argued not about fundamental principles but about the details of legislation. But above all, the social antagonisms roused in the contest for the land coloured all of politics and left a lasting impression on the Australian outlook.

3

The Struggle for Power, 1860-1880

The term 'Conservative' expresses the feeling less of a political party than of the whole of the people who have anything whatever to lose. Those who have something object to giving a share in the Government to those who have nothing.[1]

I believe the real danger to this country is in selfishness and want of education, in the want of a liberal tone in the thoughts and character that marks the very wealthy classes in this country. It is a small class, a very small class, but it is enormously powerful, and its power is derived chiefly from its monopoly of the public property.[2]

FROM 1860 there was little need for Australians to find a theoretical justification for democratic government. Its basic principles had the unquestioned adherence of the majority. Thus those who were opposed to its principles and suspicious of its consequences could have little expectation of gaining substantial popular support for the defence of positions of privilege. Conservative viewpoints were expressed, but radicals and liberals scarcely found it necessary to reply. The poverty of political thought in the Australian nineteenth century is one of the minor results. The major result was that the privileged, unshielded by any acceptable sanctions, were forced to defend themselves by entrenching in the positions of strength remaining to them. Joseph Chamberlain startled Britain in 1884 with the watchword, 'the Peers against the People'. But in 1885 there was still a heavy working-class vote for the Tories.[3] From the eighteen-fifties Australian conservatives had to resort to other means than electoral support to implement their policies.

As a class, the squatters defended themselves against the consequences of democratic political opinion by maintaining their domination of the land. Conservatives as a whole sought the maximum advantage from those institutions and practices which they

---

[1] C. Dilke, *Greater Britain*, ii. 39.
[2] George Higinbotham in an election address. *Age*, 24 October 1864.
[3] 'The Whigs can no longer call us the party of the classes. If they do, I'll chuck the big cities at their heads', cited W. S. Churchill, *Lord Randolph Churchill*, i. 472.

expected would work most to their advantage. Of these, the two most important were the legislative councils and the constitutional relationship with Britain. In practice the legislative councils proved to be preserves of conservatism, but the relationship with Britain, although it tended to strengthen the hands of conservatives, and at times was quite decisive in political crises, proved to be a much less secure bastion of conservatism than was expected in 1860. Nevertheless, both because of their actual and potential function, basic political policies of the radicals were to limit the powers of, or abolish, the legislative councils and to define and limit the ability of the British government to intervene in Australian affairs. Thus radical democrats tended towards a nationalist political position—seeking to extend the powers of the colonies over their own affairs. In this respect Australia followed one of the main trends in nineteenth century Europe. As seen by Namier,

> the political problems of the European continent in the nineteenth century were posed by the French Revolution; and the basic change which it ushered in was the transition from dynastic to national sovereignty, and a progressive widening of the 'political nation' from the privileged orders to democracy, till the nation came to comprise, in theory at least, the entire people.[4]

The main battleground was Victoria. For this there were both economic and political reasons. The problem of readjustment was most acute there, with pressure of population and extensive unemployment reaching a peak in 1865-6. Together with this, the structure of the two houses of the legislature encouraged the alignment of opposing interests and opinions. While there were divisions within each of the houses of parliament, the main line was between the houses. The Legislative Assembly, drawn mainly from the professional, small landowning, manufacturing, and trading classes, was broadly middle-class in composition. The Legislative Council was recruited from the big business, landowning and pastoral interests, with squatters the largest single group. The greatest change in its composition between 1856 and 1881 was in the ratio of its members: in 1856 fifteen of its thirty members were pastoral tenants (squatters), while in 1881 there were only nine. But to the nine pastoral tenants must be added ten landowners, the majority of whom had previously been pastoral tenants and who had presumably acquired freehold titles to their runs under the selection Acts.[5] Thus squatters,

[4] L. Namier, *Basic Factors in Nineteenth Century European History*, p. 2.
[5] J. E. Mills, 'The Composition of the Victorian Parliament 1856-81'. *Hist. Studies*, vol. ii (1942), no. v.

some of whom had changed their state from Crown tenants or licensees to landowners, still dominated the Council in 1881. Ten years later, when the number of Council members had been increased to forty-eight, there were still twenty-two members described as pastoralists, graziers, or owners of rural property.[6] The other important groups represented in the Council were importers, merchants, and bankers.

The reason for the difference in the composition of the houses is quite obvious. From the second election after responsible government, the Assembly was elected by manhood suffrage. Middle and working classes elected middle-class representatives. A tiny minority of manual workers did find their way into parliament, but by and large the working-class vote went to middle-class candidates. Before 1870 in Victoria, 1886 in Queensland, and 1889 in New South Wales, members of parliament were unpaid. This created great difficulties for working-men who might seek seats in parliament, but clearly it was not the main reason for their failure to appear in larger numbers. The fact is that until the mid-eighties, although many workers contested seats, few were returned. It was not until the labour movement reached a stage of maturity where it articulated a policy of its own, distinct from the radicalism that workers shared with the middle class, that working-men began to appear in parliament in any numbers.

The composition of the Legislative Council is still more easily explained. The qualification for membership of the Council between 1856 and 1868 was the possession of freehold property to the value of £5,000. By 1900 it had been reduced, but it still stood at £1,000. Likewise, the electorate was limited. Possession of freehold or leasehold property or specified academic or professional qualifications limited the electorate to only a fraction of the Assembly electorate. In 1866, a little over nine times as many electors were enrolled for Assembly as for Council election. By 1900, the Assembly electorate was still nearly double that of the Council.

Although the great contests between the Legislative Assembly and the Legislative Council were, in form, disagreements about constitutional principles, to contemporaries, both conservative and radical, they appeared basically as conflicts between classes. To George Higinbotham, the most outstanding leader of the Assembly in the sixties, the Council was the preserve of a selfish wealthy

---

[6] G. Serle, 'The Victorian Legislative Council 1856-1950'. *Hist. Studies*, vol. vi (1954), no. xxii.

minority. In attacking their claim to be compared with English conservatives he said:

> I believe that under the use of the name conservatism and under the abuse of what is called democracy, there is a crafty design which aims at the aggrandizement of a few by a monopoly of the public property and of political power to the exclusion of the mass of the people from political privileges. Well gentlemen, the Legislative Council, I am sorry to say, represents this class in the community.[7]

Sir Frederick Rogers, the Permanent Under-Secretary of the Colonial Office, was satisfied that differences between Council and Assembly were due to the fact that the Council represented a small and wealthy class whose interests were opposed to those of a democratic Assembly.[8] The editorial writer of the conservative *Argus*, while defending the Council, differed from George Higinbotham only in his interpretation of the consequences of Council policy. At the height of the constitutional crisis of 1866, the *Argus* compared Higinbotham's 'determination and recklessness' to that of a cornered rat. Of the Premier, McCulloch, it commented:

> He may fairly boast that he has succeeded by this chicanery in alienating the sympathies and annihilating the opposition of the wealth, respectability, and intelligence of the country ... He may dwell with peculiar satisfaction on the thought that it was he who robbed the property of its birthright and stifled the voice of intelligence—that he has elevated to power those most unworthy of it, and taken power from that section of the community which has the best right to use it, and was most likely to use it best.[9]

This impassioned identification of wealth, respectability and intelligence, however widely it may have been acceptable in Britain in the mid-sixties, was acceptable in Victoria only to the respectable and intelligent who were also wealthy; to the majority, not at all. For the majority, it was the naked defence of property too recently acquired for the justice of the acquisition to be accepted.

Permanent disagreement between Assembly and Council, which on two occasions became acute crises, was a direct outcome of these differences in interest and outlook. In a recent article Serle has summarized the record of the Legislative Council over ninety-five years. He considers that it carried out satisfactorily two of the usual functions of an upper house: initiating and fully debating non-

[7] *Age*, 21 October 1864.
[8] D. P. Clark, 'The Colonial Office and the Constitutional Crisis in Victoria, 1865-68'. *Hist. Studies*, vol. v (1952), no. xviii.   [9] 27 January 1866.

controversial legislation, and improving legislation by clarification and technical revision. But in regard to its revising and deliberative function, Serle concludes:

> It has often, both in its early and later history, done much more than merely delay legislation. Mandate or not, it has applied the veto, on long-term issues often for a decade or more, on short-term issues often finally. Resting on its unusual powers and its clear, constitutional representation of property, it could afford to neglect expressions of the popular will except when such a rare strength of popular feeling was raised that its existence was endangered by the sheer weight of opinion producing a government either prepared to force a long crisis or take extreme unconstitutional action.[10]

In the forty-five years between 1856 and 1901 nine per cent of Bills sent to the Council by the Assembly were defeated in the upper house. More important is the record of the Council in regard to liberal and radical reform legislation. It consistently rejected, amended, or delayed the more important social, political and economic reforms initiated by the Assembly.[11]

Between 1865 and 1868, and 1877 and 1881, the differences between the Council and Assembly flared into open warfare.[12] Because of the light it throws on radical attitudes and because it coloured the relations of Council and Assembly for the rest of the century, the crisis of 1865-8 will be considered in some detail.

The incidents may be stated briefly. The first crisis was precipitated in 1865 by the McCulloch Ministry's introduction of a mildly protective tariff, and was revived in 1867 by the attempt of the Legislative Assembly to make a gift of £20,000 to the wife of the ex-Governor. The tariff resolutions were passed by the Legislative Assembly in January 1865 and, in accordance with well established precedent, collection of duties began. But contrary to precedent the tariff was 'tacked' to an appropriation Bill, in the belief that, despite its known opposition to protective tariffs, the Legislative Council would not be prepared to throw out an appropriation measure. In July the Council 'laid aside' the appropriation Bill, at the same time announcing that it was prepared to pass the appropriation if it were

[10] 'The Victorian Legislative Council', p. 200.
[11] Ibid., pp. 194-7.
[12] See H. G. Turner, *A History of the Colony of Victoria;* G. W. Rusden, *History of Australia*. Of recent works the most important are: K. H. Bailey, 'Self Government in Australia 1860-1900', *Cambridge History of the British Empire*, vol. vii; F. K. Crowley, 'Aspects of the Constitutional Conflict between the two Houses of the Victorian Legislature 1864-68'; J. E. Parnaby, 'The Economic and Political Development of Victoria, 1877-81'.

separated from the tariff. The Government would not follow this course, and the lower house adopted resolutions asserting the sole right of the Assembly to deal with all taxation matters.

Left without funds, the Government adopted an ingenious arrangement with the London Chartered Bank by which the bank lent sums of money to the Governor in Council and then issued a writ for its recovery, under the Crown Remedies and Liabilities Act. By arrangement no defence was entered for the Crown, the Attorney-General confessed judgment for debts and costs, and the amount was paid out of consolidated revenue. This procedure was repeated every few weeks, thus allowing the Government to carry on without obtaining parliamentary approval of the appropriation. A total of £880,000 was freed for the Government's use in this way. In September, the Supreme Court found against the collection of duties but the Government refused to accept the decision without appeal to the Privy Council. In November, the tariff was sent separately to the Council, but the Council rejected it on the ground that it included a preamble in which the Assembly claimed the exclusive right of granting supply. Parliament dissolved for an appeal to the country. The election was a triumph for the Government. Although the Government lost two seats, the Opposition could muster only twenty in a house of seventy-eight.

In the new parliament the tariff was again sent to the Council and again rejected. The Government then resigned. The country was now without a government after a year in which the Government had been able to carry on only by the most unusual expedients. This could not continue, and Sir James McCulloch agreed that he and his colleagues would continue to administer their departments although not strictly in office. At this point, although not officially announced, it became known that the Governor, Sir Charles Darling, was to be recalled. This broke the deadlock. A conference between the houses was arranged, the Government made some concessions on the preamble, and the disputed measures were passed quickly through the Council.

On the day the Bill passed the Council, the Governor's recall was announced. This soon precipitated a new crisis or, rather, gave the old one a new form. Throughout the year the Colonial Office had criticized the actions of the Governor. Sir Frederick Rogers, the Permanent Under-Secretary, considered the financial transactions of the Assembly illegal and the Council's rejection of the 'tack' constitutional. In regard to the collection of duties not approved by the Council, Rogers pointed to the difference between collection when approval of the upper house was expected and collection after rejection by the Council. In November 1865, Darling was instructed by the Colonial Secretary, Edward Cardwell, to cease both the borrowing of money and the collection of duties. After the Colonial Secretary's dispatch had been written but before it reached the Governor, a petition was sent to the Queen by twenty-two Executive Councillors.[13] This followed a petition to the Queen signed by twenty thousand people and forwarded by the Chamber of Commerce.[14] The Executive Councillors restated the complaint of illegal acts by the Government and went on, 'these illegal acts could not have been committed, much less persisted in, if His Excellency the Governor had not given them the sanction of his authority'.[15] The petition was transmitted to the home government accompanied by a long statement by Sir Charles Darling in which he defended the legality of his actions. He bitterly criticized the Executive Councillors, recommended that they should be dismissed from their offices, and stated that he would not be prepared to work with them in future.[16] The Colonial Secretary replied immediately. He once more stated that the Governor had wrongly concurred in illegal acts and had been guilty of partisanship. The present position, he informed the Governor, had resulted 'entirely from your own acts, your adoption of a course of conduct which cannot be justified in law, and your strong denunciation, in which I am wholly unable to concur, of those who have objected to that course'.[17] For these reasons he relieved Darling of his duties and ordered him to return to England immediately.

Public demonstrations, meetings and torchlight processions in protest showed where the sympathy of the people of Melbourne lay. The Colonial Secretary was denounced in unmeasured terms and deputations and addresses of sympathy were made to the Governor. A select committee of the Legislative Assembly prepared an address of appreciation of Sir Charles Darling's services to the colony. As a material expression of its feelings the Assembly voted a gift of £20,000 to Lady Darling and adopted an address to the Queen pray-

---

[13] In Victoria all persons who had been members of a government retained the title of Executive Councillor.
[14] Vic. V. & P. (L.A.), 1867, vol. i. This volume contains papers presented to the imperial parliament, 23 March, 28 May, 28 June, 1866. The papers contain the correspondence between Sir Charles Darling and the Colonial Secretary, together with enclosures. The three references following are to papers contained in this collection.
[15] Enclosure in Despatch No. 152, Darling to Cardwell, 23 December 1865.
[16] Darling to Cardwell No. 152, 23 December 1865.
[17] Cardwell to Darling No. 25, 26 February 1866.

ing her sanction for the gift. The Colonial Secretary's reply to the address was received in February 1867. It was an emphatic declaration that the regulations of the Colonial Service prohibited such gifts so long as the officer concerned remained in the service. However, anxious to accept the gift, Sir Charles Darling resigned. On hearing of this the Government introduced a supplementary appropriation Bill including provision for the grant. This immediately precipitated the new crisis.

The Legislative Council announced that it was prepared to consider the grant only if it were sent up as a separate measure. The Assembly refused to comply and the Legislative Council rejected the Bill. Once more the two houses were locked in a struggle which continued until the end of the year. In December 1867 parliament was dissolved and in the election of February 1868 the ministerial party was returned with an increased majority—fifty-nine members in a House of seventy-eight.

The new Governor (Sir Henry Manners Sutton) was instructed by the Colonial Secretary (the Duke of Buckingham) not to recommend the vote unless the grant was submitted as a separate measure. The Government was adamant and resigned once more. For two months there was no Ministry and the administration of the colony was at a standstill. During this interval the Governor received new instructions—that he should advise the Council to withdraw its opposition to the known will of the people. At length in May a minority Government was formed. It remained in office for three months despite an overwhelming vote of no confidence at its first meeting with the Assembly, only resigning when supply was refused. At this point information was received that Darling had returned to the Colonial Service and that in the new circumstances neither he nor his wife could accept the proposed gift. Darling died in 1870. The Victorian parliament then voted a pension of £1,000 per year for Lady Darling, together with £5,000 for the education of her children.

The very triviality of the issues that paralysed government emphasizes that behind them lay matters of importance. Constitutionally there were two questions, the relative powers of the houses and the competence of the British government to instruct the Governor. Together with this was basic disagreement between the houses on land policy and the tariff. It appears certain that the constitutional issues were raised at this time because of the Council's hostility to the Government's policy on the land and the tariff.

Under the constitution, the powers of the two houses were co-ordinate except in regard to money Bills. They could originate only in the Assembly and could be rejected, but not amended, by the Council. It was in connection with the precedents provided by the imperial parliament in this regard that the Assembly and Council were at issue. The Council claimed that by 'tacking' the tariff to the appropriation Bill the Assembly was attempting to coerce the Council contrary to the established practice of the British parliament. Similarly, the preamble which claimed for the Assembly exclusive power to provide supply was regarded as coercion. Of course the Council was right. The actions of the Assembly were coercive and were quite intentionally so. The tariff was 'tacked' to the appropriation because the Assembly considered that this was the only way that it could be forced through the Council. The other actions of the Assembly were consequential.

In regard to the ability of the British government to intervene, the Assembly, led by George Higinbotham, insisted that it was not competent. The Council not only claimed that Britain could intervene but made every effort to ensure that it did. Altogether, five appeals were made to Britain. The Council twice appealed to the Queen and once to the Privy Council. The Executive Councillors and the Chamber of Commerce also appealed to the Queen. The burden of their plaint was that the actions of the Assembly were unconstitutional and illegal, and that the British government should take action to protect the constitution. Higinbotham's view, simply stated, was that from the establishment of responsible government the powers of the colonial government in respect of internal affairs were identical with those of the British government in Britain. For this purpose, then, the Governor was a 'colonial king' subject to no influence other than that of his local responsible advisers. As a statement of present law, Higinbotham's view was mistaken. But as a statement of the rights of self-government, it was unexceptionable. By the end of the century Higinbotham's views had been established by convention. In this process his assertion of rights as law was a compelling factor in having them established as law. 'Statesman rather than lawyer,' writes Bailey, 'Higinbotham had the future with him.'[18]

The Assembly attempted to coerce the Council and criticized the actions of the British government because it was satisfied that this was the only way to put into effect the policies demanded by the majority of the people. The democratic answer was that the Council must be forced to bend before the popular will. Equally, if the British government supported the Council's position, then the

[18] K. H. Bailey, 'Self Government in Australia 1860-1900', *C.H.B.E.*, xii. 397.

exercise of its powers, too, must be contested. The two major policies insisted on by the majority of the people were the opening of the land and the adoption of protective customs duties.

As we have seen, under the Nicholson Act 1860 and the Duffy Act 1862 squatters rather than selectors acquired the land. In Shann's well-known comment, Duffy's Act 'completed the transfer of Australia Felix in fee simple to the pastoralists'.[19] During 1863 and 1864, in the face of rising popular hostility, the Council rejected two amendments to the Duffy Act designed to safeguard selection. In 1865 the Council was forced to accept Grant's Act, which largely overcame the practice of dummying by making bona fide settlement and improvements precede alienation. In the Council debate on the Bill, great weight was attached to the Government's electoral mandate. The Council was forced to pass it, but was not satisfied with it. The *Age* commented:

> two bills were rejected by the Upper House; and this, the third, would have shared the same fate, had not the recent elections for that branch of the Legislature shown so decidedly the bent of public opinion even amongst the Conservatives and property-holding classes, that further opposition became dangerous.[20]

Although forced by public opinion to pass the Land Act, there is much evidence to suggest that the Council was still bitterly opposed to the policy it was forced to assist in implementing. At the height of the government crisis J. M. Grant, the Minister for Lands, asserted:

> it is from our attempts to break up this gigantic monopoly, and by every means in our power to get the people settled upon the lands, it is from our efforts to place rational men upon the lands ... for the purposes for which God intended them to be, and to employ them for the support of men, instead of for sheep and cattle exclusively—that it is, I believe, that is at the bottom of the crisis.[21]

Darling was convinced that antipathy to the Government's administration of the land was behind the Council's attitude. He wrote to the Colonial Secretary,

> the Ministry are, I have no doubt, obnoxious to many Members of the Council, and the propertied constituencies they represent, not so much on account of the active part they have taken in passing the recent Land Law as for the honesty and good faith

[19] E. O. G. Shann, *An Economic History of Australia*, p. 214.
[20] 25 March 1865.   [21] *Argus*, 8 January 1866.

with which they have endeavoured to carry out the intention of that law, and foil the efforts of interested parties, through the medium of mock lessees, to defeat the *bona fide* settlement of an independent population on the agricultural areas.[22]

Members of the Council did not move from the high ground of constitutional principle on which they had taken up their position, but it is evident in the debates that councillors were actuated by a fear of what they considered to be the dangerous democracy of the Assembly. Perhaps the radicals over-emphasized the importance of the Land Acts in deciding the Council to defend its privileges against the Assembly. But they were correct in believing that the Council was committed to opposing their whole policy, of which the Land Acts were an essential part. The tariff became the other essential largely because of the Council's opposition.

The leading members of the Government were professedly free traders. The tariff itself was only mildly protective and could have been justified, had the Government so desired, as a revenue tariff. But they were prepared to call it protective because of the popular demand for protection. Why was this demand raised at this time?

One answer that has been given to this question is that David Syme, proprietor of the *Age*, by his advocacy of protection forced governments, despite themselves, to introduce measures of protection. Undoubtedly from 1860 onwards, when he took over the direction of the *Age*, David Syme was the most considerable force in Victoria in moulding public opinion. But this was so only because the people were prepared to be influenced in the direction in which he pointed: 'The economic crisis, combined with a nationalistic, anti-English sentiment, explains why he and others came to advocate the protectionist remedy for a society faced with a sudden cessation of prosperity'.[23] Before Syme began his campaign for protection, the idea was already finding a place in democratic programmes. The Victorian Tariff League was active from early in 1859,[24] and protectionist candidates had stood in the elections of 1859. On the other hand, the pastoralists and the conservatives generally were in favour of free trade. As La Nauze points out, protection was in the circumstances a 'natural' idea that has occurred to many people beside Syme.

Like other Australian theorists of the nineteenth century, Syme added little or nothing to economic or political thought, but his

[22] Darling to Cardwell, 25 September 1865. Vic. *V. & P. (L.A.)*, 1867, vol. i.
[23] J. A. La Nauze, *Political Economy in Australia*, p. 119.
[24] *Age*, 24 March 1859.

importance lies in the fact that he gave a theoretical gloss to what most Victorians of the poorer classes wanted to believe. His views were simple and were stated and restated pungently and emotionally in the *Age*. Tariff policy, he considered, should be shaped to encourage the growth of manufactures from raw materials produced in the country. Such growth could not occur whilst Australian manufacturers continued to be exposed to the overwhelming competition of 'low-priced (not cheap) articles, made of refuse material especially for the Australian market, with which we are inundated from the crowded factories and workshops of Great Britain'.[25] So long as this continued Australian manufactures would not develop, with the result that capital would leave the country and avenues of employment would close. Australia, he said, was specially suited for the production of certain goods, as for example wines, brandy, oil, malt drinks, preserved fruits, vegetable dyes and similar commodities. As time went on the list of articles lengthened. The immediate advantage to the nation's economy that would flow from the encouragement of such manufactures appeared obvious to people whose avenues of employment were narrowing. Furthermore, in longer perspective, unless manufacturing industry were encouraged, Syme believed that Australia would become a nation of people destitute of manufacturing and scientific skill. In his words, which are typical of his forceful language:

> in a few short years hence, if this pre-arranged practice of national industrial abortion is continued amongst us, the people of Australia will be as utter strangers to all scientific skill and practical dexterity in the arts and manufactures of highly civilized nations as are the Bedouins of Barbary, or the Tartars of Central Asia.[26]

His was clearly a nationalistic doctrine.

Land policy and protection were the twin pillars of radical policy, and the country insisted that they must be implemented. If constitutional difficulties stood in the way, then the constitution must be bent to the will of the people. As the crisis developed, so far as the radicals were concerned the issues were simplified. They were stated by George Higinbotham. The Council was an oligarchy of wealth protecting itself behind its privileges and the conservative effect of the relationship with Britain. The appeals to Britain by the Council and the recall of Darling turned the issue, from the radicals' point of view, into a struggle for self-government. In this struggle the conservatives were seen as people prepared to trade the rights of

---

[25] Cited A. Pratt, *David Syme*, p. 119.   [26] Ibid.

self-government for the protection of their property. In a forceful denunciation of the appeal to the Queen, Higinbotham said:

> I believe at this moment—and I hope I do them no injustice—that the Melbourne merchants would gladly purchase a continuance of their importing monopoly by the surrender of our civil government. I believe the pastoral class would gladly, on the same terms, effect the defeat of the agricultural interest.[27]

In regard to the competence of the Colonial Office to intervene, Higinbotham's views were equally decisive. He agreed that the Colonial Secretary had power to recall the Governor but argued that he did not have power to censure the Government or comment on the legality of its acts. If he did have such powers, Higinbotham insisted, responsible government was not a reality, and so long as he continued to exercise such supposed powers, real sovereignty would rest in the Colonial Office and not with the people of the colony. In a speech which became famous because it seemed to show the realities behind Colonial Office intervention, Higinbotham declared—

> I believe it might be said with perfect truth that the million and a half of Englishmen who inhabit these colonies, and who during the last fifteen years have believed they possessed self-government, have been really governed during the whole of that time by a person named Rogers. He is the chief clerk in the Colonial-office. Of course he inspires every Minister who enters the department, year after year, with Colonial-office traditions, Colonial-office policy, Colonial-office ideas. His views form the law for his chief, while the chief writes in imperious, and almost imperial style to the representative of the Crown.[28]

There were no important immediate results of the conflict. But in long term it contributed to the reform of the Council and was an important incident in the evolution of the concept of independence within the empire. The effect on opinion was to consolidate the attitude to which both radicals and conservatives would adhere for a generation.

The crisis of 1877-81 was similar to the earlier one in that it was the result of protracted disagreement between the two houses. Throughout the second crisis, the precedents established in the first were quoted by both sides. In the minds of both voters and poli-

---

[27] *Parl. Deb.* (Vic.), 1866, ii. 240.
[28] *Parl. Deb.* (Vic.), 1869, ix. 2137. This citation is from a speech in which Higinbotham stated at length his views on the relations between the governments of Britain and Victoria. See also E. E. Morris, *A Memoir of George Higinbotham*.

ticians the main issue was the same—the relative powers of Assembly and Council. As in the previous crisis, the Governor was strongly attacked by the Council, but there was the difference that on all except one minor question the actions of the Governor were backed by the Colonial Secretary. No doubt the Governor, Sir George Bowen, reinforced by the precedents established between 1865 and 1869, acted with more circumspection than did Sir Charles Darling, but it is also significant that the Colonial Secretary did not deviate from the position that the Governor was bound to act according to the advice of his responsible ministers.

As with the earlier crisis, the incidents may be described briefly. Payment of members had been introduced in 1871 and had continued since then by a series of short-term Acts. Instead of renewing the Act in 1877, the newly appointed government, led by the radical-protectionist Graham Berry, merely included the amount necessary in an appropriation Bill. The Council rejected the appropriation on the grounds that it was a 'tack' intended to coerce the Council. The Government replied by dismissing a large number of senior civil servants including all the judges of the County Courts, Courts of Mines, the Court of Insolvency, and chairmen of Courts of General Sessions. All police magistrates, and coroners, together with a sprinkling of officers of varying grades from practically all other departments of government were also unceremoniously dismissed. Although the majority of the legal officers were restored to their positions, 'Black Wednesday' was a severe shock to Victorian society. The Government explained the retrenchment by the need to economize in face of the rejection of the appropriation.[29]

Such measures, however, could solve neither the short-term need for funds nor the long-term purpose of clipping the wings of the Council. So the Premier advised the Governor that it was perfectly constitutional for funds to be made available simply on the vote of the Assembly. The Governor accepted the advice and the Council, recognizing defeat, was forced to pass the appropriation.

The next round opened with a Bill to amend the constitution designed to deprive the Council of all power to reject money Bills of any kind. It also provided that, in regard to other Bills, the Council should have only a suspensive veto. The Bill was passed by an overwhelming majority in the Assembly, but the Council refused to consider it. Likewise, the Assembly refused to debate a rival measure initiated in the Council, which aimed to reform the Council

---

[29] The main collection of printed papers on this crisis are contained in Vic. V. & P. (L.A.) 1879-80, vol. ii.

by reducing the property qualifications for the franchise and for membership. The Government then appealed to Britain. Graham Berry led a mission to England to request the British government to legislate by Act of the imperial parliament to reform the Council. Britain refused, and Berry returned to Australia. A further attempt in 1880 to replace the elective by a nominee Council also failed. But in 1881 the Council agreed to an Act which reduced the property qualification for the Council vote, increased the number of Council members from thirty to forty-two, and reduced Councillors' terms of office from ten to six years. This was a modest reform as compared with what Berry had attempted, and had little effect on the composition or policy of the Council.

Why did the permanent disagreement between Council and Assembly flare into open battle in 1877? Basically because the members of the Council saw in Graham Berry an immediate threat to the interests they represented and the privileges they had so sedulously guarded. The policy with which Berry went to the country was centred round the by now tried radical slogans of protection and reform of the Council. To this was added a land tax of the type that he had failed to pass in the previous session. Unpopular as these policies were with the pastoralists, merchants and wealthy and conservative groups generally, Berry appears to have represented for them something even more dangerous—mob rule. Neil Black, conservative pastoralist of the Western District, and member of the Council, was voicing the fears of his class when he wrote: 'Communism is the order of the day with stump orators. We are fast heading in that direction and may reach that goal much sooner than is expected.'[30] The *Argus* commented on the 1877 election result in a bitter editorial, which read in part:

> considered as a whole, we may safely say that the new House will fitly represent the ignorance and passion of the country; and if it should be found that no particular harm follows its instalment in power, we may safely attribute the fact to its incapacity and not to its want of will to work mischief . . . the result of the elections on the whole is most disastrous and discouraging to the party whose object all along has been to preserve law and order, and secure good government.[31]

The land tax was the first important legislative act of the new parliament. It provided for a tax of 1¼ per cent on the capital value of land, the value to be estimated according to its carrying capacity.

[30] Cited Parnaby, 'The Economic and Political Development of Victoria', p. 61.   [31] 12 May 1877.

Properties of less than 640 acres, or of value less than £2,500, were exempt from the tax, and in larger estates the first £2,500 of value was not to be taxable. The Premier frankly admitted that the tax was progressive and was directed at what James Service, a more conservative and careful member, called the Assembly's 'natural enemies, the squatters'.[32] Its main immediate aim was to raise revenue, but its long-term purpose was in accord with the established policy of the Assembly, namely, to 'break up the great estates'. Berry denounced the land monopolists and espoused the cause of the small holders and potential small holders.[33] The Act is important in the evolution of radical policy towards the land. It was the first of the land-tax measures which were to become increasingly popular in all colonies in the last decade of the century and after. It provided the pattern that would be followed in the attempts to compensate for diminished revenue from land sales, as well as imposing an impost on the unpopular monopolists. Whether or not its authors really believed that it would assist in making land available for the small settler is less certain. But at least it provided a popular slogan and helped to retain the support for the Government of the diverse groups who had returned it to power.

The Assembly carried the tax by fifty-nine votes to five. The Council delayed but finally reluctantly accepted the second reading by a small majority. They were unprepared to fight the Assembly on an issue that had the clearly expressed support of the country. The crisis over the appropriation began soon after, on ground the Council considered more favourable to itself.

Council and Assembly were agreed that the crisis of 1877-80 was merely a violent phase of the political warfare that had broken out in 1865. The Council's position was most fully expressed in a statement submitted to the British government in December 1878.[34] In essence, its argument was that the Assembly had consistently misused its special powers under Section 56 of the Constitution (over money Bills) to force through other measures not intended to be covered by these powers. In this, it had attempted to exceed the powers claimed by the House of Commons. This position was the more intolerable, the Council insisted, because the Council, unlike the House of Lords, was a representative body, even though its electorate was only a minority of the community. In effect, the Council claimed for itself the function of protecting the minority against the tyranny of the majority. In the absence of an effective

[32] *Parl. Deb.* (Vic.), 1877-8, xxvi. 573.   [33] Ibid., pp. 504-5.
[34] Vic. *V. & P. (L.A)*, 1879-80, vol. ii: Paper no. 43, pp. 140-4.

opposition in the lower house it considered that it performed 'the functions which of right belong to the opposition in the Assembly'. Therefore its powers should be not less than those of the Lords, but greater.

In regard to the Governor, Sir George Bowen, the Council, like its predecessor, was full of complaint. In its view the Governor had acted in collusion with the Assembly, thus rendering possible its coercive career. This interpretation of the Governor's role, together with the refusal of the British government to intervene, strained the Council's repeatedly expressed loyalty to the Crown, a dilemma it resolved by attributing the greatest weight of blame to the Governor personally.

Graham Berry's views were stated equally succinctly in a memorandum to the Governor for transmission to Britain. In four thousand five hundred words he traced the obstructive career of the Council since 1865, stressed the fact that it had been at odds with every Governor since responsible government was established, noted that it represented a small and wealthy class, and concluded that its power to thwart the will of the people, as expressed in the Assembly, must be curbed.[35]

Thus the Council and the Assembly either directly or by implication interpreted their continuing differences as a conflict between classes. In the language of the Council, the difference resolved itself into a defence of the minority against the tyranny of the multitude. In the language of the Assembly it was the assertion of the rights of the majority against the privileges of the capitalists who were, in the minds of the Assembly, the squatters and the commercial and banking interests.

Victoria was to witness many more disagreements between Council and Assembly but none so protracted or so bitter as those between 1865 and 1880. This was less the result of reform of the Council than of the gradual disintegration of the front built up in the Assembly. Up to 1880, squatters and commercial men were more or less isolated in a community in which workers, manufacturers, selectors, and professional men accepted an identity of interest and opinion. But by 1880 fissures were beginning to appear in this front.

[35] 'When it is borne in mind that a Victorian Governor mixes habitually in social intercourse with the members of the Council and with the class from which the Council is drawn, and may have his life embittered by their hostility, the fact that Sir Henry Barkly, Sir Charles Darling, Lord Canterbury, and Sir George Bowen, our Governors since the Constitution was proclaimed, have all declined to side with the Council against the Assembly, may be taken as presumptive evidence that the Assembly is not unreasonable in its claims.' Graham Berry, Paper no. 43, p. 151. Vic. *V. & P. (L.A.)* 1879-80, vol. ii.

Manufacturers, some of them now established for twenty or thirty years, were beginning to find common interests with the commercial classes. And workers were more consistently at odds with their employers.

In New South Wales, differences between the upper and lower houses were not unknown, but were never so protracted or so acrimonious as in Victoria. The Land Act of 1861 was passed by the Council, but only after negotiation and some pressure. In 1872, Parkes attempted to reform the Council when it rejected a Bill to deal with border customs duties, but allowed the matter to lapse when the Council threw out the amending measure. No further attempt was made until 1894-5, when the Council blocked a government Bill imposing direct taxation. Again the attempted reform failed.

The explanation of this difference between the colonies will be found in a number of factors. Because the New South Wales Council was nominated, a determined Government could threaten, as it did in 1860, to swamp a recalcitrant council. This safety valve was rarely used, but the fact that it existed made for more amiable relations between the houses. More important, perhaps, was the fact that a nominated chamber was less inclined to claim powers fully co-ordinate with the representative house. It tended to be satisfied with a lesser function. Also a careful examination of the composition of the lower houses in the two colonies might reveal significant differences between them. Although both were characteristically middle-class, it seems that squatters were more consistently represented in the New South Wales Assembly than in Victoria.[36] If this is so, it would tend to blunt the edge of the difference between the houses in New South Wales.

In the last resort, however, the explanation is to be found in public opinion. Gold did not produce the same dramatic transformation of society in New South Wales as in Victoria. In the southern colony, the decade of the fifties began with separation from New South Wales and the establishment of a completely new government. It ended with a population seven times greater than it had been at the beginning, and with large numbers of people faced with the dire need to find alternative employment, from which they believed they were cut off by the squatter monopoly of the land. Politically, the decade had witnessed responsible government established five years

---

[36] This is no more than a suggestion. It can only be proved or disproved by further painstaking work of the kind embodied in the published and unpublished work of A. W. Martin and J. E. Parnaby.

after separation and a year after massive demonstrations of democratic sentiment on goldfields and in Melbourne. Thus new political institutions hardened in this mould of social conflict, in which the monopolists directly controlled the Council and the Assembly was responsive to the pressure of the masses. In effect, class differences were institutionalized in the relationships between Council and Assembly.

By the time responsible government was established, New South Wales had existed for sixty-seven years and enjoyed some kind of political institutions, operated by at least a section of the community, for a generation. Thus, the political institutions adopted in 1856 were less an innovation and more a development of existing ones. The new Legislative Council occupied an entirely different constitutional position from the old but it was, in an important sense, a continuation of the first representative body. To some degree it inherited the popular consent to its existence that was denied to the newer institution in Victoria.

Possibly more important than the causes were the consequences of their differences. Whilst in neither colony did political parties in the modern sense, or in the sense employed in contemporary Britain, emerge before the end of the eighties, the institutionalized political divisions in Victoria provided an external discipline that canalized opinion. The radical programme was a relatively integrated whole confirmed in its correctness, in the mind of its supporters, by the opposition of the Council and the classes there represented. On the other hand in New South Wales (although, as A. W. Martin has discovered,[37] there was some order behind the kaleidoscopic alliances of individuals and factions), public opinion was not so consistently arrayed against recognizable opponents, and supported a more or less consistent policy. In the short run, this meant that the atmosphere of Victorian politics up to the eighties was more radical than that of any other colony. In the long run, in the late eighties and nineties, the by now traditional Victorian radicalism impeded the emergence of a distinctive labour party. In New South Wales and Queensland, its absence was one less brake on the political and social forces that were producing such parties.

---

[37] Martin. 'Political Groupings in New South Wales, 1872-89'.

4

Trade Unions and Politics, 1855-1880

The poor docile working-classes of England had been content to labor on and permit the upper classes to think and act for them. . . . The reason why working-men had not hitherto occupied the position they should was because they did not know their best friends. Working-men must look for friends among themselves.[1]

How is the problem of the greatest possible amount of happiness for the greatest number to be effected? I will tell you; by regulating the number of hours that a man shall work in a day, sufficient to feed, clothe, and educate the population, and with a due regard to the advantages in which we should share by the introduction of labour saving machines, we should also prevent the pernicious tendency to over production which has too often proved disastrous to many of the great manufacturing centres of the world.[2]

THE permanent trades hall which Melbourne unionists built in the late seventies and eighties, to replace the temporary structure opened in 1859, was both a spacious home for the thriving trade-union movement and a symbol of solid achievement. As significant as the building itself are the men that the unionists chose to honour in their new home. In the Council Room there were four portraits and four busts. George Higinbotham, by then Chief Justice, was represented twice: by a portrait in the place of highest honour over the dais, and by one of the four busts. Sir Charles Darling, the 'People's Governor', and Wilson Grey, the leader of the convention, were there with Charles Jardine Don, the first working-man to sit in the Victorian parliament, and Benjamin Douglas, first chairman of the Trades Hall Committee.[3] With the exception of Don, the political heroes of unionists were the middle-class leaders of Victorian radicalism.

Trade unions developed as non-political institutions. In the minds of workers their function was of a different kind from the business of politics. Had this continued to be so, trade unions would have but a small place in the history of working-class politics. But the

[1] The Chairman of Melbourne Trades Hall Committee (Mr Eves). *Argus*, 25 May 1859.
[2] Charles Jardine Don, cited J. Norton (ed.), *The History of Capital and Labour*, p. 130. [3] Ibid., pp. 136-7.

69

fact is that, despite the conscious efforts of unionists to maintain the political independence of unionism, unions were impelled increasingly to participate in political activity. The final outcome of this process was the formation of the Labour Party. But this is to anticipate. Here we are merely concerned with the early development of unionism and its relationship with politics. Workers as citizens, by and large, supported the radical cause. As unionists they sought to achieve other, non-political, ends, but in the process found it increasingly necessary to employ political means.

The first effect of gold on unionism was to break up the unions that had been painfully born during the forties. But when the first gold fever was over, new unions were formed and old ones re-formed on firmer foundations than in the past.

In different countries and at different times the stimulus to union organization has varied. Intolerable working conditions or starvation wages have at times produced desperate combinations to resist the exactions of employers or advance the demands of workers. More generally, however, permanent organizations have arisen in conditions where shortage of labour or high profits have strengthened the bargaining position of employees and encouraged the employers to make concessions. So it was in Australia.

In 1855-6 large quantities of gold were still being produced, and although the day of the individual miner was rapidly passing, Australian society remained fluid from the effects of gold. The numbers on the Victorian goldfields were increasing and, despite the recession of 1854, skilled workers in Melbourne, and to a lesser degree in Sydney, were still at a premium. This was particularly true in the building industry, which was booming under the impact of the wealth produced from gold. Acute shortage of labour in the two or three years after 1851 probably doubled real wages, even though prices rose. And despite recurrent downward pressures, they were never again to fall below a level considerably above that which had prevailed before gold, or had been customary in Britain. As Coghlan puts it, before gold

> the standard of labour in England was the practical test of the conditions of the working classes in Australia, who were thought well off, simply because their earnings enabled them to enjoy comforts beyond the reach of their fellows in the Old World. Since the gold era this has been changed and the standard, which Australian workers have made for themselves, has now no reference to that of any other country.[4]

[4] Coghlan, *Labour and Industry in Australia*, ii. 706-7.

TRADE UNIONS AND POLITICS

Demands for higher wages and resistance to wage reduction have an important place in the history of Australian unionism, but the central question with which workmen were concerned in 1855-6 was the length of the working day. For various groups of workers, it continued to be so until at least 1890.

Reduction of the hours of labour had been an important component of the social programme of chartism and of the practical humanitarianism of the men who pressed the Ten Hours Bill through the British parliament. It was of particular importance for those who saw the future welfare of the working class in terms of their moral and intellectual improvement. This continued to be a major theme in the more conservative English unionism of the third quarter of the century. Typical of the attitude is the speech in 1861 of George Potter, secretary of the Council of United Building Trades and editor of the *Beehive*. Having advanced economic reasons for the nine-hour day, he went on:

> But this question was not a pounds, shillings and pence question with him, he based the demand for this reduction in the hours of labour on the *right* of the workman to have his intellectual facilities properly educated, physical toil is not the only toil in which the energies of the operatives ought to be expended. All other arguments and considerations in favour of this reduction though important in themselves, are subordinate and inferior to the sacred and God-given right of every working man to a proper moral and intellectual education.[5]

In fact, reduction in hours of work became something more than a particular trade-union policy. It was regarded as the means of regenerating the working class.

In Australia, not the nine-, but the eight-hour day, was achieved by many skilled workers in 1855-6. In Melbourne, the hours of stonemasons, plasterers, bricklayers, carpenters and joiners, slaters, plumbers, and painters, were reduced to eight per day, and fortyeight per week. In Sydney only the masons gained the reduced hours, the other building workers failing in their claim. Plasterers were successful in 1861, but bricklayers and carpenters continued to work longer hours.

In Melbourne, the demand for the eight-hour day was the result of the formation of unions in the building trades, and its achievement a stimulus to continued organization. It is not clear to what extent the separate unions arose from the initiative of the Eight Hours League, which represented all the building trades. But it is

[5] Cited J. B. Jefferys (ed.), *Labour's Formative Years 1849-1879*, p. 40.

certain that this league was decisive in having the principle generally adopted and then in maintaining firm links between the several unions. The adoption of the eight hours was the work of the league. In March 1856 a public meeting of building workers, presided over by Abraham Linacre, a master builder, decided on the motion of Thomas Smith and James Stephens, a Welsh chartist, that as from the 21st April no more than eight hours would be worked.[6] Linacre announced that employers in the building trade had met and agreed to adopt the eight hours but that some of the big contractors had refused. James Stephens was in favour of all members of the league refusing to work longer hours from the appointed date.

April 21st saw the first of what was to become the most characteristic and important of all Australian working-class festivals. A procession of building workers through the streets of Melbourne was followed by a meeting 'in honour of the day being the first on which the system of working only for eight hours was to come into operation'. It was reported to the meeting that only two contractors were refusing to accept the eight-hours principle, and it was decided that no member of the league would in future work more than eight hours.[7]

From then on the eight-hours festival with its procession and picnic became the focal day of trade-union life. It became the occasion for celebration by those who had won 'the boon' and the inspiration for those who were yet to achieve it. What the eight hours meant to workers is to be seen at the opening of the temporary Trades Hall in 1859. A wooden structure, built on land granted by the government, its erection was a result of the close co-operation between unions, achieved in the eight-hours movement. When completed, the hall itself and the committee appointed to manage it were the centre of the union movement.

At the opening ceremony speakers were lyrical on the significance of the eight hours. The toast of the evening was 'the Eight Hours' System: may its physical, intellectual, moral, and social advantages be extended to every member of the human family'.[8] The chairman of the Trades Hall Committee proudly emphasized the achievement.

> This hall [he said] was the first ever erected by working men, and the reason for this was to be found in the fact that in other countries, although working-men had struggled to obtain the boon of eight hours' labor, they had never been able to obtain it. The poor docile working-classes of England had been content to labor on and permit the upper classes to think and act for them.

[6] *Argus*, 28 March 1856.   [7] Ibid., 22 April 1856.   [8] Ibid., 25 May 1859.

While being far from an accurate picture of trade-union activity in Britain, the words of the chairman expressed an attitude that became more and more common amongst Australian unionists. They became convinced that their standards of hours and wages, which made possible a reasonably satisfying life, were better than those commonly existing in Europe. There was substance in this conviction, but the reason for the difference was perhaps as much the wealth of the country and the weak bargaining position of the employers as the manly independence of the artisans. On the other hand, the relatively favourable conditions in Australia gave to workers the leisure, the energy, and the security to build permanent organizations that were powerful factors in resisting downward pressure on their conditions in periods of economic difficulties. The firm core of unionism at this time, and for a generation to come, were the artisans who had achieved a standard of living which made possible a sober respectability that both secured, and in their view justified, the maintenance of their relatively favoured position. At the opening of the Trades Hall one of the speakers pointed to the hall itself, and to the decorous family groups seated around the trestle tables just cleared of the remains of a festive meal as evidence 'that the traducers who said, eight hours means drinking and riotous living, were wrong'. For the leaders of unionism, the eight hours meant leisure and moral and intellectual improvement.

In Britain, the collapse of the chartist movement in 1848 was followed in the fifties and sixties by the building of the great amalgamated unions of artisans, on the model of the Amalgamated Society of Engineers, seeking strength through the accumulation of funds, the avoidance of strikes when possible, and efficient organization. They aimed to achieve their industrial objectives by arbitration and parliamentary lobbying for trade-union measures. Under the leadership of the small group of full-time officials that the Webbs called the 'Junta', a powerful and permanent trade-union structure was created. Conservative in outlook and method, it nevertheless was not infrequently forced into industrial conflict to defend established standards. Similarly, the movements of national liberation on the Continent, notably in Italy, and the Civil War in the United States, together with the absence of the vote for workingmen, drew the unions into political activity on the liberal and radical side. In the early sixties, the London Trades Council played an important role in leading the union industrial and political movement on a national scale. With the first Trades Union Congress in 1868, leading to the formation of the Parliamentary Committee of the Trades Union Congress in 1871, a permanent national leadership with a continuing political function was formed. From then on an important part of trade-union activity was the agitation for legislative enactments of interest to the unions.

The Australian unions were, like their English counterparts, unions of skilled workers. The general pattern of their development towards political activity was also similar, but within the pattern there were significant differences. Industry was in the infant stage, though it expanded in the sixties and seventies. Only the building trades employed large bodies of workers from the fifties onwards. Amalgamation on a national scale was precluded by the isolation of the colonies from one another and was rendered unnecessary within each colony by the concentration of population and industry in Sydney and Melbourne. The exception to this was the Amalgamated Society of Engineers, which was established at Sydney in 1852 by migrant ironworkers as a branch of the great English union.

The general political issues for the unionists were also different, since representative democratic institutions had already been won. Workers exercised their votes, and, as we have seen, under radical middle-class leadership, particularly in Victoria, they were a considerable factor in the politics of the sixties and seventies. But perhaps the most important difference between Britain and Australia was the early success of the Australian unions. In 1860, the London Building Trades fought for the nine-hour day. Not only did they fail to achieve it, but they were forced into a defence of the right to organize against the concerted presentation of the 'Document' by the masters. In Australia four years earlier the eight-hour day had become an established fact for the then most numerous organized body of workers. In the sixties the main emphasis in Australian unionism was on the maintenance and extension of a principle that had already been conceded in respect of some artisans. Thus, in the sixties and seventies, the pressures on organized workers towards political action by unions were much less than in the old country.

Nevertheless, it would be quite wrong to imagine that there was unbroken progress from the fifties onwards towards the general application of the eight-hours principle. At the end of the fifties in Victoria a forty-eight hour week was usual for skilled building workers and some unskilled occupations associated with building, for some skilled metal workers, and for a few other skilled occupations such as shipwrights and saddlers. In New South Wales the achievement of the short hours was both less general and more ephemeral. During the sixties—a decade of readjustment and recurrent depression—the eight-hour day was not extended but rather tended to be withdrawn by employers—cabinet-makers, for example, had reverted to ten hours by 1863. Even in the building trades adverse economic conditions caused partial disintegration of many unions, and in practice the eight hours was lost even in trades where it nominally existed. In Melbourne during the sixties, however, unionists still continued to celebrate 'the boon' and agitate for its extension. By 1870, the eight-hour procession, which included only unions whose members claimed to be working the eight hours, was three thousand strong and represented eleven unions.[9] Despite the weakened bargaining position of unionists resulting from the depressed economic conditions, the eight-hour day survived in some trades and lived as a principle to be fought for in all.

The eight-hour day became a political question in two ways. Firstly, as a policy common to all unionists it was a link between organizations which in other respects were separatist, sectional, and jealous of their independence. The celebration of the eight-hour day was merely the most vivid expression of this community of interest. Secondly, from as early as 1859 unionists were beginning to seek legislative enforcement of the shorter working day. In time this became one of the more important planks in the trade-union political platform that was built piecemeal out of the industrial experience of the unionists.

In 1859, Charles Jardine Don moved in the Legislative Assembly that 'all future Government contracts should be let on the understanding that eight hours shall be considered a day's work'.[10] He argued that this would directly affect some eight thousand men and indirectly establish the principle throughout the colony. Despite some government support, the motion was withdrawn. In 1870, the Victorian government agreed that in future all government contracts should stipulate an eight-hour day. In the meantime, as a result of the activity of a Short Hours League, a Bill had been introduced into the Victorian parliament in 1869 to make eight hours the working day in the colony. It failed to pass, as did further Bills in 1871 and 1873. The eight hours was eventually to become general not as a result of legislation but by the example set by governments and by agreement between the various unions and their employers. On the other hand, the fact that unionists agreed on this single aim and supported legislation to achieve it was an important step on the road to a trade-union political policy.

The emphasis on the achievement and partially successful defence

[9] Ibid., 22 April 1870.   [10] *Victorian Hansard*, v. 111.

of the eight hours during the sixties should not be permitted to obscure the very real problems faced by the working class during the depressed sixties. From 1857 in New South Wales and Victoria there was extensive unemployment which probably reached a peak in 1866. From then until 1872 in all colonies, including Queensland, a large though fluctuating number of men continued to be unemployed. The worst affected were the unskilled, but many artisans suffered extended periods without work. The reaction of the unemployed, in the absence of the dismal apparatus of a poor law, was to demand government relief works and the cessation of assisted immigration. Artisan members of unions were to some extent protected by the unemployment benefits of their unions or friendly societies; for the rest the alternatives were destitution and private charity or government-sponsored relief works.

From the eighteen-forties onward, unemployment, downward pressure on wages and working conditions, and assisted immigration (to a lesser extent, unassisted immigration) were considered by the working class to be sides of the same coin. In Coghlan's view:

> the great body of the wage-earners have been, if not hostile, entirely indifferent to taking steps to introduce new population. They see in the newcomer a competitor for employment, and they fear that, where he is not a competitor, he may bring with him a low standard of living.[11]

If anything, Coghlan's generalization understates the opposition of the working class to immigration, particularly during periods of unemployment. For obvious reasons this hostility to immigration was directed most firmly towards state-assisted immigration.

Although during the gold decade the number of assisted migrants was a smaller proportion of the total than at other times, it was in sum a substantial number. Between 1851 and 1860 more than seventy thousand migrants reached New South Wales with government aid. In Victoria more than thirty thousand arrived between 1851 and 1853, the numbers declining in the second half of the decade. With responsible government, pressure was exerted on governments to reduce the numbers, or indeed to cease assisting migrants entirely. During the sixties the numbers at first increased and then declined rapidly although unevenly as between the colonies. Victoria reached a post-gold-rush peak in 1863, and then the numbers gradually dwindled to a mere five in 1880. For the rest of the century there were none. In New South Wales, also, migration reached a peak in

[11] *Labour and Industry in Australia*, ii. 874.

1863 and thence dropped more rapidly than in Victoria to none in 1870. However, during the seventies and early eighties the numbers gradually built up again to a peak of more than eight thousand in 1883. Queensland was more consistent than the southern colonies. With the exception of 1868, when there was a mere handful, the annual intake of assisted migrants never fell below a thousand, reached nearly nine thousand in 1874, and was on average more than thirteen thousand between 1882 and 1887, with a peak year of a little less than twenty-five thousand in 1883.

The migrants of the late fifties and sixties entered communities in which there were always some unemployed, the numbers of whom were, at times, very large indeed. From 1857, with seasonal variations, unemployment became gradually worse until 1866, when conditions began to improve. Queensland differed from New South Wales and Victoria only in that conditions were relatively good until 1866, when widespread unemployment occurred suddenly and persisted until 1872. Whereas in the southern colonies depressed conditions resulted in pressure to increase hours of work, and minor reductions in wages, in Queensland there was less unemployment but a substantial reduction in wages.

The working class reacted to these conditions by demands, organized in 1857 and reaching a crescendo in 1866, for government works and the cessation of assisted immigration. Deputations waited on the governments, public works gave temporary relief, benevolent societies set up soup kitchens, and a number of unions attempted to warn British workers of the position in Australia. One such warning, sent to Robert Applegarth, was published by him in the London *Star* in January 1867. The short-term effect, as the difficulties in Australia became known, was to reduce the attraction of Australia for potential migrants. It was also partly responsible for the changing policy of governments. For example there was no new provision for assisting migrants to New South Wales between 1867 and 1872. Although some were assisted in these years, it was with money previously voted. The long-term effect of these conditions was that the persistent working-class attitude of opposition to immigration became in due course a more or less settled policy written into union programmes.

The attitude of workers towards fiscal protection in Victoria has already been touched on. In the opinion of the working class there was a close connection between persistent unemployment and the free flow of manufactured goods into the colony. Even in New South Wales the select committee investigating 'the condition of the working class in Sydney', which reported in 1860, hinted at the desirability of protecting certain industries.[12]

Thus, by the end of the sixties the trade unions were probably weaker than they had been at the beginning. Yet, despite the depressed conditions, the principle of the eight hours had been kept alive and, except in Queensland, real wages had not fallen much below the standard attained in the fifties. The attitude towards immigration had hardened, and the belief that governments should provide relief work for the unemployed was generally held by both organized and unorganized workers. Protection had become a settled working-class policy in Victoria and had some adherents amongst working-men in New South Wales.

With the seventies began twenty years of prosperity only occasionally and briefly interrupted. Under these conditions the trade unions flourished. By 1880 the unions of the skilled trades—mainly the building workers or men engaged in the various iron trades—had consolidated their organization.[13] The core of the union movement was still the crafts, which had first effectively organized in the fifties. By 1880, however, new groups of workers had begun to form unions. In 1872, a union of gold-miners was formed at Bendigo with the aim of securing an eight-hour shift, resisting attempts to reduce wages and to employ Chinese, and advocating legislation for the regulation of mining. Two years later an important step was taken when twelve local miners' unions amalgamated to form the Amalgamated Miners' Association of Victoria. The main immediate objective of the amalgamated union was legislation to regulate conditions in mines. With the passage of the Regulation of Mines and Machinery Act of 1877, its objective was achieved and the union fell on lean days until it was revitalized in the eighties. Closer association between unions in the same industry by means of amalgamation or federation was to become a characteristic trend during the eighties; during the seventies the first experiments were made. In 1874, seamen's unions were formed in Sydney and Melbourne. A year later they federated and promptly proved the value of federation by winning a strike against the employment of Chinese on ships. But these were the exceptions. The typical union during the seventies was the small local union of skilled workers protecting the interests of its members and the standards of its craft against pressures from employers and from other workers.

[12] N.S.W. *V. & P. (L.A.)*, 1859-60, vol. iv.
[13] J. T. Sutcliffe, *A History of Trade Unionism in Australia*, pp. 27-31, contains details of unions formed or revived between 1870 and 1880.

As the unions matured, their position under the law became a matter of concern to them. This concern was heightened by the efforts of British unionists to gain legal recognition. The passage of the British Trade Union Act in 1871 and the storm of protest from the unions against the Criminal Law Amendment Act with which it was accompanied, stimulated interest in the question in Australia. Until the passage of the Trade Union Act of 1871, unions in Britain were not entities recognized by the law. The greatest disability that this entailed was that, as unions, they were unable to hold property. Thus, if an official absconded with union funds there was no legal remedy. This disability was overcome by the Act of 1871. But at the same time the Criminal Law Amendment Act (originally included as a clause of the Trade Union Bill) reaffirmed and even increased the stringency of penalties for picketing, intimidation, molestation, and watching and besetting. As interpreted by the Courts, almost any activity incidental to a strike could be brought within the meaning of these terms. Thus in the conduct of industrial disputes the unions found themselves more vulnerable than previously. For four years the demand for the repeal of the offending measure overshadowed all else in the trade-union world. The organized demand for repeal did much to break down the opposition of unionists to political action and made it a central issue in the general election of 1874. Some unions even broke completely with the tradition of non-participation in politics and voted money for 'labour' candidates. In the election, which returned a conservative majority, the first 'labour' members, Alexander Macdonald and Thomas Burt, leading officials of the National Union of Miners, were elected. Parliament repealed the Criminal Law Amendment Act, substituting for it the Conspiracy and Protection of Property Act, which removed most of the limitations on union activity that had been imposed by the repealed measure.

In due course the Australian colonies carried trade-union laws modelled directly on the British legislation. In South Australia and New South Wales, the Trade Union Acts of 1876 and 1881 were in all essentials the British Act of 1871. Victoria followed with an Act in 1884 and an amendment in 1886. The Queensland Act was passed in 1886. Acts containing the same provisions as the British Conspiracy and Protection of Property Act were carried in South Australia in 1878 and Victoria in 1891. The other colonies appear not to have followed this legislation.

These Acts are mentioned here because of the moves towards them made during the seventies. In the sixties the legal status of unions did not raise the same interest in Australia as in Britain, for two reasons. First, although the Australian unions were legally in the same position as British unions before 1871, they were not in practice subjected to the same disabilities and persecutions. Second, because they were so much smaller and poorer than the English unions, they did not encounter the same difficulties in their business affairs. Nevertheless, during the seventies, the 'legalization of trade unions' began to find a place in union programmes and in the policies of working-class political organizations that were being formed.

Trade unionists, as we have noted, generally took the view that politics were beyond the proper purposes of unionism. On the other hand, the unions, in the attempt to implement their policies, began to move towards political action. During the seventies this process was accelerated by two developments. The first was the establishment of central trade-union organizations which, by their nature, concerned themselves with questions of general interest to working-men and hence were capable of solution by political means. Secondly, in both Sydney and Melbourne associations were formed, on the initiative or with the participation of leading unionists, seeking the election of working-men to parliament or advocating a political programme of particular interest to workers.

As in so many other aspects of their trade-union and political history, there were marked differences between Sydney and Melbourne in the development of central trade union organizations. From the post-gold-rush beginnings of trade unionism in Melbourne there were attempts to establish organizational links between the unions. The Eight Hours League was father of the Trades Hall Committee, which in some degree acted as a co-ordinating agency for the unions. However, with the building of the Trades Hall and the depressed conditions of the sixties, the committee became little more than a committee of management for the hall. Thus during the seventies, when moves began to be made to transform the committee into an effective central trade-union body, these were not encouraged but resisted by the majority of a committee that had become satisfied with its limited function.[14] Exactly what happened is not clear, but apparently in the early seventies moves were made to give the committee the function of a Trades and Labour Council, co-ordinating the activities of unions and exercising some degree of control over them. Mrs Philipp is of the opinion that the Trades

[14] Norton (ed.), *History of Capital and Labour*, p. 147.

Hall Committee began to have the broader function during 1878-9.[15] In 1884 the name of the committee was changed to the Trades Hall Council, and in the following year new rules embodying this function were adopted. Until 1879 the Trades Hall Committee took no part in trade disputes, but in that year they began the practice of bringing such matters to the notice of affiliated societies. This was a small beginning which led, in the eighties, to a more definite policy of co-ordinating the actions of unions. However, the Melbourne council moved neither so far nor so rapidly in this direction as its counterpart in Sydney.

Inter-union co-operation began later in New South Wales than in Victoria, but when it did it was less complicated by existing interests. The Sydney Trades and Labour Council was formed in 1871, and from the beginning it succeeded in co-ordinating the activities of a number of unions. The building of a trades hall was one of its objectives, but it was not until 1883 that an effective Trades Hall Committee, with the task of building and managing a hall, was appointed. In this respect the sequence of events was the reverse of that in Melbourne. From the beginning it had some success in co-ordinating the activities of unions and it is perfectly true, as Mrs Philipp puts it, that in the eighties, by comparison with Melbourne,

> the Sydney Trades and Labour Council was able more effectively to compel unions to notify it of impending disputes or of actions contemplated which might lead to disputes; with some success it tried to force unions to act on its advice; and once having decided to support a society on strike, it could, when it thought fit, do so with considerable effect.[16]

These differences were to prove important when trade unions began to contemplate seriously the establishment of a political party.

A further important, but related, difference was the attitude of the two bodies towards politics. In 1874 the Sydney Council sponsored the candidature of Angus Cameron, a carpenter, for the Legislative Assembly.[17] Neither he nor they thought of this support as constituting him a delegate of the trade unions in parliament. The prevailing view that the parliamentary member was a representative of the people, making an independent and personal decision on all questions, was fully accepted. He was thought of simply as a working-man who, because of his origins and associations, would be

---

[15] J. Philipp, 'The Organization of Trade Unions in New South Wales and Victoria, 1870-90'. [16] Ibid., p. 172.
[17] *Minutes of Labour Council of New South Wales*, 10 June, 28 July 1874.

likely to express the opinions of his class and to have specialized knowledge and experience bearing on questions of particular interest to unionists. That this view was acceptable to Cameron is borne out both by his parliamentary career and by his stated objectives. In his election address in 1874 he declared himself a 'bona fide' advocate for the rights of labour. He disclaimed any aggressive feelings towards the employers but felt that it was time for the voice of working-men to be heard in parliament. Burt and Macdonald had set the example in Britain. At the same time, his return to parliament would prove that it was untrue 'that the working man's vote could be had for a pint of beer', and his performance there would demonstrate that men of his class were capable of 'giving a clear, lucid, and honest opinion upon all questions of national importance'. His behaviour, he believed, would show that working-men were able to behave like gentlemen. To these general propositions was added a four-point programme: finance for city development; free, secular, and compulsory education; the legalization of trade unions; and the stipulation of the eight-hour day in government contracts.[18]

With this outlook Cameron easily fitted into a parliament that was not divided on any great principles but in which factions provided governing majorities, in which the dominant political ideal was the 'independence' of the member, and the business of parliament was largely the administration of affairs. He appeared as a specifically working-class representative only in connection with matters of peculiar interest to unionists. Of these the most important was the legalization of trade unions. In 1876 he introduced a Trade Union Funds Protection Bill modelled on the provisional measure adopted by the British parliament in 1869. His choice of this model was dictated by his fear, shared by many unionists, that a more comprehensive measure would cause the difficulties for unions experienced in Britain after the adoption of the 1871 Acts. Cameron's Bill was laid aside by the Council. Then, curiously enough, in 1881 the Bill which became the Trade Union Act of 1881 was initiated in the Council by a member who had led the opposition to Cameron's original measure. In the debate in the Assembly Cameron's viewpoint was consistent with the position he had taken five years before. He insisted that the Bill went too far; that all the unions needed was protection of their funds against dishonest officers; and that the proposed measure would tie them up in legal technicalities.[19] Cameron was mistaken about the effects of the law, but his attitude

[18] *S.M.H.*, 5 December 1874.
[19] *Parl. Deb.* (N.S.W.), 1881, vi. 2189.

is of interest as expressing a fear of legal technicalities common amongst members of the working class.

At the election of 1877 Cameron was less closely connected with any specifically working-class body. In his first parliament he had broken with the Trades and Labour Council and had become integrated into one of the factions which were, as A. W. Martin has shown, the mechanism of order within an institution where all professed personal independence. 'An objection existed to his having joined a party,' he said. 'A man who voted like a weathercock would often find himself deserted, so he joined a party who agreed with five out of seven ideas he held himself.'[20] While the unions that had sponsored him did not wish him to behave as a delegate, they felt that he had gone too far towards identifying himself with one of the existing factions.

More important than the attitude of Cameron were the attempts made at the 1877 election to establish a working-class political organization. The key to this was the Working Men's Defence Association that had been formed some time previously. During the first week of the election campaign, a conference, with representatives of the Working Men's Defence Association, the Reform League (a Newcastle body), the Trades and Labour Council, and the Free Selectors' Association, met in Sydney. The free selectors withdrew to their own conference, being held simultaneously, which decided that amalgamation with the other bodies would be 'premature' because their immediate single concern was the amendment of the land law.[21] The others proceeded with their conference, adopted a more comprehensive political policy than had any previous working-class gathering, and supported the candidature of three men for the West Sydney seat. The policy included electoral reform, with more equal constituencies and the abolition of plural voting; payment of members; cessation of assisted immigration; and reform of the land laws. Fiscal protection was agreed to in the form of 'taxing the import of articles capable of being produced in the colony'—a form of words that was approved as avoiding the use of the term 'protection'.[22] None of the three candidates nominated was returned, but in long term the organization that took place was an important incident in the evolution of working-class politics.

In Victoria, political activity of unionists during the seventies was less independent but more immediately effective than in Sydney. The sharp divisions in Victoria had produced a degree of extra-

[20] *S.M.H.*, 19 October 1877. [21] Ibid., 16 October 1877.
[22] Ibid., 17 October 1877.

parliamentary organization that was not paralleled in New South Wales until after 1887. Graham Berry went to the elections in 1877 with the support of the most effective political organization that had appeared in Australia up to that time. Its protectionist and anti-squatter policy has been considered in connection with the constitutional crisis, but here its structure should be noted. The National Reform and Protection League was formed in 1875 by the amalgamation of the Protection League and the National Reform League, representing, respectively, the opinions of Melbourne manufacturers and workers, and of the selector interest.[23] The branches, which by 1878 numbered 150, selected candidates and then sought to persuade others of the same opinions to retire from the election. Mainly an electoral organization, it did, however, carry on between elections, pressing for the implementation of its policies. In 1878 these were to support the reform of the Legislative Council and to encourage local industry by preferential treatment as well as protective duties.

No trade-union body was officially represented in the League, but trade-union leaders were active members of it. Of the annual meeting of the League in 1878, W. E. Murphy remarked, 'the meeting was attended by many of the prominent members of the Trades Hall Committee'.[24] In effect, union leaders regarded the Reform and Protection League as their political party, thus rendering less necessary independent political action by the unions.

During the seventies trade unions, by the logic of their own development, were moving slowly towards political action. During the next decade these first tentative steps were to become giant strides.

[23] Parnaby, 'The Economic and Political Development of Victoria', p. 251.
[24] Norton (ed.), *The History of Capital and Labour*, p. 147.

5

Towards Trade Union Politics, 1880-1885

Class questions require class knowledge to state them, and class sympathies to fight for them. Land, Commerce and Capital are all cared for in our Legislative Assemblies, but Labor, the source of all wealth, is only fought for, as Labor should be, outside that body, and yet laws are made by it, and taxation imposed, which may either ruin or raise these trades on whose existence scores of thousands of laboring families depend.[1]

DESPITE the differences that have been emphasized, there was much in common in the political development of the several colonies of Australia. In all of them the essence of politics was the administration of affairs within rapidly expanding economies. Penal colony beginnings had determined that the state would be both centralized and positive. Self-government had not changed the pattern, but merely added to its complexity. Land legislation and administration, the building and running of railways, the creation and administration of centralized state education systems had become aspects of government activity in all colonies during the sixties and seventies. In carrying these out, governments had become major entrepreneurs in each of the colonies. This was not, however, the result of any collectivist or quasi-socialist theory. As we have seen, the popular houses of parliament were dominated by middle-class men, and the dominant ideas were individualistic. Victoria differed from New South Wales in its early adoption of protective tariffs. Politically, this was a result of the pressure of a radical electorate faced by economic difficulties. Economically, it became increasingly important as a source of government revenue. In New South Wales there were not the same initial problems of population, and the problem of revenue did not arise until later than in Victoria. Until 1883-4 in New South Wales, land sales continued to pour money into the Treasury, to be used both for capital investment and for current expenditure. On the other hand Victoria, with a larger population and a much smaller land area, soon exhausted the returns from land sales and was forced to find alternative sources of government revenue.

[1] I.T.U.C., 1884. *Progress Report of the Parliamentary Committee*, p. 10.

Economic historians may speculate on what would have been the results of a more negative economic policy by governments: less competition by governments on the loan market may have increased the amount of private investment, and less public investment may have meant a more competitive economy in which, amongst other things, the standards of hours and wages of the working class would have been lower, and conditions for the growth of unions less congenial. But the outstanding fact is that the political demands of an enfranchised people rendered any other course of development impossible. Australian governments before 1880 had become positive agents in economic development.

From the point of view of the growing labour movement this was an important fact in the transition to trade-union politics. Although there was a broad hiatus between the affairs of trade unionism and the business of politics, the gap was less than in communities where positive state action in regard to economic affairs had to overcome an established practice and tradition. For the Australian trade unionist and the humanitarian it was but a short step from the acceptance of the state's function in various economic fields to the demand that it should be extended to regulate a wide range of social and economic matters of particular concern to the working class. The legalization of the eight-hour day and government provision for the unemployed had become established policies of the working class during the sixties and seventies. In the early eighties the number of fields in which legislation was sought was rapidly multiplied.

Of course Australia was not unique in this. Despite the fact that different people have perceived the end of *laissez faire* in Britain at dates as widely separated as 1870 and 1926, it is apparent that between 1870 and 1880 an important change began to take place in the matters with which British governments concerned themselves. Dicey selected 1870 as the year when what he called legislative opinion had become predominantly collectivist.[2] He traced the cause of the change to development both of ideas and institutions that had taken place over the previous half century. He pointed to the fact that although before 1870 the dominant opinion was individualist, and governments were primarily concerned with limiting the area of state intervention in economic affairs, the complete individualists had never been unchallenged. Before 1850, the tory philanthropists and the working-class chartists had a social programme that implied

---

[2] A. V. Dicey, *Lectures on the Relation Between Law and Public Opinion in England during the Nineteenth Century*, pp. 64-5. (Henceforward referred to as *Law and Public Opinion in England*.)

the necessity of positive state action. After 1850, the writings of Carlyle, Kingsley, and John Mill contributed to the movement of opinion away from the negative state of Bentham. Again, D. H. McGregor points to the fact that even the political economists, whose doctrine contributed most to the policies of extreme individualism, were not themselves thoroughgoing individualists.³ Adam Smith, Ricardo, Malthus, and Senior all qualified their support for the negative state in a way that was ignored by many of the politicians who claimed them as their masters.

In institutional development the same process is noticeable. The Ten Hours Bill was contemporaneous with the repeal of the Corn Laws, and although the extension of the principle contained in it did not occur until after 1870, in the intervening twenty years changes were taking place that would make such extension inevitable. Notable amongst these were changes in economic life. Corporate action by both workers and employers was increasing. The development of trade unionism was a movement towards collective, as opposed to individual, action. It was opposed by the followers of Bentham as a restriction on the individual's freedom of contract, but the unions grew in spite of liberal opinion. Similarly, in the conduct of business itself, in spite of the dominant opinion that the first condition of successful business is unlimited competition, combination was becoming characteristic of commerce. After 1850, says Dicey, 'one trade after another passed from the management of private persons into the hands of corporate bodies created by the State'.⁴ The institutional changes threw up new questions for solution and they could not be solved in the old way. 'There could not be legislation about factories, companies, trade unions, or public health, until people had combined into groups for working or living', says McGregor.⁵ Opinion reflected the new circumstances, and governments increasingly gave their attention to legislation required by the new conditions.

In Australia, it is neither necessary nor possible to trace any change in sophisticated thinking about the proper role of governments to account for the changing attitude towards the state's responsibility. Secondary industry scarcely existed before 1860, and its rapid development began only in the seventies. Trade unions and the demand for controls grew with it, in a political environment in which governments had long been accustomed to playing an important role in economic affairs.

[3] *Economic Thought and Policy*, pp. 80 ff.
[4] *Law and Public Opinion in England*, p. 245.
[5] *Economic Thought and Policy*, p. 73.

In all colonies in the early eighties there was a spate of union organization and attempted organization. Central trade-union bodies assumed larger functions and the idea of linking the various separate local unions in an industry by amalgamation or federation was widely discussed, and some steps taken towards its implementation. Politically these organizational moves gave to union policies a weight that they had not previously exerted. The immediate results of these trends were different in the several colonies. In Victoria they stimulated some socio-economic legislation. In New South Wales and Queensland they were without immediate political results, and are important mainly as a part of the process that, at the end of the decade, produced a trade-union political party—the Labour Party.

Victoria was the first colony to adopt a factory Act. This was passed in 1873 as a result of the revelations by the *Ballarat Courier* of bad working conditions in clothing factories in Ballarat.[6] Taken up by the local member, a Bill regulating the employment of women was introduced in the Legislative Assembly. It excited little interest in the House, and was passed with minor amendments. In the Council there was no discussion, but some amendments limited its scope. The Act was virtually inoperative since, as amended by the Council, it defined a factory as a place where at least ten people worked, thus excluding from its operation the large numbers of workrooms employing a handful of workers, which it was most necessary to regulate. Factories could be exempted from its provisions by executive Act, and no proper provision was made for policing it. Nevertheless, it was important as establishing a precedent that could be called on when the pressure for more effective regulation should arise. This occurred in the early eighties.

The initiative was taken in 1879 by a group of manufacturers, moved no doubt by sympathy for the women and children employed in the clothing industry, but also concerned about the competition from the 'sweated' labour in backyard factories and workrooms. Led by a large clothing manufacturer named Parry, pressure was put on the government for the amendment of the 1873 Act to bring it into line with current British factory legislation. The proposals were: to prohibit the employment in factories of children under thirteen years of age; to limit the hours of women and of children under sixteen years to forty-eight a week; to bring all factories under

---

[6] E. C. Fry, 'The Condition of the Urban Wage Earning Class in Australia in the 1880's'. The origin and enactment of Victorian Factory legislation is covered in great detail in this thesis.

the Act and create the necessary machinery for inspection and policing. The proposal foundered on the opposition of the Manufacturers' Association.

From this time the pressure for factory legislation was exerted from a number of different directions. In the process, the long-standing political alliance between workers and manufacturers was weakened. The break was far from complete, but the initiative passed into the hands of employees, frequently in the face of opposition from their employers. During 1880, the Melbourne Typographical Association appealed for legislation to control apprenticeship and to determine minimum conditions of health and safety in workplaces. In the following year a Salesmen's and Assistants' Union took up energetically the demands of a moribund early closing association, formed in 1858, to limit the hours of work in retail shops. A Bill to enforce the closing of shops at 6 p.m. on weekdays and 10 p.m. on Saturdays was referred to a select committee. The Typographical Association kept its own agitation alive, but the event that forced the question squarely under public notice was the tailoresses' strike at the end of 1882.

The effect of this strike of women wage-earners was not unlike that of the match-girls in England a few years later. As a strike of women it was a novelty, and the deplorable working conditions revealed, when public attention was drawn to them, aroused a wave of sympathy. The Trades Hall Committee assumed the leadership of the strike and organized a union of tailoresses which was soon two thousand strong. The majority of employers soon accepted the union's log of claims on hours and wages.

The tailoresses' strike and the formation of the union commanded public attention, but it was also symptomatic of a widespread movement towards the formation of unions in many trades. Amongst those who attempted, sometimes successfully, to form unions at this time were some semi-skilled urban workers who had previously been quite outside the scope of unionism. In 1882-3, for example, steps were taken to form unions of butchers, bakers, quarrymen, draymen and carters, wharf labourers and coal lumpers, cooks, hairdressers, and male clothing factory operatives. Bootmakers as well as a number of skilled tradesmen such as coachmakers, wheelwrights and smiths organized new unions or attempted to revive inactive unions or extended existing unions.

The Trades Hall Council which, it has been noted, was assuming the wider function of a trades and labour council, became genuinely representative of the growing union movement. In 1880 no more than a dozen unions took part in its proceedings; by 1885 there were more than fifty.[7] Associated with this spate of organization was a series of strikes for higher wages or improved working conditions, in a number of which the Trades Hall Council took an active role in gaining support from other unions for the men or women on strike.

The most important of these disputes was the bootmakers' strike (or, more correctly, lockout) of 1884. Because it was a major strike and because it raised issues that were important for the whole of light industry, it will be considered in some detail. Although during the eighties the structure of industry was changing towards larger concerns, in 1881 the average number of employees in workshops in Victoria was sixteen.[8] There were a number of relatively large factories, but in the manufacture of clothing, boots, and other products of light industry there were many places employing two or three operatives. Together with this, the practice of 'outwork', typical of the early stages of industrial development in all countries, was common in those trades where it was possible. These conditions bred the characteristic abuses of apprenticeship: intolerably long hours of labour, and low and uneven wage levels. Similar conditions, at least in respect of hours, existed in the retail trades and service industries. In 1882 bakers commonly worked seventy to eighty hours a week and butchers even longer. Shop assistants generally worked from fourteen to sixteen hours a day. Strikes by butchers and bakers in 1882-3 improved their position, and the agitation of the shop assistants brought their plight before the public.

The Operative Bootmakers' Union was formed in 1879 and three years later drew up a log of claims designed to bring uniformity into the wages and conditions prevailing in the industry. After two years of negotiation, the strike or lockout began in November 1884. The Trades Hall Council supported the unions and during the thirteen-week stoppage organized financial support from both unionists and sympathizers in all colonies except Western Australia. The strike was terminated by an agreement between the Trades Hall Council and representatives of the Manufacturers' Association. This struggle was important in two respects. It was the first large-scale conflict in which a number of unions co-operated through the Trades Hall Council in a contest with employers. Also it was, with the tailoresses' strike, influential in bringing to public notice the conditions of the less fortunate sections of the wage-earning population.

[7] J. Philipp gives the figures of unions actively participating in meetings of the central body as 11 in 1880 and 58 in 1885.
[8] Computed from figures in Vic. *Year Book 1882-3*.

Nevertheless it would be wrong to imagine that the heightened awareness of unsatisfactory conditions in some branches of industry was solely due to the growth of trade unionism. From the time of the first proposal in 1879 to amend the Factory Act, the *Age* lashed the 'greed of avaricious taskmasters [and] the evils of uncontrolled competition'.[9] It demanded the limitation of hours, control of apprenticeship, minimum conditions of space and safety, and an efficient system of inspection. In particular it attacked 'sweating',[10] and insisted on a full-scale investigation of conditions in Melbourne factories and workplaces. This was in accord with its protectionist policy, which claimed to be in the interest of both manufacturers and employers. The current British interest in 'sweating' strongly influenced the *Age* in particular and public opinion in general. W. A. Trenwith, secretary of the operative bootmakers, felt no need to explain his reference when he summed up the reasons for the bootmakers' strike. He concluded,

> We are fighting for the abolition of a system which, in the old world, has reduced thousands of human beings to a condition of indescribable misery, degradation, and crime; a system which is agitating the minds of the greatest thinkers of the world, and has produced the 'bitter cry of outcast London', and is rapidly tending to the same results in our own midst.[11]

The clear implication was that such conditions had no place in a country that prided itself on its high standard of living.

Any attempt to classify the groups that sympathized with the demand for reform raised by the unions, the *Age*, and some middle-class reformers must be quite tentative. But it seems that people of humanitarian instincts in all classes favoured action to right the worst wrongs. The Legislative Council produced no Shaftesbury but was not actively opposed to the factory Bill that reached it in 1885. Certainly some manufacturers, in particular the larger ones, were influenced by a desire to limit the competition from 'sweated' labour. On the other hand, the series of strikes from 1882 clearly indicate that many employers, however much they may have sympathized in theory with the views of the reformers, were not prepared to see the mote in their own eyes. This is borne out by the reaction of the

---

[9] 16 June 1879.
[10] 'The expression "sweating", much used at the time, was a controversial term, applied loosely, needing definition in itself, though a useful meaning can be given to sweating as one type of outwork'. E. C. Fry, 'Outwork in the 'Eighties', *University Studies in History and Economics* (University of Western Australia), vol. ii.
[11] Cited Norton (ed.), *The History of Capital and Labour*, p. 161.

Chamber of Manufactures to the report of the factories commission in 1884.

This commission was appointed in 1882 as a select committee to 'enquire into . . . the best means of regulating and shortening the hours of employees in shops'. Under pressure from the unions, the *Age,* and the committee itself, it was elevated to a royal commission and its terms of reference broadened to take in conditions in factories. The commission provided a focal point for all interested in bringing about reform. The Trades Hall Council set up a special committee to prepare evidence and the commission called numerous witnesses and inspected every type of factory and workplace. The long list of recommendations included the registration of all factories, a forty-eight hour week, the specification of hours between which juveniles might be permitted to work, limitation of the number of apprentices, the prohibition of 'outwork', the adoption of regulations on space, lighting, ventilation, and the protection of dangerous machinery, and the appointment of inspectors to police the regulations.[12]

The recommendations were a triumph for the Trades Hall Council but were bitterly criticized by the Chamber of Manufactures, which referred to them as a libel on manufacturers.[13] It subsequently agreed to registration and inspection but continued to oppose the other proposals.

The Workrooms and Factories Law Amendment Bill, introduced in the Legislative Assembly by Alfred Deakin, emerged from more than a year's debate containing more of the ideas of the employers than of the unions. Registration and inspection were included, but the definition of a factory as a concern employing six or more operatives put outside its operation the workplaces that it was most important to control. In practice the Act proved to be little more effective than its predecessor, but in the history of working-class politics it is an important landmark. Agitation for regulation, and subsequently against the details of the Act, was a unifying factor in the trade-union movement, and the practical experience associated with it clarified unionists' views on their objectives. Most importantly, the increasingly active role of the Trades Hall Council was investing it with a broadly representative function.

In New South Wales, also, the early eighties was a period of rapid extension of unionism amongst workers similar to those organized in Victoria.[14] And the Trades and Labour Council likewise extended

---

[12] Vic. *V. & P. (L.A.),* 1884, vol. ii: 'Report on the Operation of the Victorian Factory Act 1874'. [13] *Age,* 1 April 1884.
[14] N.S.W., *Report of the Royal Commission on Strikes.* Appendix, L 3.

its authority, the number of unions actively participating in its work rising from twenty to thirty during the five years. On the other hand, although it was busy accumulating a policy on socio-political questions, it was much less successful than the Victorian movement in achieving any practical results. In Queensland there were sufficient unions and a strong enough demand for union co-operation to stimulate the formation of a Queensland Trades and Labour Council in 1885.

Considered on a national scale, the most important union development was the initiation of intercolonial trades union congresses. Their summoning presupposed the existence of common interests to be defended; their effect was to give definite expression to these interests and to encourage the further development of unity. The first Intercolonial Congress met in Sydney in 1879. Although it was little more than a New South Wales conference, it was intended that it should be representative of the whole of Australian unionism. Invitations had been issued by the Sydney Trades and Labour Council to unions in all the colonies, and only two colonies had declined. That there were only two delegates from colonies other than New South Wales actually present was due to financial and other difficulties. Whilst it cannot be assumed that of itself the convocation of this and succeeding conferences was an indication of the unanimous acceptance of the desirability of closer relations between unions, the enthusiasm does demonstrate that there was a growing consciousness of a need for some representative gathering, at which the matters of more general interest to trade unionists could be thrashed out and policy adopted. Even the Operative Stonemasons' Union, which had previously withdrawn from the Trades and Labour Council, participated in the Congress, voted 15s. a day to its representatives, and rejected a resolution of censure on the congress for discussing 'party politics'.[15] Allowing for a certain over-emphasis, the secretary of the first congress was not very wrong when he wrote that the fact 'was established that the labour organizations of Australasia were practically unanimous in holding certain opinions in social politics'.[16]

Before considering what these 'opinions on social politics' were, it is desirable to pursue further the developing idea of trade-union unity. In Britain, as Sidney and Beatrice Webb have exhaustively shown,[17] in spite of the extreme localism which had no counterpart

[15] Minutes of Sydney Lodge Operative Stonemasons' Society, 21 October, 8 December, 1879. These minutes are in the possession of the union.
[16] I.T.U.C. *Report*, 1879, p. 3.
[17] S. and B. Webb, *Industrial Democracy*, pp. 72-103.

in Australia, the inevitable tendency in organization was towards the unit of the 'trade', the operative motive being the desire to establish minimum conditions for the whole industry. But having achieved such a unit of organization, any further advance was extraordinarily difficult. Numerous attempts were made to establish central organizations, all of which, except those on a very limited local basis, broke down for a multiplicity of reasons. Attempts to bring about federation of the trades within the same industry broke on the rock of jealousy and particularism. Attempts at wider federations were obviously even less successful. Schemes such as the 'National Association of Organised Trades' inaugurated in 1846, the 'United Kingdom Alliance of Organised Trades', the conferences at Glasgow in 1875 and Birmingham 1876, all failed in the attempt to provide the machinery of a trade-union government.[18] On the other hand, the British Trade Union Congress in its present form dates from 1871 and had as its inspiration opposition to the penal 'third clause' of the Trade Union Bill of that year.

The summoning of the first Intercolonial Trades Union Congress in Australia indicates a level of development similar to that which produced the Trade Union Congress in Britain. And, just as in Britain, despite the desire of important trade-union leaders for a more permanent and definite organizational unity, so the same factors prevented its achievement in Australia. The desire for unity resulted from the stirring of the idea of class representation, the opposition to it arose from the idea of 'trade'; the compromise was for such organization as would provide for the expression of ideas of a limited kind, which did not run counter to any of the interests that the 'trades' considered as especially theirs. The idea of federation was to be more completely realized in Australia than in Britain, in the Australian Labour Federation of 1889, but despite its partial and temporary success, the more persistent unifying institution was to be a political party—a possibility that was not apparent to anyone in 1880 or even in 1885. The movement in the direction of federation at the intercolonial congresses was, however, an unconscious step in the direction of forming a political party—an outcome that was not only not envisaged by the men of 1880, but would also have been regarded by most of them with acute apprehension.

The first congress established the precedent. The second, which met in Melbourne in 1884 and the third, in Sydney in 1885, adopted firm policies, made recommendations on trade-union organization,

[18] G. Howell, *The Conflicts of Capital and Labour*, pp. 394-7.

and set up machinery for parliamentary lobbying. The subjects discussed at the congresses give a fair indication of the questions of social politics with which unionists were concerned. They ranged from such specialized trade-union demands as the inspection of land boilers and mining on private property to factory legislation, workmen's compensation for injuries, and the legalization of trade unions, to the more purely political topics of protective tariffs, immigration, education, and payment of members of parliament.

Only one of these questions gave rise to any serious disagreements or misgivings. For New South Wales unionists, protection was a dangerously political question. At the first congress they agreed on the need for a fiscal policy which would 'give encouragement to Australian industry', but denied that they meant protection. By the third congress, however, any subterfuge was dropped and there were only five dissentients in a congress of a hundred to the motion 'That the time has now arrived when a judicious and discriminating protective tariff should be applied in New South Wales'.[19]

It is interesting to note that the very small opposition was not based on the usual free-trade argument that the cost of protective tariffs was borne by the consumer, but along the lines of the attempt made later by the early political Labour Party to 'sink the fiscal issue'. It is significant also that such a point of view should have been expressed by an unskilled worker, because it was the influence of the unskilled workers in the trade unions and at the ballot boxes which later united the Labour movement around other issues. A representative of the United Labourers' Protective Association believed that the fundamental question was distribution. He maintained that

> there was an enormous surplus of wealth in the colony produced by the wage-earning classes, but remaining in the hands of the few; and that they must look for the remedy in the laws of distribution. Then and only then, could it be said that they were suffering from poverty. In a country of such vast resources as New South Wales, all they wanted to do was to develop their natural resources, as this would cause the population to increase and create centres for the establishment of industries.[20]

A more cynical view was expressed by one who thought that 'everything resolved itself into competition; and it did not matter whether the policy adopted was free trade or protection, wages would always

[19] I.T.U.C. *Report*, 1885, p. 19.
[20] Ibid., p. 23.

find their own level'.[21] Perhaps he had never heard of Lassalle, but here was the 'iron and cruel law'.

Important as the congresses were, they did not fulfil all the needs of closer union of which some delegates were conscious. W. G. Spence, already busy building the Amalgamated Miners' Association, which was soon to join miners in all colonies in a single powerful union, at the second congress moved:

> That the Congress recommend the federation of the Trade Unions of each colony, after the following manner: Each trade to be recommended to amalgamate the several unions of the same trade under the one head or governing body; each of the latter heads then to appoint representatives to a conference at which a Federal Council shall be elected, who shall watch over the interests of the whole, and deal with matters affecting the well-being of the working classes generally.[22]

Spence made it quite clear in his explanation of the motion that he had two distinct ideas in mind. By amalgamation he meant the linking of the various local societies covering a particular trade. He was not thinking of what he was later instrumental in creating—an industrial union that would contain all the workers in an industry. By federation he intended a loose association of amalgamated unions which would have executive authority on a limited number of general matters such as the 'Trades Union Bill and the legalisation of the eight-hour day'. In his opinion, the federal council would function in a manner similar to the Parliamentary Committee of the English Trades Union Congress.

In the following year a more comprehensive scheme of amalgamation and federation was adopted. More precise, it included some machinery proposals to implement the policy:

> 1. That in each colony each trade shall extend its organisation to the limits of such colony.
> 2. That each such trade organisation, where practicable, hold an annual conference (of delegates from its Branches) in each colony.
> 3. At the above conference a delegate or delegates be appointed to attend a central Colonial Council of delegates from every trade, which shall meet at least annually.
> 4. Such central Council to appoint a stipulated number of representatives on the intercolonial committee, which shall be recognised as the Federal Executive of the Australasian Trade Unions.
> 5. That every member of the incorporated trades contribute one penny per month for the purposes of the Federal Executive.

[21] Ibid., p. 43.   [22] Ibid., 1884, p. 53.

6. The Federal Executive to take its instructions from and be responsible to the Annual Intercolonial Congresses.
7. Representation—for every 4,000 members or portion thereof, each central council shall send one representative.
8. That the necessary work for carrying all the foregoing into practical effect, be left in the hands of the several Parliamentary Committees to be appointed.[23]

The congress closed with the optimistic instruction to the parliamentary committees to carry out the foregoing instructions within a month. But despite the unanimous acceptance of the idea, there was no definite result, even on a colony-wide scale, until the formation of the Australian Labour Federation in Queensland in 1889. Nevertheless, the acceptance of the idea, with whatever mental reservations, was an important landmark towards developing the idea that workers needed institutions to represent them as a class.

The fact that the policy remained only as an idea is quite comprehensible in the light of the comment upon it by delegates at the congresses. Many of them saw only the practical difficulties imposed by the 'trade' view of their members. It was pointed out that previous attempts to unite the Ballarat branch of the United Society of Boiler-makers and Iron-shipbuilders with the Sydney branch had failed because the Ballarat branch had insufficient funds.[24] Interstate jealousy was seen as a bar. The Victorian Book-binders' Society when it had been formed in 1878 had adopted the comprehensive title of 'Australian', but the Sydney bookbinders had refused to join because of state feeling. James S. T. McGowen, who was in 1910 to become the first Labour Premier of New South Wales, saw difficulties in the legal status of the unions in the several colonies. He believed that 'before amalgamation, they should first consider whether it was a legal proceeding. Otherwise they might, as a previous speaker had jocularly put it, be indicted for conspiracy'. James Curley, of the Hunter River Coal Miners' Association, saw 'as the only barrier to amalgamation or federation, the selfishness of the men themselves', and the representative of the Amalgamated Society of Engineers, 'feared that the difference in the organisation of each society would prevent a satisfactory amalgamation upon the broad principles enunciated'. One delegate saw an obstacle in his own inability to understand what was meant by federation and amalgamation, and a minority of delegates believed that there was not sufficient common ground between the various trades, and that, lacking a common purpose, there was no utility in federating. But despite the recogni-

[23] Ibid., 1885, p. 75. [24] Ibid., 1884, pp. 63-4.

tion of difficulties, most of the leading unionists agreed with the sentiments of John Norton, who wrote in the preface to the report of the third congress, 'unfederated, the numerous labour organizations of these colonies are, in the presence of the organized forces of capital, as weak as the undisciplined mob in the face of soldiery; but federated, the numerical and moral power of the working classes would be irresistible'. There was a *sentiment* in favour of some kind of closer union, the appeal of which was largely emotional, the need for which could only be vaguely seen, and which was, as proved by the fact, insufficiently strong to overcome the practical difficulties presented by the very nature of the organizations.

The practical outcome was the formation of parliamentary committees. At the second congress it was decided to set up a parliamentary committee consisting of six members, two from each of the states of New South Wales, Victoria and South Australia, with the further provision that it be enlarged to ten when Queensland and Tasmania saw fit to enter. Due partly to the ideas of unity fostered by the congress and partly to the English example, this unworkable committee was agreed upon. Obviously, colonial parliamentary committees were required to carry out their functions in connection with the several colonial parliaments and, despite the decision, the national committee existed only on paper. The Melbourne Trades Hall Council, acting on its own initiative, appointed a parliamentary committee and at the third congress was able to report on its activities, which included lobbying members on the Factory Act, which as we have seen was the most important question for unionists in Victoria in the early eighties.

The idea of trade-union federation had brought forth parliamentary committees—a result much less far reaching than the ideas advanced by Spence, but symptomatic of the growth of the idea of common union interests, the need for organizational forms to express them, and of political means to realize them. In the five years after 1885 the trade-union movement advanced rapidly towards the formation of political parties in all colonies—parties which would write into their platforms the policies that had been largely formulated by the central trade-union bodies by 1885.

6

The New Unionism, 1886-1890

Until the whole of the different branches of labour throughout the length and breadth of Australasia become welded into one strong union, labour organisation cannot be said to be perfected.[1]

By 1888 a European community had inhabited Australia for a century and its people had enjoyed self-government for a generation. In the thirty-odd years since the discovery of gold the ideal of economic independence had proved unrealizable for the majority of the people. No longer were there vast areas of Crown lands held under temporary title to excite the hopes of future independence. In 1891 approximately seventy-six per cent of people were wage or salary earners. In the same year thirty-four per cent of New South Wales people lived in Sydney and forty-three per cent of Victorians in Melbourne.[2] There was now both a permanent city and rural population. In New South Wales and Queensland the countryside was dominated by the squatters. Small farmers, selectors under the land Acts more persistent or more fortunate than the thousands who had failed to hold their selections in the struggle with nature and the pastoralists, had become a settled farming population. Defending their interests through selectors' associations, they frequently felt more in common with the rural working class than with the pastoralists whom they still regarded as their natural opponents. The rural workers consisted of the permanent hands employed on the sheep and cattle stations and occasionally on the larger farms, but in the main they were itinerant workers: shearers, shed-hands, construction workers, and miners, following seasonal labour. For part of the year the permanent army of itinerant workers was joined by selectors waiting for a crop to grow or attracted by the wages to be earned shearing or sinking a dam. In Victoria the picture was much the same, except that, as we have seen, the selector was more in evidence than in the other colonies.

[1] I.T.U.C. *Report*, 1888. Preface by A. Hinchcliffe.
[2] Vic. *Year Book, 1892*; T. A. Coghlan, *Wealth and Progress of New South Wales, 1892*.

The occupations of the urban population were what might be expected of entrepôt cities with small-scale but rapidly developing secondary industries. Finance and commerce provided the 'capitalists', but increasingly they were being joined by manufacturers. During the eighties the average size of factories increased rapidly, more rapidly in New South Wales than in Victoria. In 1881 the average number of employees in workshops was sixteen in Victoria and eleven in New South Wales; by 1891 it had increased to approximately nineteen in both. While the small concerns that carried on in converted houses or backyard sheds still existed in large numbers, the new-type factory built for the purpose, and employing fifty or more hands, became more common. The manufacturers, too, were changing. The founders of the business, often enough artisans who had set up on their own account, were now substantial men whose way of life was far removed from their artisan beginnings. In the sixties and seventies they had been the 'new men', politically allied with their workers in support of policies believed to be in the interests of both. In the eighties more of them were finding their level in the upper ranks of society, and while not denying their former assumptions on the identity of interest between workers and masters, finding more frequently in practice that their interests were in conflict. The professional classes differed perhaps from similar classes in older countries in that they included more who had seized the opportunities offered by colonial society to raise their social status above that of their parents. The permanent city wage- and salary-earning class was composed of the white-collar workers in finance, commerce, and government services; the artisans, occupying a key position in the developing secondary industry and forming the backbone of the trade-union movement; and the semi-skilled and unskilled workers in industry, commerce and transport.[3] This last group provided a permanent link between city and country, for it was not unusual for the country worker to drift to the cities to seek better-paid or more congenial labour and for the unemployed city worker to search in the country for the job that evaded him in the city. Mobility of labour between city and country can be exaggerated, but at least amongst the unskilled workers it was considerable.

How was this population distributed between the various types of occupation? It is outside the purpose of this book to attempt any detailed quantitative estimate of the distribution, but there may be some value in giving a rough picture. The New South Wales Statis-

[3] Fry, 'The Condition of the Urban Wage Earning Class in Australia', pp. 35 ff.

tician divided Australian breadwinners of 1891 into five categories: professional, domestic, commercial, industrial, and primary producers. He found that in New South Wales and Victoria more breadwinners were occupied in industrial than in primary production, the margin in favour of industry being a good deal greater in Victoria than in New South Wales. In Queensland there was greater emphasis on primary production, with about forty per cent more engaged in primary than in industrial production. In each of the colonies commercial pursuits were the next largest group, the number engaged in New South Wales and Victoria being between half and two-thirds of that engaged in industrial production, and in Queensland a little over two-thirds. In each of the colonies the categories professional and domestic taken together were approximately equal to the numbers engaged in commerce.[4]

By 1890, in terms of the occupations of the people and in its contribution to total national output, primary production was no longer predominant in the Australian economy. In 1891 secondary and primary industries contributed almost equally to the national output of New South Wales, with tertiary industry contributing approximately a third more than either of the others.[5] On the other hand, the economy was still underpinned by the pastoral industry, with wool providing thirty per cent of total export income in 1890. Throughout the period of rapid expansion from 1868 to 1888 the pastoral and agricultural industry had been, with residential construction and railway construction, one of the three important fields of investment.[6] And as the major contributor to export income, the pastoral industry occupied a critical position in an economy whose expansion was financed largely by British capital. Hence it is not surprising that the fortunes of the pastoral industry had a profound effect upon the economy as a whole, and the industrial relations within it an influence much greater than its contribution to the total national output or the proportion of the population it employed would suggest. For the history of the labour movement, the trade-union organization of the pastoral workers after 1885 is a central fact.

The whole decade of the eighties is marked by the rapid extension of unionism. In New South Wales there were approximately one hundred unions in 1890. Of these about sixty had been formed since 1880, forty of them since 1886. In Victoria there was a similar expan-

[4] T. A. Coghlan, *The Seven Colonies of Australasia*, p. 311.
[5] H. W. Arndt and N. G. Butlin, 'National Output, Income and Expenditure of New South Wales, 1891', *Economic Record*, vol. xxiv (1950).
[6] N. G. Butlin, *Private Capital Formation in Australia, Estimates 1861-1900*, p. 3.

sion, with the difference that there were more unions formed in the first half of the decade than in New South Wales. In Queensland there were not less than twenty-five unions by 1888, with a Trades and Labour Council established in 1885.[7]

More important than the quantitative changes, however, was the influence of the new types of workers organized in 1885 and after. As noted in the previous chapter, between 1880 and 1885 unionism extended to many of the unskilled workers in Melbourne and to fewer of them in Sydney. After 1885, further urban occupations employing unskilled men were organized. But in terms of their influence on the whole union movement, the most important new body of workers organized at this time were the bush workers. In this book emphasis has been placed on the growth of unity of the union movement through the instrumentality of central trade-union bodies and by the amalgamation and federation of local unions into larger and more comprehensive associations. This trend was accelerated by the influence of the unskilled and semi-skilled workers. The conception of special interests which deterred craft unionists from more than tentative steps towards unity of the movement as a whole did not exist for the workers who were now being brought within the union fold. For them, competition could only come from the unorganized, and strength would derive from the size and completeness of the union. So, almost from the beginning, the new unions aimed to achieve a comprehensiveness undreamed of by their predecessors.

The two giants amongst the new unions were the Amalgamated Miners' Association (A.M.A.) and the Amalgamated Shearers' Union (A.S.U.). In 1882 William Guthrie Spence, who for the next twenty years was to be the outstanding figure in Australian unionism, became general secretary of the struggling Victorian Miners' Union. He set out, in his own words, 'to unite all miners—gold, silver, copper, and coal—in one body, with an Intercolonial Council to deal with large issues and to arrange for financial aid in case of need'.[8] Within four years his ideas had been widely accepted, and seven years later branches had been established in every colony and miners of every kind were included in the organization. From 1886 Spence also played a leading part in the formation of the shearers' union. Previous unsuccessful attempts had been made to organize the shearers, but in 1886 unions were formed at various centres in New South Wales and Victoria and were immediately united as branches of the A.S.U., of which Spence became president. From its

[7] I.T.U.C. *Report*, 1888.
[8] W. G. Spence, *Australia's Awakening*, p. 33.

THE NEW UNIONISM

inception the union was thought of as an intercolonial organization. 'Before we began,' wrote Spence, 'I laid down the principle that the union must be intercolonial—must ignore political boundaries—and every member must carry his rights and privileges as a member with him.'[9]

In the first year nine thousand members were signed up, and by 1889 there were 22,500 members,[10] only a small minority of shearers remaining outside the union. In Queensland the Shearers' Union was independent of the union in other colonies, but its members worked in close collaboration with the Amalgamated Shearers' Union. The Queensland Shearers' Union had 3,000 members by 1889 and the Queensland Labourers' Union, which included rural workers other than shearers, had 6,000 members.

This record of union organization was the more remarkable because it had to overcome the barriers of distance and the political boundaries between the colonies. Contemporaries attributed the formation of the unions to various causes, none of which tell the full story. Spence himself insisted that the decision to form the shearers' union was a result of the announcement by the pastoralists of a reduction in the shearing rate.[11] A contemporary historian of the union considered that it was due to an increasing aggressiveness of the employers and an unwillingness to meet the men in conference.[12] To these must be added a number of long-standing grievances: unsatisfactory accommodation, excessive prices charged for rations from the station store, and 'raddling' were most commonly mentioned.[13]

In larger perspective, however, the particular grievances of the industries are not sufficient to explain why so many of the unskilled and semi-skilled workers were organized into unions at this time. For as well as the miners and shearers, most of the transport workers were forming unions. The waterside workers of Sydney formed a union in 1882 and were followed by those of Melbourne in 1885. Coal lumpers and trolley and draymen formed unions during the eighties and in 1885 a maritime council linked the seamen with the unions of those engaged on the various classes of work on the docks. As for the shearers, the nature of their work was peculiarly con-

[9] W. G. Spence, *History of the A.W.U.*, p. 22.
[10] *Shearers' Record*, March 1889.   [11] *Australia's Awakening*, p. 68.
[12] *Shearers' Record*, February 1889.
[13] 'Raddling' was the practice of declaring a sheep not properly shorn, in which case the shearer would not be paid for his work. Some contracts, according to Spence, included the clause that if one sheep was 'raddled' none of the day's work would be paid for.

ducive to the formation of unions. Their work was seasonal but they worked and lived together, under conditions not unlike those of factory workers in a large-scale industrial enterprise, with the difference that they had a greater sense of independence arising from the knowledge that if they lost a job in one station they could get one at the next. The success of their union undoubtedly affected others in the chain of production and transport from the station to the ship. Similarly, there was a good deal of contact between shearers and miners, many of the shearers engaging in mining in the off-season. The development of unionism in one sphere influenced others. If this interpretation of the period after the gold decade is correct, then the fundamental reason for the new unionism was the fact that the working class was becoming conscious of itself as a class.

Remarkable success attended the efforts of the new unions. For a few years the shearers won a succession of victories. The objective of the union was to reach agreements with the pastoralists of a district on working conditions in that district. The policy was to seek agreement by discussion but to back the request for an agreement by the threat of strike. So effective were the methods employed that by the end of 1889 agreements had been entered with employers in most of Queensland and New South Wales. Only in Western Victoria did the employers hold out.[14] The results had been obtained in many cases simply by negotiation, but there were also more strikes in the pastoral industry between 1886 and 1889 than in all other industries combined.[15] It was a militant unionism that sought agreement by peaceful methods, but if they failed it was prepared and sometimes anxious to fight.

The success of the shearers and the similar success of the A.M.A. confirmed the view that strength lay in unity and led to projects for still wider union organization. At the fifth Intercolonial Trade Union Congress at Brisbane in 1888 it was decided that a plan to federate all unions throughout the country should be drawn up. The task was delegated to the Brisbane Trades and Labour Council, from whose labours emerged a draft constitution of the Australian Labour Federation, which was to be a nation-wide organization of all unions with a central direction for both industrial and political activity. A programme of this kind implied that something more than the concepts of simple trade unionism lay behind the scheme— it was the notion that the working class needed organization to represent it as a class. This attitude made the organizational proposal

[14] *Shearers' Record*, March 1890.   [15] Spence, *Australia's Awakening*, p. 80.

possible, and its correctness was confirmed for many workers by the ideas of the revived socialist movement that were coming from Britain and America and were being tested against Australian experience.

Socialist thought confirmed the emergent idea of class interests and was the more readily accepted because of the trade-union experience. It justified the new attitude and was acceptable to men who had arrived empirically at the necessity for an ever-widening organization. As in Britain and America, the ideas of Henry George and Alfred Russell Wallace acted as the intellectual bridge from liberal individualism to socialist ideas.

On unionists and non-unionists alike, the theory of land nationalization and the single tax had a great influence. In a country in which land policy had been a major political issue throughout its whole history, this was inevitable. The direct influence of the theory on organized trade unionism is to be seen in the resolution adopted at the Fifth Intercolonial Trades Union Congress, the same congress that agreed to the formation of a national trade union federation. There it was resolved that

> a simple yet sovereign remedy which will raise wages, increase and give remunerative employment, abolish poverty, extirpate pauperism, lessen crime, elevate moral tastes and intelligence, purify government, and carry civilization to yet nobler heights, is to abolish all taxation save that on land values.[16]

The importance of the resolution lies not in its naïve prescription for social ills so much as in the fact that a trade union congress was prepared to stray so far from what had been considered the proper sphere of unionism. The national trade-union movement had gone far since its first tentative steps towards political action nine years before.

Although political policies flowing from George's theory continued to find a place in trade-union programmes and, later, on Labour Party platforms, the land reformers, as in Britain, popularized a line of thought that led on to socialism. In Australia the line was from George to Edward Bellamy, whose ideas reached the people in his own book *Looking Backward* and more generally from the pen of William Lane, a Brisbane journalist who, from 1887 to 1893, occupied a position of leadership that has rarely been equalled in the history of Australian radicalism. In 1887 William Lane founded in Brisbane a Bellamy Society, but it was through the columns of

[16] I.T.U.C. *Report*, 1888, p. 83.

the *Boomerang*, the *Evening Observer*, and the *Worker* that he taught to the Queensland workers the lessons he had learned from Bellamy. The significance he attached to *Looking Backward* is demonstrated by the fact that in the first issue of the *Worker*, the journal of the Australian Labour Federation, he began the serial publication of it.

Socialist ideas, then, seeped through to the working-class movement, colouring its attitude and to a lesser extent providing it with political policies. Above all they provided trade unionists with a conviction that their trade-union struggles were justified and were the stimulus that urged them on towards political action on behalf of their class. The connection between trade-union experience and the socialist ideal was the concept of co-operative action for the collective good—'to stand together that is solidarity' wrote William Lane, 'to be each for all and all for each, to move with a collective strength inspired by collective thought for the collective good'.[17] Socialist thought contrasted the collectivism of trade-union practice, in particular the trade-union practice of the new unions, with the atomism of the individualist ideal. Secondly, socialist theory sanctioned the claim of the working class for a larger share in the national wealth. Perhaps Marx's theory of value was not widely known, but in the words of a New South Wales judge of the Supreme Court, 'the idea of a great many wage getters is that the wages they get for their labour do not represent any share of the profits. Labour is the capital they possess and what they get for it is not profits any more than the hay which the horse is given to eat to keep him alive'.[18] In 1890 the president of the Sydney Trades and Labour Council would be saying that the workers generally desired some reconstruction of society but they differed as to what it should be.[19] But vague as the socialist programme was, the ideas carried a conviction that the working class had a right to a better life and that it could be achieved by co-operation. They saw, as the means, trade-union action, ever widening in its scope, and the entry of the trade unions into politics. These two conclusions were to be given organizational effect in the Australian Labour Federation.

The constitution of the Australian Labour Federation provided for a greater degree of unity of the trade-union movement than had ever existed in any country. It was to include all unions, organized in a pyramidal structure, governed by district, provincial,

---

[17] *Worker*, 1 April 1890.
[18] *Report of Royal Commission on Strikes.* Mr Justice Windeyer in minutes of evidence, q. 6468.   [19] Ibid., q. 1810.

and national councils. A degree of autonomy was to be retained by the constituent unions, but decisions on all major issues were to be taken by the higher committees of the federation. Strikes, for example, were to be decided on by the relevant committee, which would seek the opinion of the members in district or province. Although the scheme was rejected by the Intercolonial Congress in 1889 on the grounds that it left insufficient autonomy to the constituent unions, it was adopted at the Congress in 1891. In the meantime it had been put into effect in Queensland, and by 1890 the unions in six districts were federated in what was called the Australian Labour Federation and which was intended to be the Queensland province of the federation when the other colonies agreed to the organization.

On a nation-wide scale the federation was never to be an effective organization because of basic weaknesses in its proposed structure and because the events of 1890-1 directed working-class organization in New South Wales and Victoria towards the formation of parties that would be less closely linked to the unions. But the implementation of the scheme in Queensland and its adoption by the Intercolonial Congress in 1891 is of great importance in indicating the lines on which trade unionists were thinking. They were impressed by the idea of union, of co-operation that would be effective to the extent that it was comprehensive. Indicative of the same spirit was the extraordinary response to the appeal for assistance by the London dock workers on strike in 1889, when £30,000 was collected and cabled to London. William Lane called for a sympathy that extended to the ends of the earth, and leading trade unionists were thinking in terms of national trade-union co-operation, leading on to a co-operative commonwealth and perhaps even a co-operative world. The universals of triumphant liberalism in the golden age of British capitalism were being paralleled by the acceptance of cooperation, in its widest meaning, by the Australian workers in this period of successful unionism and social idealism.

In August 1890 the first general council meeting of the Australian Labour Federation, that is the Queensland section, adopted a political programme. Its preamble described competitive society as one in which the wealth of the few was constantly increasing and the poverty of the many ever becoming deeper. It was a society for the exploitation of the many by the few. 'Good times' were followed by depression, women and children worked under slavish conditions and the lives of the mass of the people could not be improved until competitive society had been replaced by collectivist society. The aims included the nationalization of the means of production and exchange, the provision of pensions for children, the invalid, and the aged, and provision from the national wealth for education and sanitation. The aims were to be achieved by forming political associations permanently connected with the industrial organization, which would stand candidates in all local and national elections.[20] In 1891 the Intercolonial Congress accepted the principle of political organization but was not prepared to adopt the political programme. This was in part due to the numerical preponderance of conservative Victorian unionists, but also to the events of 1890-1.

Up to the end of 1889 the new unions had met with very few setbacks—they had taken part in some hard and bitter struggles, but in general they had achieved their objectives. Such was their success that they were aspiring to reach agreements with employers that would cover a whole industry. This implied on the one hand the organization of the employers, and on the other the employment of unionists only in the industries where such agreements were sought. Leading unionists advocated the organization of employers so that such agreements could be reached, but found to their cost that when an efficient organization was obtained, its purpose was not to reach agreements with, but to fight the unions. Nevertheless the first round in the struggle for the comprehensive agreement went to the unions. Early in 1890 the Australian Labour Federation in Queensland gave notice to the Pastoralists' Union that wool not shorn under union conditions would be declared 'black'. They asked for a conference where an agreement binding on the whole industry might be reached. The Pastoralists' Union did not comply with the request for a meeting, and when non-union-shorn wool from Jondaryn station arrived at the wharves the wharf labourers refused to handle it. The Pastoralists' Union was forced to accept a conference and agree to the union terms, which included the clause that only unionist shearers would be employed by the members of the Pastoralists' Union. The first attempt to assert the principle of the 'closed shop' on a wide scale had succeeded and unionism had won another triumph. But it was the last for a very long time.

The employers had already decided to organize nationally, but not for the purpose of reaching an agreement with the unions on the unions' terms. They arrived at this decision because they were no longer prepared, in their own words, to accept dictation from the unions. How far this decision was influenced by economic trends is a matter of dispute, but it seems likely that there was a growing awareness that the twenty-year period of expansion was coming to an end.

[20] *Worker*, 1 September 1890, 24 January 1891.

THE NEW UNIONISM

It is more certain that pastoralists had become increasingly restive under the concessions forced from them by the unions in a period of falling export prices.[21] So pastoralists, supported by employers in the transport and mining industries, decided to fight the issue of the closed shop and assert against it the principle of 'freedom of contract'. The immediate incentive was the defeat suffered by the Queensland pastoralists in May 1890.[22] Three months later there began what was perhaps the most decisive industrial battle in Australian history. Affecting all the eastern colonies, what was known as the Maritime Strike brought out on strike transport workers, miners, and pastoral workers. For more than a month many industries were at a standstill in what had assumed the proportions of open class war. The unions were defeated and their defeat was followed by equally decisive defeats in the more violent struggles in 1891, 1892 and 1893.

The three years of depression and bitter class struggle produced a qualitative change in the Australian labour movement. Out of it emerged the Australian Labour Party as a direct consequence of the trade unions' movement towards political action before the strikes, but hastened in its formation and considerably influenced in its policy by the defeats. The three years saw the governments of the colonies more or less openly taking the side of the employing class in the war with the workers, and subsequently participating more directly in industrial relations. It cut short the development of idealist socialism, although that remained an element in labour thought, and sent its most ardent idealist and socialist, William Lane, on a hopeless venture to establish in South America the New Australia that he had believed in 1889 would be created in Australia.

---

[21] On the evidence of aggregate capital formation, N. G. Butlin suggests that the onset of the depression of the nineties may be dated 1888-9; *Private Capital Formation in Australia*, p. 12.

[22] *Official Statement of the Facts and History of the Shearing Difficulty in Australia:* Compiled for presentation to the Royal Commission on Labour (England) by the Pastoralists Federal Council.

7

Nationalism and the New Radicalism, 1885-1890

We are for this Australia, for the nationality that is creeping to the verge of being, for the progressive people that is just plucking aside the curtain that veils its fate. Behind us lies the Past, with its crashing empires, its falling thrones, its dotard races; before us lies the Future into which Australia is plunging, this Australia of ours that burns with the feverish energy of youth.[1]

Time will sanctify any encroachment and petrify any grip; hence the tendency of classes is to congeal into castes. Freedom comes back in strong convulsions, often accompanied by haemorrhage, never without strenuous battle in field or senate, waged under terrible disadvantage. Nothing is easier than for Pompey to laugh away his birthright; nothing is harder than for him to weep it back again.[2]

THE great strikes of the nineties stand out quite clearly as the culmination of a period of Australian history. In retrospect it is tempting to paint them merely as class battles, as struggles between the opposing forces that history has created. They were that, but they were also struggles between men who had a more or less clear idea of their own purposes. Those who took part in them were fighting for principles that had become accepted in the years before the strikes. Unionists fought for the principles of unionism, and against them employers posed the principle of freedom of contract. But behind these opposing principles were the attitudes and convictions that made men prepared to fight.

Between 1885 and 1890 the wide extension of trade-union organization was the visible expression of the ideas of the working class. We have seen that a unionism with a new emphasis developed in these years with the organization of the unskilled and semi-skilled workers and particularly of the bush workers. We have seen also that the leaders of the new unions departed from many of the tenets that had been fundamental to unionism previously. They believed that the whole of the working class should be organized in unions and that between the unions there should be a maximum of unity. Barriers

---

[1] W. Lane, *Boomerang* (Brisbane), 19 November 1887.
[2] J. Furphy, *Rigby's Romance*, p. 113. This book was first published in serial form in the *Barrier Truth* (Broken Hill) in 1905-6.

of trade and skill and political boundaries should not obstruct the widest co-operation.

The simple fact that a large proportion of the population was now confirmed in the status of wage earners with little prospect of ever changing that status accounts in part for the acceleration of trade-union development. But the other part of the explanation is to be found in the new ideas influencing men's opinions, for in these years there took place a marriage between attitudes moulded by the conditions of life in Australia and ideas reaching Australia from Britain and the United States.

By 1885 Great Britain had already experienced ten years of the Great Depression. Her monopoly of world trade had lasted a bare twenty years. The confident expectation that, given what liberalism understood by freedom, the world, and particularly Britain, would advance to ever new levels of national wealth and production was being questioned. The rate of progress had slackened. The world monopoly was being threatened by the competition of the new Great Powers, Germany and the United States of America. An empire that had been developed by the enterprise of individuals was under threat from Germany, France, and Russia. The liberal concept of Empire was being replaced by the new imperialism. If Lord John Russell's calm acceptance of the ultimate independence of the colonies was characteristic of the fifties, W. E. Forster's statement that 'the nations of Europe begin to find out how important it is for England to have great possessions in different parts of the world, and try to have their share in such possessions',[3] was equally characteristic of the eighties. Liberal imperialism was giving way to projects of imperial federation and other plans for retaining the unity of an empire that was threatened from without by the new powers and from within by movements for independence.

Similarly, liberal beliefs about the welfare of the people were being questioned. The greatest good for the greatest number had not been secured by free competition and the abstinence of the state from intervention in economic affairs. Recognition of this produced a new emphasis in liberal thought—a preparedness to mitigate the deplorable conditions of life produced by industrial capitalism amongst the less favoured sections of the people by state intervention. But the working class also was finding its own solutions in the rebirth of socialist ideas and in the extension of trade unionism.

Ideas and events in Australia were deeply influenced by the new current flowing in Britain, but they were by no means a mirror of

[3] Cited S. Lane-Poole (ed.), *Thirty Years of Colonial Government*, p. 5.

events on the other side of the world. Part of the effect was a reaction against contemporary English tendency, but part also was in sympathy.

The reaction to the new imperialism was a vehement expression of national feeling. This new radicalism found a sympathetic audience amongst working-men already moving in the direction pointed by the new ideas and by middle-class radicals seized by the possibility of establishing an Australian utopia. The reaction against imperialism and the belief in the possibility of creating the good society came together in a composite of ideas and attitudes that we may call radical nationalism. In its negative aspect it was a rejection of the assumptions that lay at the roots of the class societies of the old world; in its positive aspect it was the assertion of the validity of values which were thought of as distinctively Australian.

In the establishment and extension of self-government and democracy, radicals had found themselves at odds with the upper classes in Australia and with the British government. But because the society was too new to have acquired a settled way of life and a set of distinctive beliefs, and because the British government never resisted the aspirations of the colonists to the breaking-point, the continuing movement for self-government had not articulated a distinctively national position. John Dunmore Lang saw a nation in the future, developing within independent institutions. Higinbotham fought for rights of self-government. The Melbourne people who demonstrated in 1865 denounced the Legislative Council and the squatters, in whose efforts to gain British support they saw a subversion of the rights of self-government. From the fifties onward democratic opinion was coloured with the belief that there was more possibility of creating a political and social democracy in Australia than in the old world. But it was not until the eighties that there was any fully explicit statement of the principles which Australians believed were enshrined in their national outlook.

A recent writer has argued with convincing evidence that the beliefs and attitudes which in the eighties became accepted as distinctively Australian were largely a product of the life of the bush workers to the west of the Great Divide, in New South Wales, Queensland, and to a lesser extent, Victoria.[4] Convict attitudes to one another and to their masters, the contest with loneliness and an intractable natural environment, the struggle for the land, the remoteness from the evidences of state power, moulded a class of men different in important respects from those of any other country. The

[4] Ward, *The Australian Legend*.

American frontier bred the individualistic farmer. Australia to the west of the mountains, with a pastoral industry controlled by a handful of squatters, produced a rural working class characterized by ' "a manly independence" whose obverse side was a levelling, egalitarian collectivism, and whose sum was comprised in the concept of mateship'.[5] To such men 'unionism came as a new religion', and through their union they in turn influenced in greater or less degree the union movement as a whole. But their influence penetrated deeper than that because in the eighties a self-conscious nationalist press impressed their outlook on broad sections of the Australian people as the distinctively national.

The national ethos which gained more or less coherent expression during the eighties in the nationalist press, and in the nineties and after in formal literature, may be reduced to a few simple assumptions. First in importance was the dignity and equality of man. 'I cannot', wrote Joseph Furphy, 'think it is anything worse than a locally-seated and curable ignorance which makes men eager to subvert a human equality, self-evident as human variety and impregnable as any mathematical axiom.'[6] Similarly the *Bulletin* commented on the appointment of Lord Carrington as Governor, 'in growing democracies anything which fosters the belief that distinction of any description is the natural and just reward of the accident of birth is noxious'.[7] The source of infection was seen as Britain. The young Henry Lawson, soon to be accepted as Australia's first truly national poet, warned that there was a danger that Australians might find,

> the good old English gentlemen over them; the good old English squire over them, the good old English lord over them, the good old English aristocracy rolling round them in cushioned carriages, scarcely deigning to rest their eyes on the 'common people' who toil, starve and rot for them; and the good old English throne over them all.[8]

Within Australia the danger to democracy was believed to be with the upper classes. Furphy has his socialist agitator say,

> I tell you that from the present social system of pastoral Australia —a patriarchal despotism, tempered by Bryant and May—to actual lordship and peonage, is an easy transition, and the only thing that can prevent this broadening down is a vigorous rally of every man with a clear head and a heart in the right place.[9]

[5] Ibid., p. 167.   [6] J. Furphy, *Such is Life*, p. 109.   [7] 23 January 1886.
[8] *Republican*, 15 October 1887.   [9] *Rigby's Romance*, p. 98.

Furphy's Australians were the itinerant workers of the outback. Rough and unlettered, but thoughtful and useful, 'mateship' was the first article of their credo. For Lawson, too, the bushmen symbolized a way of life that he identified with Australia. 'Rugged and true,' wrote one of his friends and critics, 'his bushmen helped each other in times of difficulty and trouble. However unworthy some of them might be, they seemed to recognise the ideal of mateship.'[10]

The majority of people in Australia in the eighties did not live, nor had they ever lived, the life from which the national myth was fashioned. But many who had passed their lives in the narrow streets of Sydney or the sprawling suburbs of Brisbane saw in it something with which they sympathized, for political democracy had existed for a generation and social stratification had never been accepted by more than a tiny minority. What the nationalist writers had to say expressed something that was recognizable to all Australians, and with which many could identify themselves. Similarly, they were equally impressed by the importance of preserving Australia from influences that would undermine those values. Joseph Furphy believed Australia to be a 'virgin continent'—

> she is committed to no usages of petrified injustice; she is clogged by no fealty to shadowy idols, enshrined by Ignorance, and upheld by misplaced homage alone; she is cursed by no memories of fanaticism and persecution; she is innocent of hereditary national jealousy, and free from the envy of sister states.[11]

To keep her free of such a heritage was the express aim of the Australian nationalist.

Such a concept of the nation was essentially a class view. As Hancock puts it, amongst the workers 'it was impossible to disentangle the passions of class and of nationalism, so inextricably were they intertwined'.[12] The idealized way of life was that of the common people who, as we have seen, had become, by the eighties, a working class. On the other hand the threat to the ideal future seemed to lie with the imperialists, both English and Australian, who were seeking closer ties between Britain and her colonies—and in Australia these were drawn from the upper class.

> The squatters and their allies were not, like the great mass of immigrant settlers and their children, compelled by circumstances to break their connections with England and accept Australia as their only home. They went to and from one hemisphere to

---

[10] J. Le Gay Brereton (ed.), *Henry Lawson by his Mates*, p. 15.
[11] J. Furphy, *Such is Life*, p. 81.   [12] W. K. Hancock, *Australia*, p. 62.

another; often they ended their days in England, and sometimes they sent their sons to Oxford or Cambridge; behind them stood the powerful financial houses, controlled from London and controlling the economy of Australia; they were welcome at Government House, and met there officers of His Majesty's Navy and journalist-politicians who argued for Imperial federation.[13]

The issue between nationalist and imperialist was sharpened by the British government's handling of Australian affairs. After 1880 the defence of Australia became an immediate problem. The French in New Caledonia had always been regarded with suspicion by those Australians who were not convinced that the British Navy was sufficient safeguard for Australian shores. The forward movement of European imperialism was watched in Australia with deep apprehension. In 1883 Sir Thomas McIlwraith, with Germany's designs on New Guinea as a reason or a pretext, annexed to Queensland that part of the island not occupied by the Dutch. There were rumours, made more than credible by the presence of troops on the island, of French intentions to occupy the New Hebrides. Then there was the standing question of the immigration of Asiatics into Australia. On all these questions the imperial government appeared to Australians to be taking up an unreasonable position. The annexation of New Guinea was disavowed by the Colonial Secretary, Lord Derby, 'who treated the colonial fears of foreign aggression with chilling disdain, assuring the Australians that their nervousness was ridiculous and that Germany had no designs on New Guinea'.[14] The annexation of northern New Guinea by Germany immediately afterwards did not increase Australian respect for the understanding of the Colonial Office. The refusal of the British government to take action in connection with the New Hebrides was interpreted in like fashion, and the Victorian government made plans to occupy the islands in spite of the opposition of Downing Street. In relation to the restriction of entry of the Chinese, the Colonial Office was even more deaf to opinion in the colonies. Miss Willard comments that the apparent dilatoriness of Lord Knutsford, Colonial Secretary, was due to a lack of appreciation of the development of opinion in Australia;[15] a development which caused Sir Henry Parkes to declaim that, 'neither for Her Majesty's ships of war nor for Her Majesty's representatives, nor for the Secretary of State, do we intend to turn aside from our purpose, which is to terminate the landing of Chinese on these shores for ever'.[16]

[13] Ibid., p. 60.   [14] W. Murdoch, *Alfred Deakin*, p. 115.
[15] M. Willard, *History of the White Australia Policy*, p. 77.
[16] Cited S. H. Roberts, *Contacts between the Orient and Australia*, p. 39.

Whereas the exclusion of Chinese had originally been seen by the workers as a policy with an economic sanction, during the eighties it became linked also with Australian national feeling—the Australian future was to be white. The nationalist press carried on a campaign against the admission of Chinese, and the policy of the British government and the Australian imperialists was represented as calculated to undermine the future of the white nation. In Queensland, William Lane employed his great journalistic talents to argue that the Chinese were a danger to the social life and the moral standards of the people. He painted with heavy hand the horrors of opium dens and the insidious attractions of fan-tan with its peculiar orientalism, the inscrutable faces of the players, and the squalor and disease of the surroundings. His readers were undoubtedly with Lane when he wrote of an opium den in Brisbane:

> and it angered me to see these men so smooth-faced and plump and contented, their placid natures nurtured by the drug that kills the passionate white man, and to think that in this smoky, stifling, stinking den these Mongolians were as much at home as if it were in distant China, and that all this was in Brisbane, in the capital of the colony that we hope to make a great white state.[17]

The assumption of the racial superiority of white men was tempered in the viewpoint of the Australian nationalist by the conviction that the employing class in Australia were prepared to sell their country's birthright for cheap labour. The squatters and the British government were regarded as being in league to foist on the white democratic Australian nation a slave population that would destroy for ever the possibilities for the future they visualized. It was assumed, further, that imperial-minded Australians, who in return for favours from the ruling class of Britain were putting the interests of Britain before those of Australia, might well in the future become the traitorous associates of a dominant Chinese who would seize control of the country and enslave the white Australian workers. In a serial story, 'White or Yellow' which ran in the *Boomerang* for three months,[18] William Lane developed this theme. It is a story set in Queensland in 1908 when the Chinese, in collaboration with a minority of wealthy Europeans, have established an alien dictatorship. The native Australians have become slaves serving their brutal oriental masters. A rising of the Australians against the despots provides Lane with an opportunity of describing a

[17] *Boomerang*, 21 January 1888.   [18] Ibid., 18 February to 5 May 1888.

revolutionary race war of Australian democracy opposing the combination of jack-booted Chinese and their sycophantic European collaborators, who are pictured as being remarkably like the *Boomerang's* impression of the Queensland imperialists of 1888. The Order of Saint Michael and Saint George, which was in Lane's opinion the price demanded by Australian politicians for imperial allegiances, had in 1908 been replaced by a dragon emblem on the breasts of the associates of the new masters. Racial prejudice, brutal and at times fanatical, was perhaps an inevitable aspect of Australian nationalism developing under the conditions we have described.

The British government remained apparently unaware of the aspirations of Australian nationalism. In 1887 the Colonial Conference met in London and there it was made clear that feeling in Australia was either unknown or ignored. Richard Jebb writes of

> the original conception of the Conference as a meeting between the Colonies (collectively, sectionally or individually) on the one hand and the British Government on the other; the former being in the position of vassals invited to confer with their overlord, who would graciously listen to their representations.[19]

It was this attitude, implicit in the conference and demonstrated in relation to the question of Australian defence and the exclusion of the Chinese, that added fuel to the fires of Australian nationalism. Australians were no longer prepared to be treated as colonials. One reaction to this situation was the demand for a greater degree of independence within the empire—the objective to which Higinbotham had devoted his life and of which in the eighties Alfred Deakin became the most ardent advocate. Imperial federation was entertained as a possible solution at this time by Deakin and men who thought like him, but already Deakin was also beginning to formulate the idea of what in practice became dominion status. On the other hand, the more radical nationalists turned to republicanism, in open opposition to imperialism. The Australian advocates of imperial federation or any solution short of complete independence were regarded as prostituted instruments of British imperialism whose price in honours and titles had been paid by an imperial government that had become quite shameless in the lavish bestowal of such signs of its approval. The imperial navy scheme under which Australia was to contribute towards the upkeep of a squadron of the British Navy was received by the nationalist press with most bitter

[19] R. Jebb, *The Imperial Conference*, p. 11.

criticism. In paragraph and cartoon the Australian flag was held in contrast with the white ensign, and the United States was presented as pointing the way to Australia's destiny.[20] The refusal of the British government to agree to the complete exclusion of Chinese, on the grounds that it would exclude British subjects from a British colony, was received in the same way. The policy the colonial governments agreed to at the intercolonial conference of 1888—to restrict but not prohibit Chinese immigration—was seen as a result of pressure by the British government. William Lane characterized it as 'altogether insufficient, puerile and absurd' and typical of 'perfidious Albion'.[21]

The English republican and secularist movement provided the bullets fired in Australia.[22] A Republican Union was founded in Sydney in 1887 and a year later it became the Republican League, with branches in Melbourne and Adelaide. The annexation of New Guinea inspired its formation and Australian national feeling was its emotional *raison d'être*, but much of its propaganda was drawn direct from contemporary English sources. Republicans were advised to read the works of Morrison Davidson, Howard Evans and Max Nordau. The most prolific of the republican publicists, George Black, who later became a Labour member of parliament and still later a conservative minister, delighted in attacking the person and institutions of monarchy. 'Let us,' he wrote, 'look down through the ages, 'mongst the mists of blood, the smoke of torture fires, and the vapours of lascivious sweat that shroud the throne, in order to examine critically the character of past English rulers.'[23]

From time to time the *Bulletin* expressed itself in equally unbridled language. It referred to our own rulers, the record of whose lives 'constitutes one of the meanest and bloodiest pages in the annals of mankind. Shocking inhumanity, unbridled lust, treachery, superstition, ignorance, stupidity unfathomable, meanness immeasurable, fill the dreary page from top to bottom.'[24] But more generally, republican propaganda contented itself with opposition to imperialism. Many Australians who were not anxious to attack the Queen agreed with Henry Lawson—'Why on earth do we want

[20] *Boomerang*, 26 November 1887; *Bulletin*, 4 June, 2, 30 July 1887.
[21] *Boomerang*, 16 June 1888.
[22] It is interesting to note that in 1888 a majority in the full Supreme Court of New South Wales found that *The Law of Population* by Annie Besant was 'neither obscene in the language, nor by its teaching incites people to obscenity'. In a long judgment Mr Justice Windeyer used what was essentially the argument of the book to justify its publication.
[23] G. Black, *Why I am a Republican*, p. 5.
[24] *Bulletin*, 16 January 1886.

closer connection with England? ... The loyal talk of Patriotism, Old England Mother Land etc. Patriotism? after Egypt, Burmah, Soudan, etc. Bah! it sickens one ... We are Australians—we know no other land.'[25]

Australian republicanism was essentially one of the political forms which Australian nationalism took at this time.[26] That the workers were nationalists we know, but how far they were republican is more difficult to decide. It is probable that in Queensland republicanism was more generally accepted than in the other colonies. William Lane could not have occupied the position in the labour movement that he did if his republican views were not acceptable to great numbers of the workers. At the eight-hour celebration that accompanied the Intercolonial Trades Union Congress in 1888 the loyal toasts were replaced by 'the day we celebrate', and three cheers were given for the 'Federated Republic of Australia'. The Australian Labour Federation was frankly republican in its utterances on the federation of Australia.[27] In New South Wales the labour movement was sufficiently republican to include in the platform of the Labour Electoral League 'the federation of the Australian colonies upon a national as opposed to an imperialistic basis'. The Associated Riverina Workers, of which the Wagga branch of the Amalgamated Shearers' Union was the effective centre, had as point six of their programme 'the complete political independence of the United Australian Commonwealth on a basis of pure democratic republicanism'.[28] But on the other hand it seems quite clear that Victorian unionists were less republican than those of the other two colonies.

The upper class in Australia were economically and culturally bound to Britain; were even admitted to their circle on a basis of near equality by the ruling class of Britain. Consequently Australian national feeling was an essential part of the class feeling generated in the conflict between classes in Australia. The same conflict created the trade-union movement, in whose creation nationalism was one of the catalysts, but after 1885 socialist ideas were another.

As we have seen, the road to socialist ideas in Australia was broken by the writings of the American Henry George and the

---

[25] *Republican*, 7 January 1888.
[26] Programme of the Republican League: 'Abolition of the office of Governor; payment of members; abolition of the Upper House; abolition of all titular distinctions; revision of the penal code; the championship of liberty at all times; nationalization of the land; federation of the Australian colonies under republican rule'. *Republican*, 8 February 1888.
[27] *Worker*, 16 May 1891. [28] *Hummer*, 23 April 1892.

Englishman Alfred Russell Wallace. Henry George's *Progress and Poverty* was published in 1879 and he immediately gained great popularity as a reformer in America and England. His work became known a little later in Australia and was widely read after 1885. There was little that was new in George's book, which drew heavily on Ricardo and Mill's theory of rent and the land schemes of Spence and Dove. But it was written in a popular style and advertised by George's Homeric lecturing tour of the United States and Britain.

John Mill concluded that land differed from all other property and was not 'sacred' in the sense that other private property was. Rent he considered different from all other income, in that it increased without any effort by the owner of the land and should therefore be subject to a special tax. He was not even opposed to the state resuming the land. George accepted Mill's reasoning on the nature of rent but differed from him by attributing all the ills of modern society to rent deriving from private property in land, and posited that the solution to all social problems was to be found in society taking over the land on behalf of the people. George contrived a whole philosophic system in which the central feature is his analysis of the function of rent. By inference and analogy he 'disproved' the Malthusian theory. He accepted what he referred to as 'current political economy'—that is Mill's reasoning on rent— and concluded that because with material progress rent everywhere advances, therefore wages and interest do not increase. It is the operation of this 'law' and not, as Malthus had thought, an increase in population that keeps wages at a dead level of subsistence. It also explained to George's satisfaction the recurrence of depressions. The ethical consideration, in his opinion, pointed directly to the fact that private property in land could not be justified. Consequently the remedy he saw was for the state to take over the land on behalf of all the people. The method was to be neither by confiscation nor compensation, but by a graduated tax on land that would make the ownership of land unprofitable unless it was used to its full capacity. Whilst he was not opposed to the confiscation of land on ethical grounds, he considered that it was not necessary, since the same result could be achieved more gradually and less painfully by taxation.

George's theory was attractive in its simplicity, and since it placed the weight of responsibility for the maladies of society on the system of landholding, it could appeal to very wide sections of the people without affecting their interests adversely. Many workers, professional people, and even employers were prepared to agree that this might well be the explanation of the paradox of poverty amidst plenty. It appealed to the same groups, too, because it was an extension of the free-trade argument, the single tax being intended to replace all other taxation. The general tenor of the ideas was supported by the growing weight of opinion on the question of land reform. The Land Tenure Reform Association, numbering among its members John Mill, Professor Thorold Rogers, John Morley, Sir Charles Dilke and Alfred Russell Wallace, had been active in Britain since 1870. Its work was known in Australia and the writings, particularly of Thorold Rogers and Alfred Russell Wallace, were being read by many of those to whom George also appealed.[29] They advocated nationalization of the land, but both George and the land nationalizers contributed to the broad stream of collectivist opinion.

During 1887 land nationalization leagues were established in Brisbane, Gympie and Charters Towers; Sydney and eight central western country towns; and later in Melbourne and Adelaide.[30] At first these Leagues discussed and advocated the policies of the English Land Tenure Reform Association, but during 1888-9 the direct influence of George becomes evident. 'Out in the great bush where men have time to think,' wrote John Farrell, '*Progress and Poverty* was read with understanding and passed from hand to hand until the sublime truth of it was impressed on many.'[31] Single-tax leagues were formed, and single-taxers infiltrated the land nationalization leagues. The influence of George's theories on the policy of the trade-union movement has already been noted. It will be seen further that, in the nineties and after, the idea of the single tax contributed to Labour Party political policy. Up to 1890, however, its most important effect, as in Britain, was in initiating a line of thought that led on to socialism, even though George himself was strongly opposed to socialism.

The socialism that influenced the broad masses in Australia was the socialism of Edward Bellamy. Like George, Bellamy had little to say that was new. He merely selected his ideas from those that were common to English socialism of the early nineteenth century, the Christian socialism of the middle of the century, and the utopian socialism of Horace Greeley and that group of rebel spirits who taught and tried to practise socialism in the United States. Nor was his method of presenting his ideas new. He followed the tradition of the utopian novel which had contributed to literature More's *Utopia*,

[29] G. Black, *A History of the New South Wales Political Labor Party*, pt. 1, p. 21.
[30] L. G. Churchward, 'The American Influence on the Australian Labour Movement', *Hist. Studies*, vol. v, no. xix.   [31] *Australian Star*, 2 January 1888.

Etienne Cabet's *Voyage en Icarie*, Morelly's *Basiliade* and other works. What was new was a public prepared to accept the utopia he painted as a realizable objective for which they could work.

Briefly, Bellamy's *Looking Backward* is a utopian novel that describes the life of a socialist America in the year 2000 A.D. Rather crudely strung together is the story of a Rip Van Winkle who wakes to find himself in Boston, which had begun to be organized as a part of socialist America fifty years before. Bellamy examines this imaginary society, in which co-operation had replaced competition, and contrasts it with the Boston of 1887. Poverty has been abolished by the simple expedient of an immense expansion of mechanical power and economies of human energy made possible by eliminating the waste of the competitive system. Production and distribution are ordered and planned by the state, the whole population being organized in an industrial army and fitted into the productive and distributive machine according to their abilities and inclinations. The method of production having been satisfactorily provided for, the people can devote themselves to physical and cultural betterment. It is a society in which there is no place for the stresses of capitalist society, and man's inhumanity to man has been replaced by co-operation and love. A new kind of people has been created by the new environment, and unfettered by the social and economic controls that result in the more unpleasant features of men and women today, the human race is constantly improving. 'Hence', as one critic of Bellamy expresses it, 'the unlovely in human nature will be gradually eliminated, while "gifts of person, mind and disposition; beauty, wit, eloquence, kindness, generosity, geniality, courage" will be perpetuated'.[32]

The ethical sanction for the co-operative commonwealth Bellamy found in Christianity. Socialism, he claimed, involved 'nothing less than a literal fulfilment on a complete social scale, of Christ's inculcation that all should feel the same solicitude and make the same effort for the welfare of others as for their own'.[33] Man would be changed by a socialist organization of society and would become much closer to the Christian ideal. He would already have commenced that mutation before a socialist organization was possible, because Bellamy believed that the transition to socialist society would occur as a result of the changed attitude of people. People would become aware of the illogicality and brutality of existing society which would be gradually changed from political democracy

[32] W. F. Taylor, *The Economic Novel in America*, p. 197.
[33] *Looking Backward*, p. 62.

to social and economic equality. Socialism would be introduced not by class warfare but by the conviction in men's minds that it was desirable.

In Queensland, William Lane as editor of the *Boomerang* and later the *Worker* taught a socialism that was in all essentials the creed of Bellamy. His thought had been greatly influenced by the English Christian socialists, American social experiments, and particularly by Laurence Gronlund's *Co-operative Commonwealth*.[34] He seized on *Looking Backward* after its publication in 1888 as a book that embodied most completely the ideas that he was already teaching. He founded a Bellamy Society,[35] and wrote that in *Looking Backward* was to be found a picture of his ideal society.[36] He accepted Bellamy, but at the same time went beyond him because he saw in the trade-union organization of the working class the possibility of people working co-operatively for agreed ends—he saw in unionism co-operative socialist living in microcosm within capitalist society. But he believed that by propaganda and example people of goodwill of all classes would come to see the correctness of his viewpoint. He tried to awaken the conscience of Queensland by bringing into the light the lives of the most debased and oppressed section of the community. He scoured the slums of Brisbane and wrote detailed reports of what he had found.[37] Feeling the tragedy of the broken lives he saw, he used all the tricks of nineteenth century sentimentalism to make the improvement of their lot the responsibility of all who read his reports. The condition of the people he attributed not to their own innate weakness but to the working of a merciless competitive system. He was bitterly critical of 'charity as a business', and demanded that society be so reconstructed that there would be no need for charity. While directing his appeal in the main to the workers, he called on all people to join him in the crusade. He seemed to be winning a great victory when he was able to publish an article by the Premier, Sir Samuel Griffith, on 'Wealth and Want', an exposition of views that seemed to be very similar to Lane's own.[38]

Had Lane confined himself to journalism his influence would have been great, but it was made the greater by his active participation in the practical tasks of organization. Convinced that in trade unionism he could see the new society of co-operation in the 'womb

[34] See *Ross's Monthly*, 16 August 1919. G. G. Reeve mentions the Icarian settlement in Narvos, Illinois, as having influenced Lane.
[35] E. H. Lane, *Dawn to Dusk*, p. 12. [36] *Worker*, 1 March 1890.
[37] *Boomerang*, December 1887 to December 1888.
[38] The Christmas *Boomerang*, 1888.

of the old', he strove for a comprehensive organization of the working class. He was largely responsible for the formation of the Brisbane Trades and Labour Council in 1885, and he drafted the plan of the Australian Labour Federation in 1889, by which the Queensland political labour movement adopted a socialist objective. He was the adviser and friend of the leaders of the trade-union movement and the inspiration of the solidarity action with the London dockworkers in 1889.[39] In fact, Lane's role was to wed the labour movement in Queensland to the socialist ideal. In the other colonies there was no figure comparable with Lane to channel socialist ideas to the working class, but reach them they did. William Guthrie Spence, himself a follower of Henry George, testified in 1890 that the workers desired a reconstruction of society although they differed as to what it should be.[40]

The socialism of Bellamy was the belief that influenced the broad masses, but in Sydney and Melbourne there were small socialist groups—the nucleus from which the left wing of the labour movement grew—that were even in the eighties striving for theoretical purity. In Melbourne, an anarchist club was started in 1886 and in Sydney, the Australian Socialist League in the following year. They were really debating societies, very small in membership,[41] where the ideas of contemporary socialism were discussed. Members called themselves followers of Hyndman, Annie Besant, Karl Marx and Kropotkin, but their interpretations of these various schools of socialist and anarchist thought revealed a gargantuan confusion on what their various leaders stood for. One of the leading members, for example, claimed to be an adherent of Marx but insisted that the best exposition of his viewpoint was to be found in Gronland's *Co-operative Commonwealth,* the writings of Sidney Webb, Bernard Shaw, Annie Besant and in W. H. Dawson's *Bismarck and State Socialism.*[42]

The theoretical confusion in the revived English socialist movement was worse confounded when it was transferred half-way around the world to Australia. Until 1884 a number of fundamentally opposing viewpoints were represented in the English Social Democratic Federation because the differences between them had not been clearly worked out. Bernard Shaw wrote ten years later that the reason why 'Anarchists and Socialists worked then shoulder to shoulder, as comrades and brothers, was that neither one nor the

[39] Ibid., August to December 1889.
[40] *The Royal Commission on Strikes,* q. 1810.
[41] *Australian Radical,* 2 February 1889.
[42] *The Royal Commission on Strikes,* qq. 9499-9501.

other had any definite ideas of what he wanted or how it was to be got'.⁴³ The fissure in the Social Democratic Federation in 1884, the formation of the Socialist League, and the increasing separateness of the Fabians was a result of the conflict that emerged as the radically different socialist doctrines took shape. The Australian socialist groups, being wholly dependent on the ideas of the leaders of English socialism, who were themselves only in the course of clarifying their own position, were naturally struggling in a sea of conflicting principles.

There appears to have been little agreement in the Australian Socialist League on any question except that the distribution of wealth in capitalist society was unfair and that some kind of common ownership of the means of production was necessary.⁴⁴ On immediate political issues there was the widest divergence of opinion. The co-secretaries of the league, W. H. McNamara and J. E. Anderton, for example, held conflicting views on strikes as a means of improving the conditions of the workers. State education had its supporters and opponents. Free trade and protection were argued heatedly. In fact, the manifesto of the League gave a fair picture of its character—it aimed 'to foster public interest in the great social questions of the day by promoting inquiry in every possible manner; and to circulate and publish literature throwing light upon the existing evils of society, and the methods necessary for their removal'.⁴⁵ The league did serve the purpose of providing a forum in which people who were later to play a part in politics received their introduction to socialist ideas.⁴⁶ It also kept at least a few people in touch with events in the labour movement in other parts of the world. The Paris Commune was regularly celebrated and was pointed to as an object lesson for all workers. The execution of the four Chicago anarchists in 1887 caused a thrill of sympathy in the ranks of the league, and memorial services were held on the anniversary of their death.⁴⁷ Probably many of the members were more interested in events in other countries than those in their own. This was particularly true in Melbourne, where the anarchists were joined by a German Socialist Club in establishing a branch of the Australian Socialist League in 1888. There, as in Sydney, anarchist and socialist ideas were debated.

⁴³ G. B. Shaw, *The Fabian Society* (Fabian Tract No. 41), p. 15.
⁴⁴ W. H. McNamara in a speech, 'Land, Labor and Capital; or Pampered Parasites and Purple clad Thieves'. *Radical*, 19 November 1887.
⁴⁵ Ibid., 19 November 1887.
⁴⁶ Black, *A History of the New South Wales Political Labor Party*, pt. 1, p. 22.
⁴⁷ *Australian Radical*, 17 November 1888.

The Socialist League was a tributary of the main stream of political life in Australia, but it was also the direct predecessor of the various organizations constituting the left wing of the labour movement through which the doctrines of the International Workers of the World and Marxism reached some Australian workers. The socialism that did reach the workers was an idealist socialism on which Frederick Engels made the penetrating comment, 'socialism is the expression of absolute truth, reason and justice, and needs only to be discovered to conquer the world by virtue of its own power'.[48] The socialist commonwealth appeared to these socialists as a rational social organization which, by contrast with existing society, must appeal to people of all classes who could be brought to think about it. To these socialists, Engels remarked, 'Society presented nothing but abuses; it was the task of the thinking intellect to remove them'.[49] The socialism that influenced the Australian labour movement was of this kind.

Directly, it encouraged the extension of trade unionism, it assisted in breaking down the barriers between the trades, it fostered the growth of nation-wide unity of trade unions. It gave the workers a justification for their claims for the betterment of their position, and it provided for some trade unionists what was in the nature of a religious ideal to work towards. But because its emphasis was on the common interest of all classes in achieving a socialist society, it did not prepare trade unionists for the realities of class warfare which their very organization made inevitable. Lane was convinced that the majority of employers would see the justice of the demand for radical social and economic readjustment. He believed that only the ruthless employer would resist the just claims of trade unionists, and it was against him that strike action would be directed—he did not foresee that the employers as a class and with the backing of the state would ultimately set out to suppress the 'dangerous ideas' with which the working class had become infected. In May 1890 he was writing that it was socialism 'that is moving the world. We are all socialists only some of us don't know it',[50] and in the middle of the maritime strike he could still write that there is 'many a heart-sick employer, feeling humanity stirring within him, will come to join either openly or secretly in the fight to overthrow the wages system, to idealise labour, to conquer Want and Hate and Greed and Vice, to establish peace on earth and goodwill among men'.[51]

This attitude is also directly expressed in policy statements by

[48] F. Engels, *Herr Eugen Duhring's Revolution in Science*, p. 26.
[49] Ibid., p. 291.   [50] *Worker*, 1 May 1890.   [51] Ibid., 1 October, 1890.

the unions. Conflict between workers and employers was attributed to misunderstanding, and the union seen as a means of preventing it. 'By looking beneath the surface of labor disputes they [employers and employees] discover that their interests are identical,' said the 1889 annual report of the most militant of the new unions.[52] Records of conferences between the leaders of the Amalgamated Shearers' Union and employers' organizations clearly show that the unionists approached the conference in a spirit of compromise which arose from the belief that the rights of the workers were limited. They believed in a 'fair thing' and they believed further that in conference the employers would be able to see the fairness of their requests. W. G. Spence always insisted that he was prepared to help the employers to organize because he believed that in that way the conditions of labour for the whole country could be settled around the conference table.

Thus an idealist socialism was a profoundly important influence in the growth of the working-class movement, but as a theory it was inadequate in directing the strategy and tactics of trade unionists in the struggles that their organization made inevitable. In the course of the strikes in the nineties a very different attitude was forced on many unionists, but the conclusions which they drew from their experience were limited by the ideological concepts that have been outlined.

[52] *Shearers' Record*, March 1889. Annual Report of the Amalgamated Shearers' Union.

8

The Formation of the Labour Party

The effect of the maritime strike was to galvanise into life the hitherto latent idea that voting power carried with it not only the choice of the Parliamentary representative, but also of the work he was expected to do when sent to the Legislature. . . . The idea of self-government came to him [the worker] in a new light, and he saw that he must not only vote, but must make the platform, and select his own political war-cry.[1]

DURING the second half of 1890 and the first half of 1891, the trade-union movement suffered two shattering defeats and the Labour Party was born. The defeats in the strikes were not the single cause of the formation of the Labour Party but were the final incentive needed to launch it. The strikes were so decisive because the issue at stake was the right of the unions to act on behalf of the working class in all their relations with the employers. They were decisive also because, in the minds of both workers and employers, they were a test of strength on a wide front between forces that had been skirmishing for the previous five years.

In New South Wales during the first half of 1890 firm steps towards political action were taken by the trade unions. At the beginning of the year the Trades and Labour Council had thirty affiliated societies with a membership of 20,000. By June it had fifty-three affiliates with a total membership of 35,000. In his half-yearly report the secretary announced that 'never before in the history of the Council has such phenomenal uniform progress been made in so brief a period'.[2] The federation of labour was being considered and preliminary steps taken towards political representation of the trade unions. In January the Council decided to communicate with other councils with a view to discussing the establishment of the Australian Labour Federation. In the same month the Parliamentary Committee was instructed to consider the advisability of standing Labour candidates in the next election and to draw up a parliamentary platform. The platform was adopted in April.[3] Only three

[1] Spence, *Australia's Awakening*, p. 220.   [2] *S.M.H.*, 4 July 1890.
[3] Trades and Labour Council of N.S.W. Minutes, 7 November 1889; 16, 30 January, 3 April 1890.

members of the Council opposed the decision to draw up a platform, but the affiliated and unaffiliated unions were less than lukewarm about Labour representation. Of the sixty-five societies questioned by the Council on their attitude to representation, only one-third replied and of these only four were in favour. However, the opposition was neutralized by the events of the maritime strike. In November, at the end of the strike, the Council decided to establish electoral leagues in every electorate where practicable throughout the colony.[4]

The Melbourne Trades Hall Council was much less interested in either the federation of labour or the representation of labour. In response to a letter from Brisbane, the Council decided in May to support a scheme of federation, 'if necessary'. The Parliamentary Committee appears to have been nobody's responsibility, and the Council was without a committee until May, its appointment being adjourned from meeting to meeting.[5] When early in 1891 the Council did take some action to obtain direct labour representation, the matter was handed over to a special convention. The attitude of the Melbourne Trades Hall Council before, during, and after the maritime strike bears out Coghlan's estimate. He wrote:

> The movement in Victoria, whether federal or local, was not democratic. There was no real consolidation between skilled and unskilled labour, and the unions in many cases represented only a small proportion of the trades for which they stood.

They were, he added,

> on the whole, narrow and exclusive bodies with high entrance fees, designed to restrict the numbers in the trade, in order that constant employment at high wages might be obtained by those within the union circle.[6]

The maritime strike, which commenced in August 1890, involved transport workers, miners, and shearers in New South Wales, Victoria, South Australia, and New Zealand. Some 50,000 workers in Australia's basic industries stopped work for periods of a fortnight to two months. In the new year, after the defeat in the southern colonies, the issue was joined in Queensland, where the Australian Labour Federation found itself at war with the organized employers on essentially the same issue as had been fought in the south. It is not necessary to trace in detail the events leading to the maritime

[4] *S.M.H.*, 28 October, 29 November 1890.
[5] Trades and Labour Council of N.S.W. Minutes, 9, 23 May 1890.
[6] Coghlan, *Labour and Industry*, pp. 1494-5.

strike, but sufficient of them should be given to indicate the way in which the opposing forces aligned themselves.

The viewpoint of the pastoral workers was made clear in a manifesto issued in July 1890,[7] which asserted on the one hand that the trade-union movement stood firm on the principle that only union shearers must be employed by pastoralists, and on the other hand that the employers were organizing to break the unions. The manifesto pointed to the opposition that pastoralists had given to the union from its inception. Attempts had been made, it was asserted, to undermine the union by offering higher rates of pay to non-union men. A law weighted against the worker had consistently been brought into operation against members of the union. The government had sided with the employers against the unionists; 'free' labourers had been given free transport on the railways, and squatters had with impunity armed non-unionists with rifles and revolvers. Now a concerted effort was to be made to smash the unions. One squatter had proposed the creation of a £50,000 fighting fund to crush the unions. Meetings had been held and decisions taken to employ only non-unionists. 'The challenge has been issued by the most selfish of the capitalist class', said the manifesto. 'Let United Labour accept it, and settle once and forever the question of the right to unite for mutual benefit, and the protection of the Rights of Labour.' This objective would be achieved by 'drawing such a cordon of unionism around the Australian continent as will effectually prevent a bale of wool leaving unless shorn by union shearers'.

The shearers' manifesto was a blunt statement of a point of view that had developed naturally out of the wide trade-union organization which we have seen was created during the previous five years. It was an assertion of the principle of the 'closed shop', and behind it lay the conviction of the rights of the working class in relation to the employers. The manifesto was issued at this time because the leaders of the Amalgamated Shearers' Union believed that the employers were organizing specifically to prevent the employment of men under union conditions—in fact that the employers aimed to smash the trade-union movement. In the words of W. G. Spence, the leader of the strike, the employers 'conceived the ambition of wiping out Australian unionism at one blow'.[8] This was a very different view from the one Spence expressed a few months before, when he had said that he was prepared to assist employers to

[7] *Shearers' Record*, July 1890. [8] *Australia's Awakening*, p. 114.

THE FORMATION OF THE LABOUR PARTY

organize so that comprehensive agreements could be reached. Had the employers reached such a decision?

Writers on the period agree substantially that the aim of the employers was to break the unions. Evatt accepts Spence's statement, with the proviso that Spence 'exaggerated the element of prior deliberation'.[9] Sutcliffe[10] and Fitzpatrick[11] adopt much the same view. Ostensibly the employers merely took their stand on the right of 'freedom of contract'—the right of employers to engage unionists or non-unionists to work under union conditions or under conditions agreed to by the men. But freedom of contract was, as one unionist put it, 'like a tiger, very beautiful to look at but dangerous to handle'.[12] If it were applied, it would break the unions. But there is further evidence that employers had arrived at a decision to attack the unions. In a statement issued after the strike, the Pastoralists' Federal Council expressly stated that the demand for the closed shop made and won in Queensland at the beginning of 1890 was insupportable, and that in all colonies simultaneous meetings were held which resulted in the formation of the Pastoralists' Federal Council to fight the unions on the issue of the 'closed shop'.[13] In other words, before the publication of the shearers' manifesto, pastoralists had begun organizing on a national scale to oppose the union's claim to act on behalf of the men in all their relations with their employers.

The decision of the pastoralists was not an isolated one. The steamship owners had taken the same decision. The marine officers had formed a union and asked for a conference with the owners to put two matters before them—a request for improvement in accommodation, and increased pay. The Steamship Owners' Association agreed to the meeting but subsequently the marine officers affiliated with the Melbourne Trades Hall Council. The shipowners then refused to meet the union until the officers had disaffiliated. Here again the issue was the same as between the pastoralists and the shearers. From the unionist point of view the issue was recognition of unionism, which was defined as the right of workers to form a union, to make rules, including the rule that unionists would not work with non-unionists, and the right of all labour organizations to affiliate with one another.[14] From the employers' point of view

[9] H. V. Evatt, *Australian Labour Leader*, p. 22.
[10] *A History of Trade Unionism*, p. 74.
[11] B. C. Fitzpatrick, *A Short History of the Australian Labor Movement*, p. 68.
[12] *The Royal Commission on Strikes*. Minutes of Evidence.
[13] *Facts and History of the Shearing Difficulty in Australia, 1890-91: Compiled for presentation to the Royal Commission on Labour (England) by the Pastoralists' Federal Council*, pp. 4-5.
[14] *Royal Commission on Strikes*, Minutes of Evidence, q. 4437.

the issue was 'freedom of contract'—a principle which directly cut across that of recognition of unionism.

The strike was precipitated by the Marine Officers' Association. Notice was given that unless the employers' opposition to the affiliation with the Trades Hall Council was withdrawn the officers would walk off all ships in port. But at the same time notices had already been posted on the wharves calling for 'free labour' to load non-union-shorn wool. Within a few days, seamen, wharf labourers and coal lumpers in the eastern ports were on strike in sympathy with the marine officers or against the loading of 'black' wool. A Labour Defence Committee, representing the greater part of the trade-union movement in New South Wales, was set up in Sydney, and was later broadened into an Intercolonial Conference, with W. G. Spence as secretary. The Pastoralists' Federal Council met in Sydney two days after the issue of the shearers' manifesto and was, with the steamship owners, the core of the Australasian Conference of Employers which had its headquarters at the Sydney Chamber of Commerce. As the strike assumed the proportions of a straightout struggle between combined employers and the trade-union movement, more unions came out on strike. Coal miners struck in support of the transport unions, and a month after the ships' officers had walked off, more than twenty thousand shearers were called out, the vast majority of them immediately obeying the call. Simultaneously, many miners were locked out by the mine owners at Newcastle and Broken Hill.

The large numbers involved and the mass demonstrations, such as the meeting fifty thousand strong in Flinders Park, Melbourne, and the procession, a mile and a half long, through the streets of Sydney,[15] were quite different from anything that had previously occurred in the history of Australian unionism. In fact, the strike became a mass movement in support of specific trade-union demands, but also implicitly, and in part consciously, a political movement in support of vaguely defined political objectives. The unions were defeated by lack of funds, by the employment of non-union labour, and by the lack of a definite political objective.

The union successes of the years immediately before the strike had given unionists a highly inflated view of their own strength.[16] In spite of the extension of unionism between 1886 and 1890, probably less than twenty per cent of men working for wages and salaries

[15] *S.M.H.*, 1, 8 September 1890.
[16] For contemporary comment see: H. H. Champion, 'The Crushing Defeat of Trade Unionism in Australia', *Nineteenth Century* (1891), vol. 29; F. Adams, 'The Labour Movements in Australia', *Fortnightly Review* (1891), vol. 56.

THE FORMATION OF THE LABOUR PARTY 133

were members of unions.[17] Furthermore, unemployment, which mounted as the strike spread, provided a reservoir from which non-union labour could be drawn. Despite extraordinary measures, such as the provision by the unions of barracks and food for unemployed non-unionists, on condition that they did not replace strikers, enough men were found to work some of the wharves and ships. Seven weeks after the outbreak of the strike the shipowners refused offers of mediation on the grounds that there was no need to confer with the unions since all their ships were running with non-union labour. The inevitability of the defeat of the unions was evident in the middle of October with the disbanding of the Intercolonial Labour Conference, but it was not until nearly a month later that the Labour Defence Committee, which had taken over leadership from the Intercolonial Conference, agreed to return to work unconditionally. As the strike collapsed, many employers made sure that unionists drank to the full the gall of their defeat. Striking marine officers were required to apply for re-employment in such terms as:

> I respectfully beg to call your kind attention to the fact of my resigning from one of your company's ships on the 17th August, and having seen the folly of so doing, I beg to be reinstated in your company's service. I ask you to kindly consider my case, having served 15 years in the company's and your service.[18]

For unionists and their supporters the bitterness of defeat was further aggravated by the attitude of the several governments during the strike. From the beginning of the strike, steps were taken by the union leadership to maintain order. In Sydney, pickets appointed by the unions served four-hour shifts. The *Sydney Morning Herald* reported that 'the system adopted by the Defence Committee in the appointment of the pickets has been found to work admirably'. However, the government decided to increase the police force by appointing special constables. The Labour Defence Committee immediately offered union members to serve in this capacity, but this offer was apparently rejected. In fact, it appears that steps were

---

[17] This does not pretend to be more than the roughest approximation arrived at by comparing the approximate number of unionists with the total number of male wage- and salary-earners at the 1891 census. A rough estimate of the number of unionists can be made by taking into account the numbers affiliated with the Labour Councils, unions not affiliated, such as the members of the Sydney Building Trades Council, and contemporary estimates, which vary greatly. The numbers of wage- and salary-earners in N.S.W. and Victoria in 1891 are given in T. A. Coghlan, *The Seven Colonies of Australasia*. The *Year Book of the Commonwealth of Australia*, 1953, gives the figure 63·5% of male wage- and salary-earners as union members in 1950. [18] *S.M.H.*, 25 October 1890.

taken to ensure that special constables should not be union members.[19] Altogether the police force in Sydney was increased from 559 to 3,952 by drawing police from country districts and the appointment of over three thousand special police.[20] The employment of such large numbers of police, and the dispatch of permanent military forces to the coalfields was interpreted by the unions as evidence that the government sided with the employers. In Melbourne, military forces under the command of Colonel Price were equally regarded as a force to intimidate strikers rather than to maintain order.

The attitude of the daily press, which had in the beginning reported some aspects of the strike sympathetically, rapidly hardened against the unionists. When the shearers were called out, the *Sydney Morning Herald* commented editorially under the heading, 'Class War—the Commune'. The editorial warned that

> twenty years ago the civilized world was struck with horror on seeing the defeated Communards of Paris in the frenzy of discomfiture trying to destroy the national monuments of greatness and the treasures of art, and to involve society in one common ruin. Little was it then supposed possible that in the happy Australian colonies our working classes—the most fortunate, the best paid, and the most prosperous body of workers in the world—would be summoned by their leaders to take part in a ruinous war against society, inspired by similarly desperate feelings and just as destitute of any rational purpose.[21]

The manifesto published by the defeated Labour Defence Committee summed up the forces that had, in the mind of the unionists, been brought into action against them. The government, the press, and the pulpit were condemned. The condemnation of the government was equally applied to the opposition. 'Whilst we have no cause for gratitude to the government for their attitude during the strike,' ran the manifesto, 'we have no reason for believing that the opposition, had it been in office, would have acted more fairly.' As for the press—

> its opinions were the opinions of the land shark and the tramway grabber, of men responsible for the management of companies working their employees almost double the number of hours prescribed by the rules of Trades Unionism, nay, of men largely interested in the very steamship companies whom the Unions were fighting.[22]

[19] *Parl. Deb.* (N.S.W.), ser. 1, xlviii. 3834, 3933, 3952, 3990.
[20] 'Report of the Inspector General of Police', *S.M.H.*, 9 December 1890.
[21] *S.M.H.*, 16 September 1890.
[22] N.S.W. Labour Defence Committee, *Report and Balance Sheet*, pp. 15-17.

The clergy, with but four exceptions, according to the manifesto, left the people 'to grope amidst the gloom of sacerdotal clap-trap'.[23] The major conclusion drawn from this estimate was that the working class needed direct political representation. However, although the defeat in the strike confirmed this need, it did not resolve the political differences amongst the workers, or amongst those who were soon to be their representatives.

The political programme adopted by the Trades and Labour Council was itself a compromise. It was a composite of trade-union policies that had been formulated over the previous ten years by labour councils and intercolonial congresses, some specific proposals for constitutional reform, and a provision for the taxation of the unimproved capital value of land. The last clause was extensively debated, with attempts being made to substitute for it land nationalization and a vague 'land reform'. It was finally carried by a narrow majority.

On the principle that divided existing parties—free trade and protection—the platform was silent. Unionists were divided on the question but were still united by the agreement that the essential difference between Parkes and Dibbs was that Parkes 'had sent Gatling guns to Newcastle and Mr George Dibbs condemned him because he did not send them a week sooner'.[24] But the fiscal issue could not be avoided and soon became the occasion of deep division in the parliamentary party.

While the feelings fired by the strike were still hot, a by-election was necessary in West Sydney, due to the death of Alfred Lamb, who had played a leading part in the strike as a member of the employers' committee and in the courts, where he had successfully prosecuted four of his striking employees for breach of contract under the Masters and Servants Act. The election resulted in the return by a large majority of A. G. Taylor, who stood on the Trades and Labour Council platform. At the declaration of the poll, Taylor declared that it was a victory for the 'holy and divine cause of Labour as against Capital'.[25]

Early in 1891, on the initiative of the Parliamentary Committee of the Labour Council, Labour electoral leagues began forming in the industrial suburbs of Sydney, in Newcastle, and some country centres. Under the rules proposed by the Trades and Labour Council, the constituency leagues were empowered to select their own candi-

[23] The exceptions were Cardinal Moran, Dr Roseby, the Reverend Mr Jackson and the Reverend Mr Walters.   [24] *S.M.H.*, 21 July 1891.
[25] Ibid., 27 October 1890.

dates, but only such candidates as fully accepted the whole political programme of the Trades and Labour Council. Qualification for membership of the league was acceptance of the programme.

There was no lack of potential candidates. In West Sydney there were twelve nominees, and in Redfern twenty. Before going to the pre-selection ballot, candidates were required to pledge themselves to the platform, and to agree to withdraw if not selected. Here the first warning of future division was given. Two sitting protectionist members for Redfern, Schey and Howe, having already been selected by the protectionist organization, sought Labour selection also. Not able to agree to withdraw if not selected by the Labour Electoral League, they were finally permitted to enter the ballot by a meeting that became a riot. They were duly selected in a group of four, the other two members of which were W. H. Sharp, the president of the Trades and Labour Council, and J. S. T. McGowen, chairman of the Eight Hours' Committee. Sharp and McGowen were then endorsed by the protectionists. However, although their names were published with Schey and Howe as members of the protectionist four, they sought the withdrawal of their names from the protectionist election advertisements. In the result the two protectionists were returned at the top of the poll and the two L.E.L. candidates third and fourth. This incident was typical. The attempt was being made to establish a completely independent party, but the men who were making it retained strong links with established parties and the policies they represented.

At the other fiscal extreme were the supporters of the single tax. Frank Cotton, representative of the Wagga branch of the A.S.U. on the labour council, member of the Parliamentary Committee and L.E.L. member for Newtown in 1891, was an executive member of the Single Tax League. Early in 1890 he had attempted to collaborate with Parkes against the labour protectionists.[26] Similarly Dr Hollis, elected for Goulburn on the L.E.L. platform, had previously been selected by the Goulburn branch of the Single Tax League. The differences between protectionists, single-taxers, and conventional free traders were reflected in the labour and pro-labour press. The *Democrat*, edited by Cotton, attacked the protectionist *Workman*, official organ of the Trades and Labour Council, which in turn fulminated against the single-taxers. A further potentially divisive influence was the number of candidates who climbed on the labour band-waggon for purely opportunist reasons. As one writer puts it,

[26] F. Picard, 'Henry George and the Labour Split of 1891', *Hist. Studies*, vol. vi, no. xxi.

'men, who had never been suspected by their most intimate friends of knowing anything of politics or having any leanings towards democracy, suddenly received a "Call" to do battle for the poor, down-trodden, workers'.[27] Nevertheless, despite the differences of opinion and the pressure of existing political organizations, the class polarization brought about by the maritime strike was sufficient to precipitate the formation of a political party that professed to be the representative of the working class. In the June elections of 1891 thirty-one nominees of the L.E.L. were returned and five other members were admitted to the first caucus.

The basic assumptions of the Labour Electoral League, clearly stated before the election, were that the Labour members were delegates of the extra-parliamentary movement, that they would seek to hold the balance of power, and they would unitedly support any government that promised a substantial number of the reforms included in the platform of the League.[28] The delegate status of the party, combined with the wide divergence of opinion amongst its members, created the need for some tight disciplinary procedure. The pledge to vote on all questions as a majority of caucus decided was the means adopted. However, in the absence of agreement on policy and before the interplay of parliamentary and extra-parliamentary forces had developed a disciplinary machinery with effective sanctions, the pledge proved to be insufficient to hold the party together. The history of the L.E.L. in its first parliament is essentially the story of how the disciplinary machinery was evolved out of disagreements between the parliamentary members and under pressure of the Trades and Labour Council and the constituency leagues.

At the first caucus the pledge was adopted, but eight members refused to sign, not because of any objection in principle to the pledge but because they claimed they were pledged to protection. Thus began the division of the party. On three issues, all of which included a tactical reference to fiscal policy, the party split and was evenly divided on the amendment which Parkes made a question of confidence. With G. R. Dibbs in office, Reid's tactical use of the same wedge split the Labour Party even more completely. The only member who voted for the majority decision of caucus and against his fiscal faith was J. S. T. McGowen.

A divided party was completely incapable of forcing the passage of those points in its programme most urgently demanded by the trade unionists, and soon there was bitter hostility between unionists

[27] R. G. S. Williams, *Australian White Slaves*, p. 19.   [28] *S.M.H.*, 5 June 1891.

and many of the parliamentary members. This was aggravated by mounting unemployment. In the first six months of 1892 nearly 14,000 men registered as unemployed at the Sydney labour bureau. In the summer of 1892-3 there was a brief improvement, but by the winter of 1893 the number of unemployed was greater than in the previous year. Wages were falling, and some of the smaller unions collapsed entirely. During 1892 a number of unions withdrew from the Trades and Labour Council because they had either dissolved or were so poor financially and in membership that they were unable to maintain their affiliation. In March 1893 the Council decided that future withdrawals of unions would not be notified to the press.[29]

The dissatisfaction of the Council with the failure of the parliamentary party to take any effective action to deal with the economic crisis or to implement its policy came to a head over two matters, one trivial in itself, the other important. In May 1892 J. T. Houghton, M.P., a member of the Trades and Labour Council, and, before his translation to the higher sphere, its secretary, obtained employment for some unemployed labourers at less than the accepted wage rate. He was trenchantly criticized, and his explanation that 'he thought he was putting a few shillings in the pockets of members who were starving'[30] did not endear him to the unionists. His explanation was followed by a resolution, not finally adopted, which would have prohibited members of parliament retaining their seats on the Council. The second matter was the Broken Hill strike or lockout, precipitated by the company's termination of a wages agreement made in 1889. The strike reduced the majority of unionists to complete destitution[31] or drove them from Broken Hill, some never to return. The unions were finally defeated by hunger and the action of the Dibbs government in arresting and prosecuting the leaders. On the arrest of the leaders, the Council demanded that the Labour Party turn out the government. Two weeks later, 'the Council viewed with contempt the execrable conduct of Messrs Fitzgerald, Kelly, Sharp and Johnson in supporting the government in the late political crisis'.[32] Sharp had been president of the Trades and Labour Council and Fitzgerald its representative in Britain during

---

[29] Trades and Labour Council of N.S.W., Minutes, 9 March 1893.
[30] Ibid., 9 June 1892.
[31] The destitution of miners is revealed in a report to the Labour Council: 'The men were very hard up for clothing, some of them being confined to their homes, whilst others got about by borrowing boots, etc., and in a few cases one goes out while the other stopped at home. The women were worse than the men, and the children worst of all', Minutes, 10 November 1892.
[32] Ibid., 20 October 1892.

the maritime strike. Already divided on tariff policy, the parliamentary party was losing the support of the unions.

In 1893 the unemployed were demonstrating in the streets, regular meetings at Queens Square were followed by deputations to parliament, but in parliament the Labour Party had been reduced to futility by division—in W. M. Hughes's words it had become 'an aimless, spineless, legless, headless party'.[33]

In mid-1893 a temporary reunion of the parliamentary party was effected under the leadership of Joseph Cook. However, at special conferences of the Labour Electoral League, held in November 1893 and March 1894, biting criticisms were made of the parliamentary members. A reworded pledge for the parliamentary party was decided upon, and this brought the breach between parliamentary members and extra-parliamentary organization into the open. The parliamentary party repudiated the decisions of the conference. In a published manifesto it was asserted that the pledge could not be interpreted and that it subverted the representative function of the member. The central committee appealed to the branches to state their opinions on the pledge. Of the eighty-four branches, seventy-two endorsed the pledge and only four did not require it. Strengthened by this result, the central committee informed Joseph Cook that only those members who accepted the pledge would be endorsed for the forthcoming election.

Only four of the sitting members consented to sign and hence received endorsement. The majority of the others stood as independent labour candidates or, like Joseph Cook, as the selected representative of his league, which had been declared 'bogus' by the central committee. Fifteen 'solidarities' and twelve independents were returned in 1894. Four of the independents rejoined the party, having agreed to sign a slightly modified pledge. The rest of the independents gradually merged with the other parties. Though much smaller than the nominal party of 1891, the party of 1894 was much nearer to the kind of party that the trade unions had imagined they had formed then.

The Victorian story is quite different. As has been seen above, the Melbourne Trades Hall Council in the months before the maritime strike was much less concerned than the Sydney Council with either the broad projects for federation of labour or direct parliamentary representation. During the maritime strike great public demonstrations were organized by a special committee set up by the Council, but the Council itself carried on its normal activities.

[33] *New Order*, 19 May 1894.

Motions of protest were carried against the government's action in calling out the military forces, but on more than one occasion at the height of the struggle decisions concerning the strike were deferred from one meeting to the next.[34]

Similarly with the Queensland shearers' strike: two months after it had begun, the strike had received little direct assistance. The Council found time to discuss at length the appointment of a deputation to advocate a free lending library, but deferred to the following meeting consideration of urgent messages from the Australian Labour Federation. Representatives were sent to the Ballarat conference of April 1891 to consider the formation of the Australian Labour Federation, but as late as November the Council had to reply to the Sydney Labour Council that no decisions had been made as the report of the delegates had not been received. The report was made at the following meeting, where it was decided to print it.[35] The attitude of the Council to the unemployed further reveals its preoccupation with its own special concerns.

The unemployed were refused use of the Trades Hall, but were permitted to meet in the courtyard, although this privilege was later withdrawn. In 1893, when unemployment was at its worst, the Council refused to be represented on a central unemployment committee. In reply to its critics the Council denied that it was against the unemployed, insisting that its efforts were being devoted to helping unemployed members of its affiliated unions.[36] In all, the Melbourne Trades Hall Council did not regard itself as a representative institution of the working class, but as the close preserve of its constituent unions. This same unconcern with the general interest of workers is reflected in its attitude to broad political policies. Resolutions with any socialist implications, such as proposals for nationalization of specific industries, were given short shrift by the Council. Similarly, the predominant protectionist opinion qualified support for land taxation, which was in the political context of the time one of the most distinctive working-class policies.[37] Even a proposal that the governments should initiate productive works to cope with the unemployed was amended to read that the government should 'use extraordinary measures to relieve the existing distress'.

On the other hand the Council gave strong support to the proposal to form an Australasian Federation League which would popularize

[34] Melbourne Trades Hall Council, Minutes, 2 September 1890.
[35] Ibid., 10 April, 13, 20 November 1891.   [36] Ibid., 14 April, 23 June 1893.
[37] Ibid., 23, 30 June, 14 July 1893.

the idea of national federation. It agreed to participate in a preliminary conference with the Chambers of Commerce and Manufactures and the Australian Natives Association. In brief, the Trades Hall Council was generally suspicious of, and at times frankly opposed to, anything that appeared to be a specifically working-class political viewpoint. The absence of the optimistic faith in a collectivist future is no more marked than in the Trades Hall Council debate on the Progressive Political League. As reported, 'one speaker complained that the Convention had not stuck to purely labour questions, but had gone outside to advocate points in the socialistic programme'. Mr Trenwith, M.L.A., combated the objection by saying that 'however much the Labour Party will have achieved, they will still go on grumbling, whilst others had more of this world's goods than they had'.[38]

The difference between New South Wales and Victoria is largely to be explained, as has been suggested above, by the differences in the central trades-union bodies. By mid-1890 only twenty-one of the fifty-three unions affiliated to the Sydney Trades and Labour Council were craft unions, whereas the craft unionists were still a majority on the Melbourne Council. This preponderance of craft unionists was accentuated by the inequality of representation that left such powerful bodies as the A.S.U. with less representation than some tiny Melbourne craft unions.[39] Thus, the only institution in Victoria capable of creating a political party was, by its structure, weighted against such a departure.

Further, certain features of Victorian political history, as contrasted with New South Wales, made the birth of a Victorian Labour Party more protracted. In the constitutional, land, and fiscal struggles of the sixties and seventies a liberal party, relatively coherent in membership and consistent in principle, at least by contrast with the kaleidoscopic factionalism of New South Wales, had won the regular support of the working class. And despite the growing friction between workers and employers, reaching its climax in the maritime strike, faith in liberals and liberal policy was merely weakened, not destroyed. Hence there was a strong tendency to think of any party that the trade unions might originate as a wing of the Liberal Party, and not as separate from it. On the other hand, in New South Wales permanent political parties were not formed until the very time that the trade-union movement was itself rapidly moving towards a political party of its own. Distinctive free-trade

---
[38] *Age*, 10 June 1891.
[39] Philipp, 'Trade Union Organization in N.S.W. and Victoria', p. 185; also Appendices 37A, 38A thereto.

and protectionist parties developed between 1887 and 1889,[40] each of which was concerned to win the votes of the working class, but neither had succeeded by 1890 in gaining the degree of working-class support that liberal and radical protectionists had long enjoyed in Victoria. This state of affairs in New South Wales strengthened the tendency to form a separate party, even though it did not prevent the early division of the party on the principle that the non-labour parties were attempting to make the dividing line between themselves.

However, partly under the influence of events in New South Wales and Queensland, the Melbourne Trades Hall Council decided that some political action was necessary. In May 1891 the Council appointed two representatives to help organize a political labour convention. The convention, at which the trades councils of Melbourne, Ballarat, Bendigo, and Geelong, the A.S.U. and the A.M.A. were represented, founded the Progressive Political League of Victoria. The programme adopted by the convention was very similar to that of the New South Wales Electoral League, except that the Victorian programme placed more emphasis on democratic reform and less on the extension of the social and economic functions of the state.[41]

Much more important differences are to be found in the relations between the political party and the trade unions and in the prevailing view of the proper relations between the new party and the older political parties. In New South Wales the Trades and Labour Council had quite simply created the L.E.L. Under revised rules adopted in July 1892 the attempt was made to secure to the Council continued substantial influence in the central direction of the League. The president of the Council was to be *ex officio* president of the L.E.L. The central committee of the L.E.L. was to include six representatives of the Council and one delegate from each branch of the League. One trustee of the L.E.L. was to be elected by the Trades and Labour Council and one by the central committee of the League. Finally, the Council retained the power of veto over any proposed alteration in the political platform.[42] On the other hand, in Victoria the Trades Hall Council had not played a decisive part in the initiation of the P.P.L., nor did it retain any special rights in the new organization.

These differences were matters of substance. If it is true, as has

[40] Martin, 'Political Grouping in New South Wales, 1872-89'.
[41] *Age*, 6 June 1891.
[42] Trades and Labour Council of N.S.W., Minutes, 5 July 1892.

THE FORMATION OF THE LABOUR PARTY 143

been argued here, that the formation of the L.E.L. in New South Wales was the result of a compromise between opposing tendencies in the labour movement, the creation of a permanent, distinct political party could only be achieved by a continuing close organization connection between the central trade-union body and the political party. The only other possible basis for a permanent political organization would have been a commonly accepted coherent body of political ideas. This was absent in both New South Wales and Victoria. The fact that in New South Wales the history of the first three years of the party was one of internal division and conflict between the unions and the politicians does not invalidate this view. The essential thing is that the dissension took place within a complex institution in which a permanent and substantial interest was represented by the Trades and Labour Council. If that had not been so, it is probable that in 1894 the party would have been completely broken under the influence of parliamentary pressures, instead of emerging smaller but more or less united. This contention is borne out by the course of events in Victoria.

The P.P.L. was at pains to minimize the differences between itself and the liberals. 'Our programme contains nothing,' said the *Commonweal*, 'despite the assertions of the Conservatives to the contrary, more than has been advocated for years past by economists and liberals.'[43] This view was accepted by the *Age*,[44] which commented: 'The Labour candidates are nothing more than Liberals under a new name. There is nothing whatever in their programme to distinguish them from the men who made the Liberal Party the power it has been since 1877'. The Trades Hall Council itself did not make any clear distinction between liberal and labour.[45] At the 1892 election nine members who associated themselves with the P.P.L. were returned. The *Commonweal* exhorted them not to make the mistake of New South Wales.

> It is clearly understood that our Party is to avoid the serious mistakes made by the Labour Party in New South Wales, notably that primary error which placed the party in a position of hostility to all other sections in Parliament. The Victorian Labour Party constitutes itself a wing of the Liberal Party, and is prepared to support a Liberal Government so long as that Government promotes genuine democratic legislation in the interests of all

[43] *Commonweal*, 16 January 1892. This paper was the semi-official organ of the Trades Hall Council: Minutes, 23 September 1892.
[44] 18 April 1892.
[45] Melbourne Trades Hall Council, Minutes, 10 February 1893, 21 August 1894.

classes, workers included. New Zealand should furnish us a model.[46]

Of the nine members of the P.P.L. elected to the Assembly in 1892, four had been members of the previous parliament. In parliament the nine behaved as a not particularly unified faction of the Liberal Party.[47] The extra-parliamentary organization was so ineffective that five months after the election of 1892 a question was asked in the Trades Hall Council whether the Progressive Political League still existed. Before the 1894 election a further attempt was made to revive the organization by calling a new conference which established the United Labour Party of Victoria, which differed in no essential from the P.P.L. An electoral alliance was made with the Deakin liberals. In explanation, the labour *Boomerang* stated that 'the Labour and Liberal Parties do not intend to repeat the mistake of previous years by splitting the votes and allowing the Tory candidates to slip in with an actual minority'.[48] The return of a liberal majority, including ten members of the United Labour Party, was greeted by the Trades Hall Council with 'thanks to the Liberal press for its assistance to the Labour and Liberal Cause during the recent contest'.[49] In effect, although preliminary steps towards the formation of a labour party had been made, no independent party had as yet been created.

A labour party of the type in New South Wales did ultimately emerge in Victoria, but under different economic and political conditions from those that fashioned the Labour Party in New South Wales. By the time the labour movement in Victoria seriously began to construct an independent party, the New South Wales party had already established a parliamentary and extra-parliamentary machine sufficiently cohesive to be concerning itself with the problem of broadening its electoral appeal and finding its way to the Treasury benches. That the Victorian party did this later, and under different political conditions, accounts in part for the differences in the history of the labour parties in the two states in the twentieth century.

In Queensland, five months after the adoption of the political programme by the central council of the A.L.F., the A.L.F. central executive drew up a scheme for the political organization of labour. The organization was to be firmly based on the trade unions. The

---

[46] 14 May 1892. The reference to New Zealand, while apposite, is in part explained by the fact that the editor, W. Freeman Kitchen, was a New Zealander.
[47] See S. M. Ingham, 'Some Aspects of Victorian Liberalism 1880-1900'.
[48] *Boomerang*, 1 September 1894.   [49] Minutes, 21 August 1894.

scheme provided for a 'labour caucus' in each electorate, to consist of all members of the A.L.F. and all members of unions and associations not affiliated to the A.L.F. but recognized as sympathetic to its aims, resident in the electorate. The 'caucus' would be entitled to select official labour candidates by a two-thirds majority at a 'caucus meeting' or, in districts where a meeting was not possible, by a majority in a plebiscite of 'caucus members'. Candidates would be required to accept the political principles of the A.L.F., and to agree to resign their seats if they lost the confidence of two-thirds of the members of the 'caucus' in their electorate.[50] The A.L.F. leadership continued to press for an organization which incorporated these principles. However, the Queensland shearers' strike, which broke out early in 1891 and which left the trade-union movement weakened and to some extent disillusioned, in conjunction with regional, sectional, and personal interests, resulted in a development somewhat different from that envisaged by the A.L.F. leaders at the end of 1890.

The shearers' strike was contested with even greater bitterness than the maritime strike had been. The issues were essentially the same—the 'recognition of unionism' v. 'freedom of contract'. But in Queensland, partly as a consequence of the socialist opinions of the union leadership, and partly because of the only thinly disguised partisanship of the government, the strike was, from the first, pictured by unionists as resistance to an attack on unionism by a combination of pastoralists and government.

Thus the steps to form political organizations were taken in an atmosphere of deep class antagonism. In the strike struggle itself, the political moral was consistently pointed by the *Worker*. As the strike was beginning, William Lane announced that 'capitalism understands thoroughly that its real fight with labour is at the ballot box'.[51] In the middle of the strike a special general council meeting of the A.L.F. prepared an electoral programme, which potential labour candidates would be urged to accept. The programme included electoral reform, educational reform, state intervention in agriculture, industry, and finance, old age pensions, and the repeal of various Acts considered contrary to working-class interests. Throughout the colony, but particularly in Brisbane and its environs, local political organizations were founded usually on the initiative of the A.L.F. Variously known as People's Parliamentary Associations, Workers' Political Associations and Workers' Political Organizations, they were based in varying degrees on the principles

[50] *Worker*, 27 December 1890.   [51] Ibid., 24 January 1891.

of organization laid down by the A.L.F. executive. That all was not going smoothly from the point of view of the trade-union leadership is, however, evident from comments in the *Worker*. In August it commented:

> Loose methods of selecting parliamentary representatives must be dropped and a workable method of choosing representatives, who, though coming from different localities, will unite solidly in supporting generally agreed upon measures, must be inaugurated ... Nor is it good enough that any man should be able to call himself a Labour candidate and weaken the political power of the Labour Party by splitting up the Labour vote.[52]

Similarly, the A.L.F. organizer wrote disparagingly of various types of prospective labour candidates who would be of no benefit to labour. At the top of the list was 'the self-assertive, loud-mouthed, obstinate man who knows nothing except that he is determined to run whether he is selected or not'.[53]

The authority of the A.L.F. had been weakened by the strike defeat. Eleven of its leaders were in prison and the unions were £5,000 in debt at the end of the strike. The Defence Committee in its final manifesto called for political representation. Events in New South Wales at first encouraged the Queenslanders and then emphasized the dangers to be avoided. William Lane had hailed the New South Wales elections with, 'New South Wales has retrieved the maritime disaster by sending her Labour Defence Committee into Parliament, there to hold watch and ward over the rights of citizens who toil'.[54] Ten months later the *Worker* was commenting sadly, 'a surprising success placed in Parliament a Labour cohort stronger than ever seen before in History—and this cohort of Labour delegates went to pieces without accomplishing anything'.[55]

Impressed by the danger of labour disunity, the delegate meeting of the People's Parliamentary Association of Queensland in December 1891 decided to elect a central political committee to bring about uniformity of programme and method of selecting candidates. The executive appointed consisted of leading unionists, with William Lane as secretary. It was further agreed that its policy and methods should conform with the decisions to be arrived at by the central council of the A.L.F., which was to meet early in 1892.

The meeting of the central council of the A.L.F. reaffirmed the position they had previously adopted on selection of candidates. They decided 'that, to secure unity, no candidate shall be recognized

[52] Ibid., 8 August 1891.
[53] Ibid., 31 October 1891.
[54] Ibid., 27 June 1891.
[55] Ibid., 30 April 1892.

THE FORMATION OF THE LABOUR PARTY

as an official labour candidate at the next elections unless he has been put forward by the recognized Labour organizations and approved, on their recommendation, by the General Executive, A.L.F.'.[56] On matters of political policy, however, this meeting made an important departure that confirmed a tendency that had been increasingly in evidence during the previous year. While formally reaffirming the political programme, including the socialist objective, it also decided that the whole strength of the labour movement should be concentrated on winning 'one man one vote'. Thus commenced the process by which the ultimate aims of the movement were progressively pushed into the background and the immediate programme became the effective policy of the party.

At a by-election in March 1892 T. J. Ryan, who had the support of the general executive of the A.L.F., won Barcoo on the programme of 'one man one vote'. Later in the year G. J. Hall won Bundaberg with a programme in which the main emphasis was on the exclusion of black labour. His victory was greeted by the *Worker* with 'Bundaberg goes white'. In the House, Ryan and Hall joined Thomas Glassey and J. P. Hoolan, who regarded themselves—and had been accepted by the extra-parliamentary movement—as labour representatives. On their initiative a Labour Party Convention was convened in August 1892.

The August convention was a turning-point in political organization in that it marked the arrival of the labour politician as a significant member of the extra-parliamentary movement. The A.L.F., the People's Parliamentary Associations, the Workers' Political Organizations, as well as the Amalgamated Workers' Union of Queensland,[57] were represented, but the chair was occupied by Thomas Glassey and the secretary was G. J. Hall, both members of parliament. The platform adopted by the convention differed little from the previous platforms except that it placed great emphasis on the exclusion of coloured, Asiatic, and contract or indentured labour —a matter with which the labour movement in Queensland was becoming increasingly concerned.

However, the executive appointed reflected the new importance of the parliamentary member. It consisted of the parliamentary party, the president and general secretary of the A.L.F., and seven members elected by the convention. This executive was to have the power of ratifying the selection of labour candidates, thus taking

[56] Ibid., 6 February 1892.
[57] Formed by the amalgamation of the Queensland Shearers' Union, and the Queensland Labourers' Union in December 1891.

over a function previously claimed by the executive of the A.L.F. This decision meant that the organizational unity of the political and industrial sections of the labour movement, for which the leaders of the A.L.F. had striven, was weakened. In fact, experience of two years had shown that under the existing conditions the all-inclusive industrial-political organization was not practicable. The weakening of the trade unions by strike defeat and unemployment and the New Australia venture, which was already draining off some of the most able unionists, combined with the authority of the parliamentary members, determined that there should be development towards an organization in which the parliamentary members, rather than union officials, would play the leading part.

Nevertheless, the open division between politician and unionist that had occurred in New South Wales was less evident in Queensland at this period. The unions retained representatives on the central executive, and the constituency organizations were firmly based on the unions. But, after August 1892, the political party was much less identifiable with the A.L.F. The view that the political party was becoming separate from the industrial movement and that the unions must be secured from excessive influence by the politicians was expressed in a resolution of the general council of the A.L.F. in February 1893. The conflict between the Sydney Trades and Labour Council and J. T. Houghton had produced a suggestion that members of parliament should be ineligible for membership of the council. The resolution had been withdrawn, but in Queensland the A.L.F. decided that no labour member should be allowed to hold any official position in the industrial movement.[58]

The Labour Party entered the election contest of April 1893 with an election manifesto that bore little evidence of the socialist theory incorporated in the political programme of the A.L.F. It advocated economies in government expenditure to meet the financial crisis, and opposed the government policies of land grant railways and the recruitment of South Sea Island labour. Electoral reform, including the formula of one man one vote, and a tax on the great estates were the two most distinctively 'labour' policies, although opposition to coloured labour was one of the themes most frequently stressed in the election campaign.

Sixteen labour members were returned and the new party found itself the effective, although not the official, opposition. The defeat and illness of Thomas Glassey deprived the party temporarily of an experienced and able leader. J. P. Hoolan was elected leader because

[58] *Worker*, 11 March 1893.

of his parliamentary experience, but he demonstrated few of the qualities necessary for the position. For two months he was the unofficial opposition leader and then cheerfully discarded his pretentions to that office, to be replaced by Charles Powers, who commanded the support of only a handful of members, but who was promised the general support of the Labour Party.

In its first parliament the Labour Party confined itself to criticism of various government measures and to the support of one. The party had no real alternative to the government's policy to deal with the financial crisis, which was at its most acute stage in 1893. Civil service retrenchment, wage and salary reductions, and stabilization of the Queensland National Bank were the chief measures proposed by the Premier, Sir Thomas McIlwraith. The Labour Party demanded that government economies should be directed towards the higher salaried civil servants, and criticized the tenderness of the government towards the Queensland National Bank, which included a number of government supporters amongst its shareholders. The advocacy of a 'real' national or state bank was the positive alternative suggested by a number of labour members. In its criticism of the government's attitude to the unemployed, the Labour Party gave emphatic support to the idea of state-aided village and community settlements. The introduction of the Co-operative Communities Land Settlement Bill was greeted with an enthusiasm that was scarcely justified by the nature of the proposal. Labour thought was strongly influenced by the New Australia movement, and the community settlements appeared to be both a solution to unemployment and a project of wider social implications. Criticism of the introduction of island labour and an abortive attempt to reform the electoral system were the only other important contributions of the party in the first session.

In the second session Thomas Glassey, elected to the seat vacated for him by J. P. Hoolan, took over the leadership of the Labour Party, but the exact position of the party in relation to Charles Powers and other opponents of the government remained indefinite. Powers resigned the leadership of the opposition and Glassey announced that he was merely the leader of the Labour Party, which would retain a free hand to support or oppose the government as it saw fit. Henceforward there was no official Leader of the Opposition, but the Labour Party continued in practice to be the opposition. The great issue in the second session was the Peace Preservation Bill under which the government acquired exceptional powers to deal with actions incidental to the second shearers' strike. By argument and obstruction the Labour Party opposed the grant of these exceptional powers to the point where half of the party had been suspended and escorted from the House.

Thus out of a trade-union movement for which an idealist socialism had acted as a cohesive ideological force emerged labour parties whose political policies bore little evidence of the socialist objective. It will be seen that the function of the labour parties was to put into effect policies of a kind that had been supported by radicals before the development of militant trade-unionism made a labour party possible. They were able to do this because their trade-union origin and connection gave them a cohesion that no political parties had previously had in Australia. Their further function was to deprive the trade-unions of the class militancy which had given the Labour Party birth, but this also led in time to a revival of militancy and a constant struggle between the political labour party and sections of the industrial movement.

9

The Foundations of the Welfare State

Australian socialism is distinguished from Continental socialism by the same features that distinguish the Magna Charta and the Bill of Rights from the crystallisations of political theory in the documents of the French Revolution. It has been called a 'socialism without doctrines'. Its object is to secure instruments by which workers may control industry. It seeks tools rather than proclaims theories, and does not try to harmonise practical attainments with a preconceived ideal of society. Therefore the socialism of Australasia is unique, and worthy of study as a phase—though still incomplete, and possibly not abiding—of Anglo-Saxon history.[1]

IN THE twenty years after 1891 far-reaching experiments were made in socio-economic legislation which both laid the foundations of that complex relationship between the state and the producers that has become characteristic of the Australian economy and also determined the issues with which political parties would be concerned for the next fifty years. Up to 1900 the colonial governments accepted ever-widening responsibilities in encouraging economic development and in regulating conditions in industry. This new function of the state was a compelling motive in bringing about the federation of the colonies into the Commonwealth of Australia in 1901, and in turn it ensured that the new commonwealth governments would be preoccupied with legislation of a similar kind.

Fitzpatrick points out that these twenty years, by contrast with the previous thirty, are not remarkable for the development of new industries or for increases in the volume of production, but rather 'for the experiments which were then made in the direction of redistributing, or regulating the distribution of, the national income'.[2] In the course of attempting this, the state began to intervene on a wide scale in economic relationships. Some of the forms of intervention were worked out in the last ten years of the nineteenth century, applied piecemeal in the several colonies, and then applied on a nation-wide scale by commonwealth governments. Other forms

---

[1] V. S. Clark, *The Labour Movement in Australasia*, p. ix.
[2] Fitzpatrick, *The British Empire in Australia*, p. 340.

were initiated by the Commonwealth itself. The keystone of the arch was the system of industrial arbitration, but closely related to it was legislation directly controlling conditions in industry and encouraging its development. Colonial governments passed industrial arbitration Acts, factory Acts, mining Acts, old age pensions Acts, and Acts to assist in the small-scale settlement of the land. The Commonwealth extended the function of industrial arbitration and integrated it with a whole system to protect and encourage Australian industry. The instruments that were evolved for this purpose were the 'New Protection', the White Australia policy, and the schemes for national defence.

These changes did not spring ready-made from any theory about society; they evolved under the pressure of the actual conditions existing after 1890. Arbitration emerged as the answer to the militant demand of trade unionism to share in framing the conditions of labour, which we have seen arose out of an economic situation in which the majority of the people had become wage workers. Arbitration was regarded as a means of disarming and controlling militant trade unionism without continuous resort to industrial warfare. But as developed by the Commonwealth it became more than a method of settling disputes between workers and employers. Linked with the 'new protective' legislation, arbitration acquired a legislative function and became the means by which the state attempted to distribute between workers and employers the product of a protected economy. Substantially it failed to satisfy the working class in this respect, but it succeeded to some extent in changing the emphasis of trade-union activity. For a time dependence on arbitration and the political labour party resulted in policies of moderation by the union movement. After 1906 this was challenged by a new militancy which questioned the efficacy of arbitration and placed little faith in the efforts of the Labour Party. State assistance to farmers was a direct result of the failure of private banking to provide the finance to encourage the development of small-scale farming. It was also a recognition that, if the violent division of society that had occurred in the early nineties was not to continue, it was necessary to create a productive middle class on a much greater scale than had previously existed. In short, in the early nineties Australian society had been sharply divided in class conflict in which the very basis of the capitalist system had been brought into question. For the whole of the decade economic difficulties, in contrast with the previous twenty years of prosperity, seemed to indicate that the economic system was running down. If the system were to be preserved, ways had to be found to stabilize it, to satisfy the working class, and at the same time bring about far-reaching changes in the class structure of Australian society. The 'new protection', regulation of industry, social service legislation, and industrial arbitration were intended to restore prosperity and satisfy the workers, and state encouragement of a class of independent farmers was to bring about a change in the class structure.

The Labour Party grew to maturity while these important changes were being made in the function of the state. The existence of the Labour Party was partly responsible for them, since in the main the changes were carried through by parliamentary alliances of the Labour Party with liberals. Because of its relatively greater unity, the Labour Party was often the decisive factor in having such policies adopted, but it was not usually the initiator of such legislation. During this period the Labour Party was finding a policy, and it found it in the course of its parliamentary experience, frequently adopting as its own ideas that had been developed by middle-class liberals. Policies were hammered out under the pressure of making practical political decisions. Inevitably, because it was not directed by any coherent political theory, it became a party of practical politics, suspicious of theory and increasingly alienated from the militant trade unionism and idealist socialism that had given it birth. As its policy thus took shape there was conflict within the party and between it and the industrial movement, but by 1910 the Labour Party had become firmly established as a party with a liberal rather than a socialist theory. The Labour Party grew out of a movement that was implicitly directed against the basis of the capitalist system, but it became a party whose function was to modify the capitalist system and make it acceptable to the movement of which it was a part.

From 1891 to 1893 the whole financial structure of Australia was in a state of acute crisis. Bank failures were followed by reconstruction, the writing down of capital, and other emergency measures. Depositors, including governments, were hard hit by the failures, and many banks were not able to re-establish their stability until after the turn of the century. The failure was a direct result of over-investment in a period of falling prices, and recovery was made the more difficult by dry seasons from 1896 to 1902. Despite emergency measures by all colonial governments, the whole decade was one of economic difficulties. Victoria was more acutely affected than any other colony, the banking crisis being more severe there and considerable unemployment continuing until the end of the century. It lost population to Western Australia and New South Wales, and the new century found New South Wales, as measured by population, again the leading colony.

Although it was a depressed decade with some industries severely affected, this was to some extent offset by greater productivity in others. The industry most affected by the adverse conditions was the staple—wool. In 1901 there were only 72 million sheep as compared with 104 million ten years before. In 1891 wool had made up fifty-five per cent of the value of all exports; in 1901 it was only thirty per cent, and the total return from wool exported in 1901 was twenty-four per cent less than ten years before. With the return of more favourable seasons and higher prices early in the new century, however, the pastoral industry was restored. Mining did not suffer the same set-back as the pastoral industry. The Broken Hill Proprietary Company was able to compensate for the low prices of the middle nineties by expanding its field of operations and by applying new processes. Similarly, gold continued to be produced in large quantities. To the rich Queensland mines were added the new deposits in Western Australia and the finds of individual fossickers in Victoria, whose numbers increased with the onset of the depression. Gold exported, in fact, rose from £5·7 million in 1891 to £14·3 million in 1901.

In agriculture there were important advances, particularly in New South Wales. Between 1891 and 1901 the area under crop there trebled and the total for Australia nearly doubled. Improved methods of production, including the use of drought-resistant wheats, was one factor in this increase. The extension of railways was another. And the efforts of governments to assist small-scale farming was yet a third. These factors also had an important bearing on the history of the sugar industry in this period. Intensive cultivation by small producers was greatly assisted by the Sugar Works Guarantee Act of 1893, under which central crushing mills were established, free from the control of the big planters. Government assistance to small producers also took the form of advances to settlers and improvements in the available varieties of sugar.

Secondary industry did not change its character in any fundamental way. It was still an industry for the processing of raw materials and the provision of commodities for the home market. Nevertheless, it accounted for quite a large proportion of the total of Australian production. In 1893 secondary industry contributed approximately thirty per cent of the total Victorian production and twenty per cent of New South Wales. In Victoria the number of

THE FOUNDATIONS OF THE WELFARE STATE 155

factories increased from 3,141 in 1891 to 3,249 in 1901 and 5,126 in 1911, and the number of employees rose from 53,800 in 1891 to 111,900 in 1911. In New South Wales there were 50,900 factory workers in 1891 and 108,700 in 1911. An important difference between New South Wales and Victoria was the relatively greater development in Victoria of industries in which large numbers of female and child labourers were employed. In 1911, Victoria had 1,407 factories engaged in the manufacture of clothing and allied products, as against 981 in New South Wales. The greater number of such concerns had an immediate bearing on the early factory legislation in Victoria and was also an important factor in shaping the factory legislation passed in 1896.

Thus the picture is of an economy based on the production and export of wool, which had reached a peak of development in 1890. In the crisis and depression that followed, the staple industry was severely affected and the repercussions were felt throughout the whole economy. Other industries, by their increased productivity, compensated in some measure for the decline in the wool output, but in general the twenty years after 1890 witnessed a decrease in the rate of economic expansion. To meet this situation and to find means of overcoming the crisis in the relations between workers and employers, the state began to intervene in economic affairs to a greater extent than had ever been attempted in any other country, with the possible exception of New Zealand.

Industrial arbitration became the method by which the state interposed itself between workers and employers. The royal commission set up by the New South Wales parliament to investigate the causes of the maritime strike recommended the establishment of conciliation and arbitration machinery by the government.[3] In 1891, after the report of the Royal Commission on Strikes had been tabled, the Premier, Sir Henry Parkes, introduced a Bill which ultimately became the first Arbitration Act in New South Wales. It provided for a council or councils of conciliation consisting of two representatives of the Trades and Labour Council and two of the employers' Union. If unable to effect a settlement, the council would refer the dispute to a council of arbitration consisting of three members appointed

[3] British experiments in arbitration were well known in Australia. Also there had been various instances of arbitration in Australia before 1890. But in all cases it had been by agreement between unions and employers. The first attempt made by an Australian government to set up machinery of arbitration occurred in 1887 when J. Carruthers introduced a Bill into the New South Wales parliament to provide for an industrial tribunal with equal representation of workers and employers and a chairman appointed by the Governor in Council. It was referred to a select committee from which it did not emerge.

by the Governor in Council. One of the members would be appointed from a list submitted by the Employers' Union, one from a list submitted by the Trades and Labour Council, and the president was to be an impartial person not directly connected with either employers or employees.

The Act failed to achieve any of the results expected of it, and the failure was obviously due to the disinclination of opposing parties to refer a matter to the court while there was still a chance of outright victory. Added to this there were the technical deficiencies of the court. It was unable to call witnesses or compel the production of books and accounts. As one writer has said, 'the Act was a not inexpensive piece of waste paper, that Parliament ended by refusing to vote money for'.[4] It was, nevertheless, an important incident in the evolution of arbitration. In 1894, in New Zealand, William Pember Reeves piloted a Bill through parliament that overcame the deficiencies of the New South Wales Act and became in turn the prototype of future legislation in Australia. It was to be more or less faithfully copied in New South Wales in 1900 and later by the Commonwealth parliament. But in the meantime another experiment was made in New South Wales, and one of a different type in Victoria.

In 1895, G. H. Reid introduced a Bill into the New South Wales parliament which provided for compulsory investigation of industrial disputes although no award could be made without the consent of both parties. It was rejected by the Legislative Council. In the following year the Victorian Factories and Shops Act became the first measure in Australia which actually did provide a workable method of determining the conditions of work by legislative and judicial means.

It was a comprehensive Act which directly specified minimum conditions of space, safety, and health in a number of industries, but it also provided for the establishment of tribunals that would have a continuous existence and that would fix wages for the industries in which they were established. These tribunals, to be known as wages boards, were immediately set up in the clothing, furniture making, baking, and butchery trades and could be established in any industry if a resolution were passed by either house of parliament declaring it expedient to do so. The boards were to consist of between four and ten members, half to be representatives of employers and half of the employees, the chairman to be elected either by the board or failing that by the Governor in Council.

[4] W. P. Reeves, *State Experiments in Australia and New Zealand*, ii. 99.

The wages boards established in Victoria differed in one important particular from the arbitration machinery adopted in New Zealand and later adopted in New South Wales and Queensland. Whereas the arbitration system to be adopted in New South Wales was to settle disputes between unions and employers or organizations of employers, the Victorian wages boards were to establish conditions for an industry and could take action on the request of an employer, a union, or a meeting of employees. Under the arbitration machinery the effective unit was the union, but the wages boards made the unions unnecessary. This difference was to have an important bearing on the development of unions. In New South Wales the arbitration system was to encourage their growth.

The New South Wales Act of 1901 was believed by its framers to have overcome the deficiencies of the previous measures. It was an Act solely for compulsory arbitration, no provision being made for conciliation. The court was to consist of a judge appointed by the government and two assessors who were to be elected by delegates representing unions of employers and trade unionists respectively. The employers, for the purpose of the court, might be organized or not, but only trade unions of the workers would be recognized. Unions or employers could be cited to appear before the court, but only registered unions would be able to vote in the election of the assessor. The court could become cognizant of a dispute by application from either a union or an employer or by the reference of the industrial registrar. The powers of the court were very wide. They included the power to make awards in settlement of a dispute and also to make a 'common rule' binding on the industry as a whole. The court could compel the production of books and accounts, but trade secrets were to be confined to the court. Strikes and lockouts were prohibited during the reference of any disputes to the court, and any strike or lockout entered upon without time being given for reference to the court was a misdemeanour, the maximum penalty prescribed being a fine of £1,000 or two months' imprisonment. The intention of the Act was clearly to provide an alternative to the strikes and lockouts that followed unsuccessful collective bargaining. It failed to do this, but it is profoundly significant as marking the acceptance by the state of responsibility for deciding issues between workers and employers. The state had accepted responsibility for the organization of important economic relationships.

Compulsory arbitration was one of the methods of state intervention in industrial relationships, and during the first ten years of the Commonwealth the ramifications of the system spread throughout the economic life of the country. But before the end of the century direct legislation defining conditions of work was also being adopted by colonial parliaments. In 1896, factory acts were passed in New South Wales, Victoria, and Queensland. The most comprehensive of these was the Victorian Factories and Shops Act 1896, which made it compulsory for factories to register with the appropriate government department. Factories were defined as any place where goods were prepared for sale and in which four or more persons were working; where steam, water, gas, oil or electric power was used; where one or more Chinese was working; where furniture was made or bread or pastry baked for sale. Factories had to conform with minimum requirements of health and sanitation and were subject to inspection. A minimum wage of 2s. 6d. per week was prescribed, and children under the age of thirteen were prohibited from working in factories. No person under sixteen years of age and no female could be employed for more than forty-eight hours a week except that on one day a week three hours' overtime could be worked. The purpose of the legislation was to deal with the problem of 'sweating', to protect women and children against the rapacity of employers who, from natural inclination or under pressure of competition, were prepared to work them for excessive hours, and to eliminate the menace to the health of the community of unhealthy workrooms. The special provision for Chinese was aimed at decreasing the 'unfair' competition from that quarter. It was provided that Chinese and European furniture manufacturers should not work before 7.30 a.m. or after 5 p.m. on Saturdays. All other factories in which Chinese were employed were subject to the same regulation, and all furniture was to be stamped with the maker's name and address.

The New South Wales Factories and Shops Act of 1896 contained provisions very similar to those of the Victorian Act. It provided for minimum conditions of sanitation, and for the fencing of dangerous machinery, and it limited the hours of work of children and females. The provisions of the Act were to be implemented by registration and inspection. The need for such legislation was revealed very clearly in the reports of the factory inspectors appointed under the Act. One inspector reported that only in a very few instances had any attempt been made to fence dangerous machinery.[5] The sanitary conditions revealed in many factories were disgusting and dangerous, and lack of air and overheating were normal. Although the Act did not provide for supervision of 'outwork', in which the worst abuses

[5] Department of Labour and Industry, *Report on Working of Factories and Shops Act*, 1897.

THE FOUNDATIONS OF THE WELFARE STATE 159

occurred, factory inspectors reported that average wages from such work amounted to from 5s. to 8s. a week. One inspector naïvely concluded that 'outwork' was not a serious problem since the rates were so low that no one could live by work of that kind; therefore, it could only be done by women with other sources of income. The Queensland Factories and Shops Act was of the same pattern as those of New South Wales and Victoria.

Closely related to the factory Acts was the legislation directed towards limiting the hours during which shops could remain open and employees could work. In Victoria a section of the Factories and Shops Act of 1885 had fixed 7 p.m. as the closing hour for shops on five days a week and 10 p.m. on Saturday. In 1896 this regulation was extended by giving the Governor in Council power to proclaim a weekly half-holiday in any trade on receipt of a petition of a majority of shopkeepers engaged in it. The working hours of women and boys under sixteen were limited to fifty-two a week, with a maximum of nine hours on five days and eleven hours on the other. The Factories and Shops Acts of New South Wales and Queensland, although differing in their scope, contained the same principle with respect to hours. The New South Wales and Queensland Acts proved to be impossible to police and were amended in 1899 and 1900.

There were a great number of other Acts dealing with the regulation of industry, but only a few of them need be mentioned here. One was the Employers' Liability Act of 1897, which extended the liability of the employer for injuries received by workers in the course of their employment. Under the Act the employer was liable for damages if the injury was sustained as a result of defects in the plant and under certain other conditions, but the Act was so framed that it was difficult to establish the employers' liability and did not give nearly the same protection to workers as the English Workers' Compensation Act of 1897. However, Acts comparable with the English Acts were passed in Queensland in 1905, New South Wales in 1910, and Victoria in 1914. Acts regulating mining were not new but were extended during the nineties in New South Wales by an Act of 1896 which was amended in 1900 and again in 1902 and 1912. In Queensland there was a Mines Regulation Act in 1898 and amendments in 1901 and 1902. Their provisions were too highly technical to be described here, but the extended application of the principle of regulation is important. In 1901 another important regulative Act was the Shearers' Accommodation Act, which laid down minimum conditions of accommodation for shearers, thus righting one of the wrongs that had been instrumental in forming the Shearers' Union.

The banking crisis in 1891-3 had forced the colonial governments to take action to deal with the emergency. In New South Wales, government action was one factor in preventing the panic associated with the crisis reaching the proportions it did in Victoria. However, the most important long-term result of the crisis was the recognition that private banking had failed as a means of providing credit for expanding settlement of the kind the land Acts were intended to encourage. In Victoria a royal commission on state banking recommended the establishment of a state bank. This was not done, but attempts were made by the governments in all colonies to find means to assist in the small-scale settlement of the land. As Fitzpatrick puts it,

> in the 'nineties all colonies legislated in this field, forced thereto by the private banks' failure to solve the problem, how to make money by lending it to farmers who would not be able to repay it, or even pay interest on it, in a world whose system of exchange would only work sometimes.[6]

The result was a spate of Advances to Settlers Acts, Closer Settlement Acts and so on.

The earliest form of these attempts to assist small-scale settlement were Acts which provided for co-operative and welfare settlements. In Queensland the Co-operative Communities Land Settlement Act was passed in 1893. Under it, land would be leased to groups of thirty or more people who would be assisted financially to the extent of £20 per person, provided that for each quarter of the period of the lease improvements to the value of 2s. 6d. an acre were made by the settlers. An interesting feature of the Act was the powers of self-government given to the groups, which were empowered to divide the land according to any principle acceptable to the members, and the government would intervene only in the case of a deadlock. Further, the groups were given powers to settle civil disputes without reference to the general courts of the country. In these last aspects, at least, the Acts were influenced by the utopian socialist ideas at that time being given great publicity by the expedition led by William Lane, which had just left to found the 'New Australia' settlement in Paraguay. The New South Wales Labour Settlements Act 1893 was similar to the Queensland Act except that it did not provide for the same degree of autonomy for the settling group.

[6] *The British Empire in Australia*, p. 360.

The Act empowered the Governor in Council to appoint a board of control which would be a corporate body capable of holding a lease of lands made available for the purpose. The government was empowered to advance £25 for each married man with a family and £15 for a single man, to be repaid at the rate of eight per cent of the total per year until the whole plus four per cent interest had been recovered. The board was empowered to make regulations concerning the work to be done in the settlement and the distribution of wages, profits, etc., and also to carry on a limited civil government of the settlement and to impose penalties not exceeding £2 to be recovered summarily in any Court of Petty Sessions. The comparable Victorian Act was the Settlement of Lands Act 1893, which provided for the establishment of village communities, homestead associations and labour colonies. It made little provision for the autonomy of the communities, which were to be financed by a combination of government finance and private charity.

The immediate motivation of all these Acts was to find some way of dealing with the unemployed, but in larger perspective it is clear that they were part of the process by which the state was accepting the necessity of concerning itself directly in the organization and development of industry. In general, the co-operative settlements were not successful.[7] They provided some measure of relief in the period of depression, but the form of government assistance to small-scale settlement that was to become characteristic was that of closer settlement Acts and money advances to farmers. In all the eastern colonies there was a series of closer settlement Acts between 1895 and 1906. Under this legislation governments repurchased land and let it on easy terms to settlers, with conditions of residence and improvement. Financial assistance was provided under legislation adopted in Victoria in 1896, New South Wales in 1899, and Queensland in 1901.

Another new field of legislation was the provision of old age pensions. In New South Wales the Old Age Pensions Act 1900 provided a pension of ten shillings a week for men and women over the age of sixty-five who had resided in the colony for twenty-five years, or had resided there for the ten years prior to application, if the previous fifteen years had been spent in another colony with a similar pension scheme. The preamble to the law made an important statement of principle, namely that the pensions were not in the nature of charity but were the just reward for those who had spent their life in useful work: 'it is equitable that deserving persons, who,

---

[7] *Australian Association for the Advancement of Science. Report, 1909*, p. 557.

during the prime of life have helped to bear the public burdens of the colony by payment of taxes, and by opening up its resources with their labour and skill, should receive from the colony pensions in their old age'. A similar pensions scheme, modelled directly on the New Zealand example, was put into effect in Victoria.

Further steps were taken in the nineties to seal the door against immigration by non-European peoples. The Chinese had been effectively excluded by 1888, and thereafter governments were mainly concerned with legislation that would prevent 'unfair' competition from Chinese already in the colonies. The Victorian Factories and Shops Act, for example, included special provisions for the furniture trade in which many Chinese were employed, and special regulations were made for other factories owned by Chinese or in which Chinese were employed. In Queensland, however, the problem was the Pacific islanders, the Kanakas, as they were known. In 1892 Sir Samuel Griffith, the Premier who had in 1886 set his face against non-European immigration, reversed his policy and agreed to the importation of indentured Pacific islanders. In that year there were 8,627 Kanakas in Queensland,[8] and in the next ten years approximately 11,000 more arrived.[9] The reversal of policy was undoubtedly brought about by pressure from the plantation owners who had customarily conducted their large-scale enterprises with cheap indentured labour, and whose profits had fallen with the drop in the price of sugar from £27 a ton in 1872 to £8. 10s. a ton in 1893.[10] Sir Samuel Griffith justified his change of heart by arguing that Europeans could not do the work on the plantations and, since it was important to maintain the industry, it was better to carry it on by indentured labourers who would not stay permanently in the colony and would not be absorbed into the population. The force of his argument was not seen in the other colonies, however, and pressure was put on the Queensland government to end a policy that would allow the continuation of this plantation type of economic organization.

In 1896 a conference of colonial premiers decided to bring down uniform legislation to extend the provisions of the Draft Restriction Bill of 1888, which had excluded Chinese, to all coloured people, including coloured British subjects. The Queensland representatives at the conference agreed with the decision, with the proviso that

[8] Qld. V. & P. (L.A.), 1892, vol. ii: 'Annual Report of the Department of Pacific Island Immigration'.
[9] Willard, *History of the White Australian Policy*, p. 182.
[10] Shann, *An Economic History of Australia*, p. 247.

THE FOUNDATIONS OF THE WELFARE STATE 163

they intended to continue with their policy towards Pacific islanders. The conference also decided that the colonies should not adhere to the Anglo-Japanese Commercial Treaty of 1894. The Queensland government took no action on the Draft Restriction Bill and in the following year, despite the decision of the conference, adhered to the Anglo-Japanese Treaty—with a consequent influx of 3,248 Japanese into the colony by the end of 1898. New South Wales, South Australia, and Tasmania passed the Restriction Bill, but in all cases it was reserved for consideration by the imperial government, which refused to accept the Bill in the form in which it had been passed. The Queensland refusal to co-operate and the refusal of the British government to agree to the Bill passed by the other colonies were important factors in carrying through the last stages the federation of the colonies.

Thus by the end of the nineteenth century, the governments of all colonies had written into the statute books a great deal of socio-economic legislation, the common factor in all of it being the idea that the state had a responsibility to concern itself directly with the economic life of the country. This was one of the decisive facts in bringing about the federation of the colonies, which was put into effect on the first day of the new century. Greenwood sums up the motive forces leading to federation as 'the necessity of fiscal union, a more adequate organization of the defence forces, the desire to speak with authority on questions concerning the Pacific Ocean, the determination to restrict the entry of aliens and the need for uniform legislation on social, industrial and transport questions'.[11] In fact, the forces that induced the various colonies to pass the kind of legislation that we have described equally induced them to establish a national government that would legislate along similar lines for the whole nation. Commonwealth parliaments could carry further the tendencies manifested in the colonies.

In the first ten years of the Commonwealth, governments were occupied erecting a wall against the outside world behind which the white Australian people could develop their wealth and productivity. The White Australia policy, a system of national defence closely linked with empire defence, and the 'New Protection' were intended to achieve this. Within Australia the means by which this hot-house-produced wealth was to be 'fairly' distributed was a comprehensive system of industrial arbitration which became increasingly integrated with the 'New Protection'.

One of the first Acts of the Commonwealth parliament was the

[11] G. Greenwood, *The Future of Australian Federalism*, p. 31.

Immigration Restriction Act 1901. It provided that any intending immigrant could be submitted to a dictation test of fifty words in any European language, and failure was sufficient grounds for exclusion. It was made quite clear in the debate on the question that its purpose was to exclude non-Europeans—a purpose with which all parties were agreed. The subterfuge of the dictation test was adopted at the instance of the Colonial Secretary, Joseph Chamberlain, who had explained when the Bills of 1896 were rejected by the British government that some such procedure, which had already been tried in Natal, would be acceptable to the British government. A further Act, the Pacific Island Labourers Act 1901, dealt with the question of the Pacific islanders in Queensland. It provided that all Pacific islanders in Australia after December 1906 would be deported, no more would be introduced after 1904, and only a limited number of licences would be issued in 1902-3. Thus, despite strong opposition from the Queensland planters, and except that the details of the deportation of the Kanakas necessitated a royal commission and an amendment to the Act in 1906 and amendments to the Immigration Restriction Act in 1905 and 1908, the question of White Australia had been resolved by the end of 1901.

Having erected a prohibitive barrier against the people of Asia, the next problem was to find a means to defend the barrier. The movement to establish military forces will be treated in some detail in a subsequent chapter; here it is sufficient to say that under the Defence Act of 1909 a system of compulsory military training was introduced. Naval defence was another matter. There had always been the argument that Australian shores would be defended by the might of the British Navy. In 1907, however, the Prime Minister, Alfred Deakin, announced the termination of the naval agreement under which a squadron of the Royal Navy was stationed in Australian waters. Australia was to have its own navy. The government's defence policy envisaged two lines of defence—the high seas, and the coastline. The defence of the seas would remain the responsibility of the Royal Navy, but to protect the coastline Australia would build a flotilla of light vessels. They would be standardized in every way with similar vessels of the Royal Navy, and in case of war would be put under the command of the British Admiralty. The plan was at first received coldly in Britain, but at the defence conference of 1909 it was accepted and even expanded. The plan for a flotilla of light vessels was replaced by the policy of building complete fleet units, including one battleship, three cruisers, six destroyers and three submarines. From the time that the keels of the first two vessels were laid until the fully equipped ships arrived in Fremantle in 1910, their construction, launching and sailing was eagerly followed by the Australian press.[12] In 1910, Australia had a navy, albeit a very small one.

The policy of the New Protection was to exclude from Australia the products of the labour of those whose persons had been excluded by immigration restrictions. It differed in one important particular from simple protective legislation in that it aimed both to protect industries and to ensure that the workers benefited from the growth of the protected industry. In 1907, Alfred Deakin explained the differences between the 'New' and the 'Old' protection.

> The 'Old' Protection contented itself with making good wages possible. The 'New' Protection seeks to make them actual. It aims at according to the manufacturer that degree of exemption from unfair outside competition which will enable him to pay fair and reasonable wages without impairing the maintenance and extension of his industry, or its capacity to supply the local market. It does not stop here. Having put the manufacturer in a position to pay good wages, it goes on to assure the public that he does pay them.[13]

The New Protection was put into operation by a series of Acts in 1906, but from the first days of the Commonwealth, governments had shown an inclination towards protective legislation.

The first customs tariff adopted by the Commonwealth parliament was essentially a revenue tariff but it contained elements of protection. Division VIA of the schedule, listing metals and machinery, was

> to come into operation on dates to be fixed by Proclamation, and exempt from duty in the meantime, except as to Iron, Galvanised, Plate and Sheet. Proclamation to issue as soon as it is certified by the Minister that the Manufacture to which the proclamation refers has been sufficiently established in the Commonwealth.

That is, it provided for protection for the steel industry when it was sufficiently established to supply some of the needs of the Australian economy. More important as a pointer of the direction in which tariff policy would develop was the Excise Tariff Act 1902. Amongst other things it imposed an excise duty on sugar of 3s. per hundredweight, but allowed a rebate of 4s. per ton in the case of sugar cane produced solely by white labour. Complementing this was

---

[12] *Daily Telegraph*, 11 February, 16, 24 September 1910.
[13] Cited W. Murdoch, *Alfred Deakin*, p. 236.

the provision in the Customs Tariff Act for an import duty of 6s. per hundredweight on sugar manufactured from sugar cane. The production of sugar was to be protected and employers encouraged to use white labour exclusively. The method of encouraging the production of sugar grown by white labour was slightly amended by the Sugar Bounty Act 1903, but the principle remained the same. The changed method was made necessary by the disproportionate burden that had been thrown on some states and the relative immunity of others under the previous Act. Under the new Act, a bounty of 4s. per ton on sugar cane and 40s. per ton on beet sugar, produced by white labour, was provided. This was the pattern of encouraging Australian industries, under certain conditions, that was amplified in the Excise Tariff Act 1906, the Customs Tariff Act 1906, and the Australian Industries Preservation Act 1906.

The Excise Tariff Act provided for excise duties on agricultural machinery manufactured in accordance with specific conditions as to remuneration and employment. The conditions were to be such as—

(a) are declared by resolution of both Houses of the Parliament to be fair and reasonable; or
(b) are in accordance with an industrial award under the *Commonwealth Conciliation and Arbitration Act 1904;* or
(c) are in accordance with the terms of an industrial agreement filed under the *Commonwealth Conciliation and Arbitration Act 1904;* or
(d) are on an application made for the purpose to the President of the Commonwealth Court of Conciliation and Arbitration, declared to be fair and reasonable by him or by a Judge of the Supreme Court of a State or any person or persons who composed a State Industrial Authority to whom he may refer the matter.

Import duties equal to twice the excise duty were provided by the Customs Tariff Act, thus ensuring double protection for the manufacturer who complied with the conditions as to employment. The Australian Industries Preservation Act carried further the principle contained in the Excise Tariff Act. It aimed to prevent 'unfair' competition which would result in their being produced with an inadequate remuneration for labour. Unfair competition was defined as existing in the case of a commercial trust, if the competition resulted in inadequate remuneration in the Australian industry, or where there was 'dumping' by a foreign competitor.

The Bounties Act 1907 and the Manufacturers Encouragement Act 1908 combined the principles contained in the Sugar Bounty Act and the Australian Industries Preservation Act. The Bounties Act provided for a bounty to be paid for the production of cotton, flax, jute, hemp, oil materials, rice, rubber, coffee, tobacco, preserved fish, and certain kinds of dried fruits. It required that the articles should be produced by white labour only and by labour enjoying conditions of remuneration and employment that were not below the standard of the district in which the goods were produced. The Manufacturers Encouragement Act gave similar encouragement to the steel industry—bounties being payable on pig iron, puddled bar-iron and steel until 1914, so long as certain conditions were complied with.

Various changes in procedure and operation of the Acts were made necessary by difficulties in their application and by decisions of the High Court on the powers of the Commonwealth parliament to pass such legislation. In fact, some of the legislation was made quite ineffective by the decisions of the High Court, with the result that the question of amendment of the constitution became a burning issue very early in the life of the Commonwealth. But since the decisions of the High Court were closely related to the operation of the arbitration system, it is necessary first to look briefly at the arbitration machinery adopted by the Commonwealth.

The Commonwealth Arbitration and Conciliation Act of 1904 was passed under powers conferred on the Commonwealth parliament by section 51 (xxxv) of the Constitution, which enabled it to legislate to deal with industrial disputes that extended beyond the limits of any one state. The court set up was similar to that established in New South Wales in 1901, except that it had powers to act as conciliator as well as powers of compulsory arbitration. Since the most important unions were interstate in character, it was apparent from the beginning that the Commonwealth Arbitration Court would be an important institution. It was made more important and its function somewhat changed by the new protective legislation, which, as we have seen, provided that a decision on whether the conditions in an industry were 'fair' could be made by the court. In fact, under the Excise Tariff Act the court was to become a quasi-legislative body with power to make decisions with the force of regulations under the Act.

In the first few years the commonwealth court sent down a number of very important judgments. In 1906 the court made an award very favourable to the Australian Workers' Union, followed, in the next year, by the famous Harvester judgment, from which the whole concept of the basic wage was evolved.[14] The judgment arose out of an application by H. V. McKay, manufacturer of agricultural implements, to have the wages paid by him declared fair and reasonable so that his products could be granted rebate of excise duty provided by the Act. In giving his decision on what a 'fair and reasonable' wage was, Mr Justice Higgins outlined the principles that had directed the court. He stated that it had nothing to do with the rate of profit, whether it was 100 per cent or nothing at all. It was not a wage produced by the 'usual but unequal combat, the higgling of the market for labour, with the pressure for bread on one side and the pressure for profits on the other' but was 'a wage sufficient to ensure the workman food, shelter, clothing, frugal comfort, provision for evil days etc., as well as reward for the special skill of the artisan'. This same concept was applied in the Marine Cooks'[15] case and the case of the Barrier Branch of the Amalgamated Miners' Association v. the Broken Hill Proprietary Company.[16] Indeed it became the principle on which all decisions of the Arbitration Court were based, at least so long as Mr Justice Higgins remained on the Bench.

By the linking of protective legislation with the machinery of arbitration and the adoption by the court of principles on which decisions could be based, it seemed that an answer had been found to the problem of how to encourage industry and at the same time ensure that its product was fairly distributed. But difficulties were soon encountered. In a series of judgments the High Court found that the court and the Commonwealth parliament had gone beyond their powers under the Constitution. In the Railway Servants case the High Court found that the section of the Act which empowered the Arbitration Court to make awards for workers employed by state governments was invalid. In the Broken Hill case and more importantly the Bootmakers case, the High Court decided that section 38(b) of the Arbitration and Conciliation Act 1904, which purported to authorize the court to declare any condition of employment included in an award to be a common rule for the industry, was beyond the powers of the Commonwealth parliament. Then the whole basis of the new protection was jeopardized in a further case that arose out of the Harvester judgment. The Arbitration Court had found that H. V. McKay did not pay 'fair and reasonable' wages,

[14] *Ex parte* H. V. McKay (1901), 2 C.A.R. 1.
[15] Marine Cooks, Bakers & Butchers Association of Aust. *v.* Commonwealth Steam-Owners' Association (1908), 1 C.A.R. 55.
[16] (1909), 3 C.A.R. 1.

THE FOUNDATIONS OF THE WELFARE STATE 169

and therefore he could not benefit under the Excise Tariff Act. McKay refused to pay the excise duty, and in the ensuing action a majority of the High Court found that the Act was invalid. The reasoning in the judgment of the majority of the court—Griffiths, C.J., and Barton and O'Connor, JJ.—was that the Excise Tariff Act was not an Act imposing duties of excise but an Act to regulate the conditions of manufacture of agricultural implements. Since the Commonwealth parliament had no such power under the Constitution it followed that the parliament could not by delegation to the Commonwealth Arbitration Court do what it was forbidden to do directly. Thus the structure of protected and regulated industry was seriously undermined by the decisions of the High Court on the powers of the Commonwealth parliament. The conclusion drawn from it by those concerned with making effective the legislative principles we have noted was not that they were inapplicable, however, but that the Constitution would have to be amended. It was from this time that the Labour Party's determination to extend the powers of the Commonwealth parliament was heightened.

In the twenty years under review, the Labour Party had grown to maturity. It had been in power for a short time in Queensland in 1899 and in the Commonwealth in 1904. In 1910 it became the governing party in New South Wales and the Commonwealth. Its policy as a parliamentary party had been fashioned during the period when the legislation we have described was being written into the statute books—in part it was responsible for the legislation. We must now turn to an examination of the way in which the policy of the Labour Party evolved.

10

The Labour Party Finds a Programme

> We have not come into this House, then, to make or unmake ministries.
> We have not come into this House to support governments or oppositions.
> We have come into this House to make and unmake social conditions.[1]

THE first years of the parliamentary labour parties in New South Wales and Queensland were marked, as we have seen, by the painful adoption of principles of organization of the party and a machinery of authority within the labour movement. In this process two principles were established, at least formally: that the parliamentary party must act as a unit on all questions affecting the party platform, and that the extra-parliamentary organization had considerable powers of control over the politicians. The Labour Party was to be a pledged party and subject to control by the movement. In practice, the formal position did not always reflect the real power relations within the party. In 1899, for example, the 'solid six' led by W. A. Holman and W. M. Hughes were able to force the party to act contrary to a decision of caucus. And as the parliamentary party increased in strength and experience the parliamentary members acquired an authority from their position that could not be matched by non-parliamentary members. The tendency was, in fact, for the parliamentary party to become the effective leadership of the labour movement, but it was to do this within a framework in which the principle was accepted that the conference and the central committee were the governing organs of the party.

The struggles within the party were due in part to the necessary difficulty of developing a machinery of authority, but they were accentuated by the lack of any comprehensive political theory acceptable to all sections of the movement. If the parliamentary party were to function as a delegate body of an extra-parliamentary movement, such a comprehensive theory would have made it easier. The Labour Party was never to have such a theory, but in the course of its political experience it agglomerated a policy that acted as a cohesive force in the movement. In its first ten years the ideas and

[1] G. Black, *Parl. Deb.* (N.S.W.), 1891, lii. 126.

interests that would continue to mould this policy were more sharply in evidence than in later periods, because the parliamentary party had not yet acquired the authority in the movement that it would later have. In 1891, Labour Party policy in New South Wales was confined to the sixteen points, which can be summarized as ten demands for the regulation of industry, five for democratic constitutional reforms, and a vague collectivist land policy. These represented the common denominator of opinion in the labour movement, and it became the function of the Labour Party to attempt to confine the policy of the whole movement within bounds set by such a common denominator. In large measure it succeeded. But before it could do so, the sections of the movement which saw the Labour Party as a party of leadership in the radical, political and social transformation of society—that is, the forces that had played a large part in establishing the party—made a strong bid for leadership. At least until the end of the century attempts were being made to fashion the Labour Party as a socialist party with a socialist objective.

In the struggle for the united party, socialist ideas temporarily played an important part. The socialist concept of the Labour Party as the party of the working class justified the demand that the party should accept direction from extra-parliamentary organizations of the working class. Against it was the idea that the party was simply a parliamentary grouping of men who had certain ideas in common, specifically the ideas contained in the party programme. On all other matters it was held that the parliamentary member should be free to make his own decisions. As the results of this second view became apparent in the crisis of the first few years, the demand for the 'solid' Labour Party won general support within the labour movement. Holman and Hughes attacked the existing parliamentary party for its ineffectiveness and at the same time preached the need for the collective ownership of the means of production and the necessity of a united Labour Party to achieve it.[2] A socialist objective was for a time linked with the idea of the unity of the party. This was reflected in the programme of the Political Labour League Conference of 1896, when there was added to the general platform 'the nationalisation of all coal, silver, copper and iron mines'.[3] And then in the following year the conference included in the programme 'the nationalisation of land and the whole means of production, distribution and exchange'.[4]

[2] *New Order*, 14 April, 12 May 1894.   [3] *Worker*, Sydney, 1 February 1896.
[4] Ibid., 30 January 1897.

In 1897 and the following year there was an attempt to have the nationalization proposal made the objective of the party and the other points of the programme the steps to it, but it was retained merely as one of the points of the programme. This was the closest that the Labour Party in New South Wales would go, until after 1920, to adopting a socialist objective. In the meantime the politicians were deciding in practice that the Labour Party would be less a socialist than a party of trade-union politics and democratic reform. From militant trade unionism and socialist theory the Labour Party acquired a unity, but it used the strength springing from that unity to put into effect policies that were neither militant nor socialist.

In Queensland the problems of unity and relations with the extra-parliamentary organization were not so acute as in New South Wales. The extra-parliamentary party was more highly organized before the sixteen members elected in 1893 gave the party any substantial representation in parliament. Also, as we have seen, from the beginning the Labour Party found itself the effective opposition and soon became the official Opposition party. Consequently it was not faced with the same tactical problems. It was important, too, that it did not have the same uncertainty on matters of policy. From 1890 the party had a socialist objective, but by agreement this was moved into the background and the party concentrated on the 'fighting platform' of constitutional reform and regulation of conditions in industry. The transition to this policy was facilitated by the argument that the fighting platform had to be achieved before the ultimate objective could be realized. In due course the fighting platform became the only platform, and the policy of the Queensland party did not differ in essentials from that of New South Wales. But because of the means by which the transition to it was made, it did not result in the same conflicts as in New South Wales. By 1898 the Queensland party, too, had become a party of practical politics. As Sir Timothy Coghlan aptly remarked of its members, 'scarcely a word fell from them that would lead their hearers to suppose that they had ever learned the alphabet of socialism'.

A further fact that was both cause and effect of the transition from socialist idealism to less inspiring programmes of trade-union politics was the departure of William Lane and a band of faithful followers to found a socialist community in Paraguay. This venture is important in the history of the Australian labour movement because its conception throws light on the thought of one of its leaders at a decisive period, because it deprived the Australian movement of some of its most dynamic leaders, and because the failure of the venture had some influence in dissipating the idealist socialism of the nineties.

No aspect of early Australian labour history has received the same detailed attention as the pilgrimage that William Lane led to Paraguay. Opponents of socialism eagerly seized upon the failure of New Australia to prove that socialism does not work and that its advocates are at best misguided.[5] Others have attempted a sympathetic analysis of the causes of failure. Some have even denied that it was a failure. However, little consideration has been given to an explanation of why the attempt was made.

The simple reason why Lane made the attempt to found a socialist community is that he was a utopian socialist. His thought was strongly influenced by the utopian experiments and ideas in the United States, where he had spent some time before coming to Australia. Theodore Hertzka's utopian novel *Freeland* has been cited as Lane's inspiration, as also has the Icarian settlement in Illinois,[6] but it seems clear that no single book or experiment was responsible for his decision. His thought was influenced by the whole stream of socialist thought and the numerous experiments in socialist living made in the United States. Horace Greeley, who publicized in the *New York Tribune* the Fourierist experiments in the United States, was greatly admired by Lane. Lane knew of Robert Owen and also of the Icarian settlements. As we have seen, English Christian socialism was an important influence on his thought, and as early as 1887 he was interested in the idea of setting up model socialist communities. He co-operated with Carl Fileberg, editor of the Brisbane *Courier,* and R. H. Roe, headmaster of the Brisbane Grammar School, in forming a society to advocate state-aided village settlements in Queensland.[7] The idea soon developed in Lane's mind to a communist settlement, and the project was being discussed in detail in 1889. But it was not until after the defeat in the shearers' strike that it became Lane's main objective, because until then he felt that the New Australia could be the whole of Australia.

To Lane, socialism was an ideal way of life as much as a political and economic system. In the days of successful unionism, the socialist way of living, as Lane understood it, seemed to be developing in Australia. Solidarity, mateship, and co-operation were the creed of trade unionists. Lane considered that this gave promise of a future for the whole of Australian society in which co-operation

[5] E.g. S. Grahame, *Where Socialism Failed.*
[6] *Ross's Monthly,* 16 August 1919.   [7] *Worker*, Brisbane, 8 July 1898.

would replace competition. His thought went no deeper than this. Because of their emotional intensity, his writings had a profound effect in convincing unionists of the justice and even the virtue of their cause. But his ideas were naïve and superficial. He made no serious analysis of the society in which he lived, nor did he have more than a hazy vision of the society to which he aspired. He was satisfied that the behaviour of trade unionists was similar to that of the idealized people of Bellamy's utopia and that in some obscure fashion this would lead to the establishment of such a utopia in Australia. Consequently when he found that the unions were defeated by the employment of strike breakers, he concluded that he had been wrong. Socialism apparently could not grow out of the co-operative action of individuals living under a capitalist system, at least within the foreseeable future. He concluded that the good life—the co-operative socialist life—was corrupted by the forces existing in capitalist society. Therefore those who wished to live as socialists should must isolate themselves from the contagion of existing society.[8]

Thus his first motive in seeking to establish a socialist community was to set up conditions under which people could live in his idealized fashion. 'Those who want to do right,' he wrote, 'who hunger after a happy life not only for themselves but for all who are unhappy, must, we think, make an effort to live, themselves, as they should live.'[9] Secondly, the racialism that had made him a violent opponent of Chinese immigration and that later led him to uncritical acceptance of Anglo-Saxon racial superiority, encouraged his belief in the barbarian virtues. Civilization was decaying and affecting the 'race-vigour' as he called it, so it was necessary to escape to a more primitive environment.[10] He had thought that Australia would be such a pure primitive setting in which to build a society free from the diseases of the old world, but in 1892 he was saying sadly that there was nothing new in Australia except the land itself. It followed from this, he believed, that it was necessary to create a new society. Thirdly, there was the urge to show by example that socialism was possible and desirable. Although the personal, almost religious, desire to live the good life was probably the strongest motive in urging Lane on, he thought of the New Australia as living proof of the truth of his viewpoint. In 1892 he wrote,

[8] *New Australia,* Journal of the New Australia Co-operative Settlement Association, 19 November 1892; *Worker,* Brisbane, 22 October 1892.
[9] *New Australia,* 19 November 1892.
[10] Rose Scott Papers: Arthur Rae to Rose Scott, 11 May 1892.

'we can best help our fellow workers here by showing them what can be accomplished by having faith in each other and courage enough to try',[11] but at the same time it is evident that he was pessimistic about the influence of New Australia on the Australian future. As he was preparing to leave the country he said that, 'if by our movement we can make a fresh hope and make them [the workers] feel like having another try for the right way out before giving up in despair, New Australia will not have been in vain'.[12]

Why should Lane have imagined that his socialist experiment would be more successful than the many that had failed? Perhaps the answer lies partly in the fact that he saw it as something he was driven to attempt if he were to satisfy his personal ideal of living; partly in that he believed in the possibility of success because the community was to be established in a remote place insulated against the influence of the outside world and to which only zealots would venture with him; and partly in the fact that he staked the success of the venture on his estimation of the character and ability of the Australian bushmen who would accompany him. One who knew him wrote that Lane had said, 'those tall straight men, they are the finest in the world. Give me those men and the right kind of women for them and I will do anything with them'.[13]

The experiment in Paraguay failed, of course, and the causes of its failure lie beyond the scope of this work. But for the history of the Australian Labour movement its significance lies in the fact that it was attempted. The enthusiasm for an ideal that sent William Lane to Paraguay was the same emotion that contributed to the formation of the Labour Party in Australia. And as Lane's hopes crumbled in the failure of his socialist settlement,[14] so the Australian Labour Party shed its idealism and settled down to practical political problems. The idealist socialism of the nineties was able to give birth to a Labour Party and a utopian socialist settlement, but it was not an ideology capable of solving the practical problems of either. These were solved under the pressures of parliamentary experience.

By the mid-nineties in New South Wales and Queensland, labour parties had emerged with a degree of organizational unity that no other political parties had. This unity gave the party a tactical advantage which, particularly in New South Wales, gave it a strong

---

[11] *New Australia*, 19 November 1892. [12] Ibid.
[13] W. Nelson, *Foster Frazer's Fallacies and Other Essays*, p. 110.
[14] Lane spent the last years of his life as the editor of a conservative newspaper in New Zealand.

influence on legislation. In New South Wales from 1895 to 1903, when the Labour Party became the official Opposition, all governments carried on their administration with labour support. This meant that the party was under constant pressure to decide what policies it would support. In the course of this experience the Labour Party charted the course that it would continue to follow. To see what this course was, the Labour Party attitude on specific issues must be examined.

Broadly speaking, the two fields in which the party influenced legislation were in carrying through democratic constitutional reforms and in widening the social and economic functions of the state. In New South Wales it supported liberal governments in passing such legislation and, because after 1894 it was a united party, was the decisive factor in pressing it through. Labour's point of view differed from the government's only in seeking a wider application of the measures than the government was prepared to give. In Queensland the Labour Party advocated policies similar to those being put into effect in New South Wales. In Victoria the party functioned less effectively as a unit and played a less important part in writing such legislation into the statute book.

The abolition of plural voting was the first question to which the Labour Party turned its attention. From 1888 the trade-union movement had made much of this demand. It was the first point in the parliamentary programme of the Labour Party in all colonies. The demand for it was widened by the visit to Australia in 1891 of Sir George Grey. This remarkable imperial statesman came from New Zealand to attend the Federal Convention, where his main contribution was the insistence that the federal constitution should embody the principle of 'one man one vote'. After the Convention he toured Australia lecturing on the importance of the principle. The Labour Party claimed him as theirs and, as a contemporary historian of the party puts it, even if the meeting were not organized to discuss this question, 'it would surely be inquired about at the close, an overwhelming vote would be taken in favour of the reform, and volleys of cheers would go up for Sir George Grey'.[15] To the supporters of labour, abolition of plural voting appeared to be the one reform necessary to enable the working class to carry its due weight in parliament.[16]

In the first parliament in which the Labour Party sat in New South Wales every opportunity was taken to press the demand. Its

[15] T. R. Roydhouse and H. J. Taperell, *The Labour Party in New South Wales*, p. 14. [16] *Shearers and General Labourers Record*, 15 June 1891.

THE LABOUR PARTY FINDS A PROGRAMME 177

members moved to delay any decision on the fiscal issue until an election was held on the basis of 'one man one vote'. Womanhood suffrage was made conditional for the Labour Party on the amendment of the electoral law to abolish plural voting.[17] Success was achieved in the Electoral Act of 1893, which abolished plural voting in New South Wales. In Queensland it was kept constantly before the parliament by the Labour Party, and as late as 1899 the party moved that it should be accepted in principle before they would support the draft federal constitution. Plural voting was not abolished in Queensland until 1905 and in Victoria until 1899.

Closely related to plural voting was residence as an electoral qualification.[18] Further, the Labour Party regarded the holding of elections on a single day that would be a holiday and on which public houses would be closed as a matter with which the full enfranchisement of the workers was linked. The requirements of six months' residence in an electoral district effectively disfranchised many workers, and the holding of elections on a working day made it difficult for workers to cast their votes. Under the New South Wales Act of 1893 the residence qualification was reduced to three months, but this was still unsatisfactory to the Labour Party. As a result of their alliance with G. H. Reid, an amendment was passed in 1896 reducing the residence qualification to one month and extending the franchise to the police. In the other colonies these reforms were made more slowly.

Womanhood suffrage became an issue of first-class importance during the nineties, and although the Labour Party in New South Wales did not give it undivided support until 1896, sections of the labour movement played an important part in popularizing the idea before then. From the late seventies, individuals had fought for the vote for women, but it was not until the late eighties that organizations began to interest themselves in it. It was first agitated in the Women's Christian Temperance Movement, in which Quakers took a leading part.[19] But in 1891 a Womanhood Suffrage League was formed in Sydney and Rose Scott, who became the recognized champion of the vote for women, led an energetic campaign. It was taken up by liberal members of all parties, and Sir Henry Parkes made a half-hearted attempt to have the principle adopted by parliament in 1891.[20] The movement continued with Rose Scott as

[17] *Parl. Deb.* (N.S.W.), 1891, lii. 508.
[18] See programmes N.S.W. Labour Electoral League, the Australian Labour Federation, the Progressive Political League.
[19] O'Connor (Mrs), 'History of the Suffrage Movement'.
[20] *Parl. Deb.* (N.S.W.), 1891, lii. 500 ff.

the centre of an expanding circle which included G. H. Reid, who had succeeded Parkes as the leader of the Free Trade Party, as well as the most radical members of the labour movement. In Queensland, a Women's Suffrage League was formed in 1890, although there is some evidence of a similar organization before that time. In Victoria the campaign appears to have been conducted by various organizations until towards the end of the century. Then Vida Goldstein organized the Women's Federal Political Association, which devoted itself to winning the vote for women in elections to the Commonwealth parliament.

From 1890, leaders of the labour movement played an important part in the campaign, and sections of the movement adopted it as part of their policy. In Brisbane, William Lane applied himself to the cause of women's emancipation. He wrote a weekly article over the name of Lucinda Sharpe, a delightful American woman living in Brisbane, who in letters to a friend in America gently satirized the foibles of womanhood and advocated political equality for women. As Lucinda Sharpe, William Lane felt 'a certain inexpressible satisfaction' in knowing that he shocked the prejudices and 'trod on the corns of every fossilised and antiquatedly ideal dame' with whom he came in contact.[21] He directed his shafts at the narrow prejudices of women as well as the prejudices of men about women. Lucinda Sharpe read Burns, Shelley, Fielding, Smollett, and Voltaire at a time when Brisbane women didn't read 'such books'. She was an enlightened woman but not a blue-stocking. She was her husband's companion, the manager of the home, but could have been equally a woman with a profession.[22] She was opposed to 'tight lacing' but didn't approve of the 'women's righters' who, 'instead of being narrow minded, cold and submissive were narrow minded, cold and pugnacious'.[23]

Lane popularized the claims of women for political equality and also played a part in organizational moves to secure it. The Australian Labour Federation included womanhood suffrage in its programme, and took the practical step of assisting in the formation of women's unions. It subscribed sufficient money to originate a women's union and support it for six months.[24] In 1891 there were reports of women's unions at Hughenden and Blackall, the centres of shearers' union strength.[25] The women's unions were seen as a necessary step in winning economic equality and subsequently political equality.

[21] *Boomerang*, 11 February 1888.
[22] *Worker*, Brisbane, 1 April 1890.
[23] *Boomerang*, 11 February 1888.
[24] *Worker*, Brisbane, 1 September 1890.
[25] *Dawn*, 6 April 1891.

In Sydney, Louisa Lawson, mother of the poet, set out to convince the labour movement of the need to support womanhood suffrage. In 1889 she established the Dawn Club and began publication of a women's paper—the *Dawn*. She regarded the suffrage as only a part of the legitimate claims that a woman might make on society. She used the club and the journal as a means of opposing social customs where they restricted women's freedom and advancing the claim of women for economic equality. She wrote that

> the cause of women's enfranchisement is a movement closely allied to that of Labour Reform, and should have the sympathies and assistance of all true friends of labour. It is impossible to raise labour as a whole without securing justice to working women. The low wages paid for female labour, which are a disgrace to our civilisation, continually tend to keep down the rate of pay for all classes of workers.[26]

Louisa Lawson ran her paper solely with female labour but she was not 'a narrow minded suffragette' and denied that the woman who wanted economic and political equality with men was necessarily one who hung 'halfway over the bar which separates the sexes, shaking her skinny fist at men and all their works'.[27] She saw suffrage as part of a general claim for equality for women.

William Lane and Louisa Lawson did much to convince the labour movement that the position of women was a matter of concern to the working class. At the Intercolonial Trade Union Congress in 1891 a motion to adopt womanhood suffrage as a part of the programme was narrowly defeated on the grounds that it would prejudice the claim for 'one man one vote'. In New South Wales for the next three years this remained as the reason the Labour Party gave for not adopting it.[28] It is apparent, however, that some unionists were opposed to it for more than tactical reasons. Arthur Rae, a radical member of the party, explained the reluctance of some trade unionists to adopt it as due to 'that narrow conservative trades unionism which seeks only to establish a more or less close monopoly or trade guild'. He considered that 'most of the city unionists seem as narrow as the streets of the city and uncharitable as it is to say so, some of them are as crooked and as dirty'.[29] Craft prejudices, which had induced the typographical union to boycott and persecute the women typesetters employed on Louisa Lawson's journal, existed in many of the older unions and prevented them

---

[26] Ibid., 5 September 1890. [27] Ibid., 1 July 1889.
[28] *Parl. Deb.* (N.S.W.), 1891, lii. 579 ff; Rose Scott Papers: John Riddle to Rose Scott, 28 February 1892. [29] Ibid.: A. Rae to Rose Scott, 11 March 1894.

giving full support to the women's case. Nevertheless the secretary of the Labour Party wrote in 1895 that the majority of the members were in favour of giving the vote to women,[30] and in the following year the conference agreed to include the principle in their programme. Thus by 1896 womanhood suffrage had become an integral part of labour policy in New South Wales and Queensland, but it was not adopted in Victoria until somewhat later. Acts granting the franchise to women were passed by the Commonwealth in 1902, New South Wales in 1903, Queensland in 1905, and Victoria in 1909.

The abolition of the Legislative Council was included in the first political programme of the Australian Labour Federation but did not appear in the New South Wales platform until 1894. In Victoria it appeared somewhat later. It was not pressed in New South Wales, but after 1905 it became the matter uppermost in the mind of the Queensland party, and the campaign was largely responsible for the passage of the Parliamentary Bill Referendum Act. Under this Act a Bill that had been passed by the Legislative Assembly in two successive sessions and rejected by the Legislative Council in the same sessions could be submitted to a referendum, and if it received a majority of affirmative votes could be presented for the Royal Assent. By 1909, abolition of the Council was the first point in the constitutional programme of the Labour Party in New South Wales and Queensland and was included in the programme of the Victorian party. That the policy has not yet, except in Queensland, resulted in the abolition of the Council is a matter of more recent history than is covered by this work.

After 1895, the constitutional issue that overshadowed all others in importance was the drafting of the federal constitution. The Labour Party did not play an important part in drafting the constitution, but as H. V. Evatt has shown,[31] it exerted some influence in making the constitution more democratic than it might otherwise have been. If the evolution of labour policy is followed from 1891, it becomes clear that the consistent factor in it was the attempt to make the federal legislative and executive government as representative as possible. Though that policy often ignored the essential nature of a federal state and was often contradictory, yet there was in it a consistency that arose from the basic proposition that the new government must be representative.

Since the issue of federation was decided in New South Wales, greater attention will be paid to the development of labour policy

---

[30] Ibid., letter to Rose Scott, 17 July 1895.
[31] Evatt, *Australian Labour Leader*, pp. 96 ff.

there than in Victoria and Queensland. To the parliamentary party in 1891 federation was a subsidiary issue. Although the platform included support for national as opposed to imperial federation, the party cannot be said to have had any real policy until 1896. By and large, the attitude of the party could be summed up as opposed to federation, at least until a substantial part of their social programme had been won in New South Wales. By 1896, however, the movement towards federation had gone so far that it was impossible for the Labour Party to refrain any longer from taking up a position, so they issued a manifesto.[32]

The manifesto centred on criticism of the proposed senate. Under the constitution framed in 1891 the senate was to be a 'States House' with equal representation by the states forming the union. Opposing this, the Labour Party proposed a senate elected by the states voting as a single constituency but with representation according to population. This continued to be the central point in the Labour programme. Labour was afraid that a senate composed of equal numbers from states of greatly differing populations would be unrepresentative and would be a stronghold of anti-labour interests.

By January 1897 the attitude had become even firmer. In the manifesto drawn up then a unicameral parliament became the second point of the federation platform. The adoption of this position was certainly not due to ignorance of the structure of contemporary federations but was a demand arising from the current attitude of opposition to all second chambers as seats of privilege and conservatism—'a safe resting place to give the gentlemen who want to dull their ears to the turbulent cries of the people'.[33] The Labour Party made it quite clear that they were primarily concerned with the probable effects of federation on the principles of democratic representation to which they adhered and upon which they considered the future of the Labour Party depended. They were quite sincere when they said, 'we are prepared to clothe the federal legislature with these colossal powers only on the condition of its constitution being such as will ensure its being a true reflex of the will of the Australian people. Under any other conditions we are opposed to federation'.[34]

The Labour Party also pressed for the maximum appeal to the people before any decisive steps were taken. They supported a referendum to decide for or against federation, and demanded the inclusion of the principle of the initiative and referendum in the

[32] *Worker*, Sydney, 1 February 1896.   [33] *Parl. Deb.* (N.S.W.), lxxxviii. 646.
[34] Manifesto of the Political Labour League 1897.

constitution. Universal adult franchise and no plural voting were further elements in the programme. One apparently contradictory aspect of the programme was the position taken on the separation of powers. The argument in opposition to the senate was based on the assumption that the senate would, as in the United States, become the 'strong house'. It is also true that the strength of the American senate is in no small measure due to the separation of powers. However, the Labour Party supported such a separation in opposition to the draft constitution provision for responsible government. Ministers, according to the 1897 manifesto, should be directly elected, thus, although not paralleling the United States system, effecting a similar division of powers. The reason for this stand was simply that they wanted both legislature and executive to be as representative as possible.

Although the Labour Party in New South Wales did not realize the full implications of their attitude, in fact it implied a demand for a more unitary constitution than the 1891 draft proposed or the constitution actually adopted. Secondly, under the conditions in which the question was decided—that is that the most ardent supporters of union were also extremely jealous of states' rights—the Labour Party attitude amounted to opposition to federation. In Victoria these implications were brought out sharply by the criticism of the constitution by H. B. Higgins, who later, as president of the Commonwealth Arbitration Court, became the executor of Commonwealth industrial policy. He attacked the proposed constitution on the grounds of its rigidity. 'The machinery of government', he said, 'should be mobile, and free from complications and embarrassing restrictions.'[35] The proposed constitution, he said, did not meet this requirement, as it would be practically impossible to amend it. He pointed to the fact that there had been only one major change in the American constitution in ninety-four years, and this had been made possible only by war. He leaned towards a unitary system, and regarded the proposed senate not only as an organ of minority rule but also as a means of perpetuating the provincialism which it was an express purpose of a national government to eradicate. He was quite aware that the adoption of a unitary state was impossible in the existing conditions. In the circumstances, therefore, his criticisms amounted to complete opposition to union. This appeared to him a necessary sacrifice if the more important principles were to be upheld. In Queensland the Labour Party showed little interest

---

[35] *The Manifesto of the Victorian Anti-Bill League*, 28 May 1898.

THE LABOUR PARTY FINDS A PROGRAMME 183

in federation but, in general, it supported a position similar to that of the party in New South Wales.

The criticism by the Labour Party in New South Wales and by H. B. Higgins, leading the opposition in Victoria, was an important factor in having the federation proposals submitted to a national referendum. It also contributed to amendments in the proposed constitution in the direction of making it more amenable to future amendment. Labour's positive achievement was, as H. V. Evatt has shown, in liberalizing and democratizing the constitution.[36] Thus on this, as on other constitutional issues, the Labour Party adopted an advanced liberal position and advocated policies that were not simply in the interests of the working class but that ultimately proved acceptable to sections of all classes in Australia.

The second distinctive category of labour political thought is the conception of the state as an instrument for the legislative and judicial control of economic relationships. In this the place of conciliation and arbitration is the most important, not only in the results it has produced in social conditions but also in the total attitude of the labour movement to which it has contributed. Before 1890 trade unionists generally accepted the view that some specific kinds of industrial legislation were in their interests, but they did not favour the judicial settlement of industrial disputes. Defeat in the strikes of 1890-1 brought about a sharp change in their attitude. By 1895 it had become an article of faith of the political labour parties and acceptable to the majority of trade-union leaders that the state should act as arbitrator between employers and employees. The labour parties have retained this attitude unchanged, but after 1905, in a new phase of prosperity, the faith of some trade unionists in arbitration procedures began to weaken.

Before 1890, conciliation and arbitration by agreement had settled a number of industrial disputes. In 1884 the Victorian bootmakers' strike had been settled by arbitration, and in 1886 the Melbourne wharf labourers and employers had submitted their dispute to Professor Kernot of Melbourne University for arbitration. There were also a number of agreements between unions and employers of the type that had become quite common in Britain. In 1884 the Steamship Owners' Association entered into an agreement with the Seamen's Union which provided that disputes should be referred to a board of conciliation consisting of four representatives of the union and four representatives of the employers.[37] In the case of failure to

[36] *Australian Labour Leader*, pp. 96-100.
[37] *Report of Royal Commission on Strikes*, Literary Appendix.

agree, an arbitration tribunal was to be set up consisting of a nominee of the employers and of the workers. In the event of their disagreement an umpire would be selected by the two arbitrators. Essentially this was an arrangement for collective bargaining, the arbitration step being so remote from the ordinary procedure that in practice it proved quite useless. The employers in due course realized that they had merely opened a channel for ready access to themselves by the union and terminated the agreement, having given the three months' notice required in the instrument. Another type of agreement was that which provided for the variation of wages according to the selling price of the product. There were numerous examples of this in Britain, where it was applied in the iron trade in the north after 1869 and in the mining industry in south Wales, Northumberland, and Durham. In New South Wales the Hunter River Miners' Mutual Protective Association entered a similar agreement with the associated owners in 1874, and renewed it in 1888. Under these agreements it was provided that disputes should be referred to a board of arbitration with an independent chairman.

In all these cases arbitration was provided for by agreement between the parties concerned, without the intervention of the state, and in general trade unionists were opposed to the idea of state intervention. In 1882 G. R. Dibbs put a comprehensive scheme, based on his understanding of the French *conseils de prud'hommes,* before the Sydney Trades and Labour Council. The reaction of the Council to his proposals is most interesting. Some speakers supported the principle of conciliation but were opposed to the details of Dibbs's proposals, and others opposed the whole conception. One speaker noted with approval that successful conciliation had made strikes obsolete at Nottingham. Another was of the opinion that all strikes were ultimately settled by some form of conciliation. In opposition to the whole proposition were those who believed that while strikes were evil they were the only method by which workers could make any gains. Dibbs's proposals were rejected, the Trades and Labour Council thus officially adopting a policy opposed to quasi-governmental boards of conciliation.

A profound suspicion of government participation in conciliation continued to characterize trade unionists' attitudes. They were apprehensive that state intervention would weight the procedure against the workers.[38] This was revealed very clearly in the evidence of the trade-union witnesses who appeared before the select com-

[38] Cf. S. and B. Webb, *Industrial Democracy*, pp. 224 ff.

mittee on Joseph Carruthers' Trade Union Conciliation Bill in 1887. James Curley, secretary of the Newcastle miners, explained his opposition to a tribunal with a government appointed chairman as follows—'we, the miners, assume, correctly or not, that the Executive, more or less no matter what government is in existence, is to a great extent composed of coal owners and you put them in the happy position of appointing their own chairman'.[39] Another witness, while not insisting that the government was composed of coal owners, believed, 'that these gentlemen composing the Executive Council are as a rule interested in all kinds of industries'. The president of the Sydney Trades and Labour Council agreed with the witnesses cited and went on to say that above all he was opposed to any move which would make arbitration compulsory.

However, this opposition in New South Wales should be weighed against the fact that there appears to have been a greater support for both conciliation and arbitration in Victoria. In 1886 William Trenwith, who later became the leader of the Victorian Labour Party, moved a resolution at the Intercolonial Trade Union Congress in support of the establishment of boards of conciliation and arbitration. The motion was adopted by thirty-seven votes to twenty-one, the support coming mainly from Victorian and South Australian unionists, who were in a majority at the conference.

The influence of the unions of the unskilled and semi-skilled workers after 1886 was away from the position adopted at the Adelaide conference, and contributed to the attitude which we have noted in New South Wales in 1888. The experience of the Amalgamated Shearers' Union and the Amalgamated Miners' Association inclined them to put their faith in collective bargaining backed by the strike. Their confidence that by meeting the employers around the conference table they could secure their ends was confirmed by experience. It was not until after the maritime strike that unionists generally were anxious to have the government compel the parties to a dispute to reach an agreement or subject themselves to arbitration.

Of the twenty-five trade unionists who gave evidence to the royal commission set up to report on the causes of the maritime strike, twenty were asked for an opinion on conciliation. They were unanimously in favour, and the majority were emphatically in favour. Of the trade-union witnesses questioned on arbitration to follow unsuccessful conciliation, nine were in favour and one against. On the other hand, of the employers questioned, four supported conciliation, three opposed it on any conditions, and seven gave it

[39] N.S.W. *V. & P. (L.A.)*, 1890, vol. viii.

qualified support which would be more correctly termed opposition. The qualifications they imposed were: if the unions would be reasonable; if it dealt only with details and not principles; so long as it did not proceed to arbitration in case of no agreement; if there were no 'labour agitators' included.

The attitude of the unionists is obviously an outcome of their analysis of the causes of their defeat. They had tried to obtain a conference with the employers but it had been refused. If the state enforced conciliation, then a refusal would be impossible. The acceptance of arbitration to follow unsuccessful conciliation was due to the same causes. On the other hand the employers who opposed conciliation did so from the conviction that any other course would be a concession to a defeated foe.

Although not included in the first platform of the New South Wales Labour Party, the Bill to provide for voluntary conciliation and arbitration introduced in 1892 by Barton received its whole-hearted support. The only criticisms made of the Bill by labour members were of the method of selecting the representatives of the labour movement and of certain other aspects of the proposed machinery. One member was doubtful whether a truly impartial person could be found to act as president, and was afraid that the proposed salary of £2,000 a year which it was intended both to procure the 'best' man and secure his independence would alienate 'his sympathy from the one class who will be the main factor in every dispute'. J. T. Houghton was, however, expressing the opinion of the Labour Party when he said, 'everyone is agreed about its main principles'.[40]

The failure of the Act of 1892, which had provided for voluntary conciliation and arbitration, encouraged the labour movement to take the further important step of throwing their weight behind the adoption of full-scale intervention in industrial disputes. At the conference of the Labour Party in 1895 compulsory conciliation and arbitration was written into the party platform and has remained as an article of faith ever since.

The decision was most important, because those who made it felt that they were making a decision to replace the strike as a working-class weapon, in favour of judicial settlement. Although experience has shown that compulsory arbitration has not had the effect of ending strikes, to the men who made the decision it appeared in that light. W. A. Holman, who was in no small measure responsible for the adoption of the policy of compulsory arbitration in 1895, summed

[40] *Parl. Deb.* (N.S.W), lvii. 6483.

up this viewpoint quite incisively in speaking of the Arbitration Bill of 1900 when he said, 'Today there is one way of settling that dispute; if the bill passes there will be another way of settling it. All that the passing of the bill will do is to substitute the method of reason, arbitration, common sense, and judgment for the methods of brute force.'[41] The Labour Party had departed fundamentally from the position of trade unionists that was characteristic in 1888. Then, trade unionists relied upon their own strength and were suspicious of the state. By 1900 the Labour Party had not only forgotten that suspicion but had elevated industrial peace into the position of the supreme social good. Both W. M. Hughes and W. G. Spence agreed that, in the conditions of the rising market that New South Wales was then experiencing, trade unions could obtain more for their members by direct action than by arbitration. But on behalf of the workers they pledged them to self-denial in the interests of peace. Hughes commended the unions for loyally abiding by previous arbitration decisions although, with one exception, the decisions had been against them. In emphasizing the point that industrial peace must be maintained at any cost, W. A. Holman said of the Bill of 1900 that 'it is very much more important that the decisions of a court should be believed to be just than that they should be just'.[42] In pursuing this idea he lamented the fact that in Australia there was no leisured class from whom an arbitrator, who would have the confidence of both workers and employers, could be drawn. The kind of person that Holman believed was necessary was 'a member of the aristocracy, a member of the diplomatic body, a member of the cultured and leisured middle class who happens to be in public life . . . and [who] has the absolute confidence of all sides in an industrial dispute'.[43]

In Victoria the Labour Party supported the Factories and Shops Bill of 1896. In the discussion of the Bill the labour leader, Trenwith, made a very important statement of principle. He stated that the motive actuating the government in bringing down the Bill was to help those least able to help themselves. But he insisted that working-men as a whole were unable to protect themselves except 'by combination and struggle', and although strikes were, in the absence of more scientific means of defending their interests, inevitable, they were prejudicial to the welfare of the people. Therefore, to him, and in this he was supported by the party, the wages board principle was not one to be confined to the 'sweated trades'— the trades employing the most oppressed, exploited, and un-

---

[41] Ibid., cv. 2227.   [42] Ibid., p. 2233.   [43] Ibid., p. 2232.

organized workers—but should be extended to all trades, irrespective of the degree of trade-union organization.[44] In New South Wales the Labour Party expected that arbitration would change the function of trade unions. In Victoria it advocated a policy that would make the trade unions unnecessary, for, as we have seen, the wages boards set up under the Factories and Shops Act did not allow direct appearance of the union.

In Queensland the Labour Party convention of 1898 included compulsory arbitration in its political platform. In June 1900 the *Worker* stated that 'all over New South Wales the demand of the labour bodies, political and industrial, is for a conciliation and arbitration Bill'. A month earlier it had published the full text of the New Zealand Act of 1894, and when B. R. Wise moved the second reading of his Bill in the New South Wales parliament, a special edition of the *Worker* contained the full text of the Bill and a verbatim report of the speeches. In June 1900 a representative meeting of Brisbane unionists passed a resolution 'that in the opinion of this meeting it is advisable in the interests of industrial peace that the government be approached with a view to having a measure of conciliation and arbitration similar to the New Zealand Act made law in Queensland'.[45] The deputation that was sent by the meeting to the Premier argued along lines similar to those being followed in New South Wales. The suffering imposed on the community by strikes was emphasized and the point made that direct action was, for unionists, a last resort. The minority report of the British Labour Commission was cited in support of the argument.

The influence of the support for compulsory arbitration as against wages boards in time affected Victoria. By 1902, although not discarding the wages board principle entirely, the Victorian Labour Party was favourably disposed to compulsory arbitration. A royal commission, appointed in 1900 partly as a result of labour influence, reported in favour of compulsory arbitration. In 1902 a deputation of trade unionists led by W. G. Spence interviewed the Victorian premier and put before him a request to set up an arbitration court to cover those industries not provided with wages boards.[46] The wages boards have, however, been retained in Victoria, the original Act being amended in 1902 by the addition of a Court of Industrial Appeals, and again amended in 1910.

For the labour movement as a whole the party policy on arbitration was of the utmost importance. It clearly indicated that the

---

[44] *Parl. Deb.* (Vic.), lxxviii. 3147. [45] *Worker*, Brisbane, 30 June 1900.
[46] *Age*, 28 June 1902.

Labour Party was moving away from the concept of industrial struggle as the means by which the working class could obtain economic advantages. In place of industrial struggle they had put the idea of economic justice to be obtained by judicial procedures. The state was to intervene to redress the balance in favour of the workers. Nevertheless it was to be found that in practice arbitration did not function as it was expected to do. The Labour Party was increasingly forced to elevate industrial peace into the position of the supreme good, with the result that deep fissures appeared within the labour movement. Many trade unionists returned to a belief in militant trade unionism—a belief that after 1905 was reinforced by the revolutionary doctrines of the Industrial Workers of the World, which reached the Australian labour movement through the minority organizations.

The Labour Party claimed as its own the mass of regulative legislation that was passed in all colonies between 1890 and 1900 and that has been outlined in the previous chapter.[47] Although the claim that the Labour Party was responsible for this legislation is an exaggeration, as evidenced by the fact that similar legislation was passed in colonies in which the Labour Party was a negligible factor, it is true that in New South Wales the Labour Party played an important part in its passage. What is of greater importance, however, is the fact that the Labour Party identified itself with legislation of this kind. The regulation of industry and the provision of social services became the characteristic labour tendency. Just as the Labour Party acquired a policy of democratic constitutional reforms and the intervention of the state in industrial relationships—policies that were quite acceptable to liberals in a period when the trade unions were demanding a greater share in government and a larger share in the product of their work—so the Labour Party also identified itself with social services and the regulation of industry—policies that were equally acceptable to many liberals. The only point of difference was that the Labour Party sought a wider application of regulation than the liberals were prepared to agree to. For example, to G. H. Reid, who introduced the New South Wales Factories and Shops Bill of 1896, it appeared as a measure to deal with the worst abuses. The Labour Party demanded the extension of its protective machinery to all workers. J. S. T. McGowen, leader of the party, put the matter squarely when he said, 'everything that can be said in favour of limiting the hours of labour of females, and of young men under 18 years of age, can be said with equal force

[47] See G. Black, *The Labor Party in New South Wales*, p. 17, n. 2.

with regard to male employees generally'.[48] Political labour desired a maximum of regulation; liberalism was prepared to protect only those least able to help themselves. It would be labouring the point to discuss the party attitude to all of the legislation of this kind—sufficient to say that labour policy was to extend the area of regulation and increase the number of people brought within the orbit of social services.

The basis of labour policy on the land had been laid before the formation of the party. The question that the Labour Party had to answer was the same as the one with which radicals had been faced since 1860. How was the land to be unlocked to the people? A collectivist answer was implied in the programmes of the Labour Party at its formation, and for the first few years it saw the means in state-assisted community settlements. As with all other aspects of policy, however, the tendency moved increasingly away from socialist solutions towards policies similar to those advocated by liberals before the Labour Party was formed. In fact, the Labour Party was instrumental in making effective policies of small-scale settlement which had been advocated from the fifties onward. Because of their greater unity, the labour parties were instrumental in achieving some success where liberals alone had failed. This success contributed to the development of the middle class of small-scale producers, the desire for whose political support had in turn important effects on Labour Party policy—effects that were not seen fully, however, until 1912.

In 1893 Acts to encourage co-operative settlement were passed in Queensland, New South Wales and Victoria. In all colonies the Labour Party received the measures enthusiastically. The Queensland Co-operative Land Settlement Act 1893 was greeted by a member of the party as 'a beautiful measure; one of the most liberal and progressive land measures the colonies have ever seen'.[49] The *Worker* acclaimed it as a necessary means of building a new Australia: 'The Government practically says to every kind of social reconstructionist, "Here is your chance, go out onto the land. Live your own life in your own way. Show the world, if you can, that you are right" '.[50] The New South Wales Labour Settlements Act 1893 was similarly received. George Black, on behalf of the Labour Party, regarded it as far in advance of anything that the Labour Party could have hoped for, and Arthur Rae saw in it the oppor-

---

[48] *Parl. Deb.* (N.S.W.), lxxxiii. 1590.
[49] *Parl. Deb.* (Q'ld), lxx. 400.
[50] *Worker*, Brisbane, 12 August 1893.

tunity of co-operative or socialist living.⁵¹ The co-operative settlements were not a success, but even before it was evident that they did not provide the solution, the Labour Party was giving its support to liberal measures whose aim was the same as that of earlier legislation but whose method was somewhat different.

In 1894 G. H. Reid's government introduced two Bills, the aims of which were to make land available for small-scale settlement and to ensure that settlement did actually take place. They were the Land and Income Assessment Bill and the Crown Lands Bill. In introducing the Crown Lands Bill, Joseph Carruthers made a significant analysis of the position of landholding in New South Wales. He insisted that previous legislation had failed and its failure was expressed by the fact that only nine per cent of government transactions in land were with occupiers—'this is the record, in so many words, of the achievement of our past legislation', he said, 'dummying has become a fine art in this colony; and even Ireland itself presents fewer derelict homesteads than New South Wales'.⁵² He proceeded to prove beyond question the truth of the assertion that previous legislation had failed.

The two measures passed with the warm support of the Labour Party proposed to overcome the weaknesses of their predecessors. The Land Tax Bill, reminiscent of Berry's 1877 measure, imposed a tax of 1d. in the £ on the unimproved capital value of all land, with an allowable deduction of £240. The labour attitude of support was most forcibly expressed by W. M. Hughes—'I am here tonight,' he said, 'advocating one particular form of land-value taxation, not because land-value taxation is direct taxation, but because what I am aiming at is the bursting up of large estates and monopoly in land'.⁵³ Strongly influenced by George's theory, the Labour Party was anxious to test his method. Land taxation was to force the squatters to relinquish land that was lying idle, and the Crown Lands Bill was to ensure that smaller settlers acquired the land that became available as a result of both the land tax and the powers taken by the government under the Bill itself. The Bill provided for the withdrawal of land from pastoral lease, but its more important provisions were for the establishment of homestead selections on Crown lands granted subject to a perpetual rent and a perpetual obligation to maintain a home upon the selection, which was secured against being taken in execution so long as the obligation of residence was performed.

These two Acts were certainly the most vigorous attempt that had

⁵¹ *Parl. Deb.* (N.S.W.), lxvi. 8019.   ⁵² Ibid., lxxii. 546.   ⁵³ Ibid., lxxiv. 2846.

yet been made to provide a solution to the problem that all except the squatters admitted to exist. In supporting it, the Labour Party crystallized the land programme that was to be in the forefront of their policy for many years—they sought to attack the land monopolists in the interests of the small settler by fiscal means, and to provide a leasehold tenure for small producers. Their fundamental reason for supporting such a policy was perhaps expressed by W. M. Hughes, who frequently saw more clearly than his fellow members the implications of his party's policy. He said of the land tax,

> I believe that the imposition of this tax will result in the growth of a class of yeomanry—the most desirable class of men in any country. The yeomanry have been the backbone of England. It is only now that they are being threatened with being driven off the soil of England that the country bids fair to become a second class power.[54]

The Acts did in fact have a result of the kind indicated by W. M. Hughes—they did assist in the development of a class of independent farmers which on the one hand resulted in the great increase in agricultural production in New South Wales and on the other provided a class of people whose vote the Labour Party was always anxious to retain.

By the end of the century, then, when the formation of the Commonwealth brought new issues to the forefront of politics, the lines of policy which the Labour Party would continue to follow had already been drawn. Its form of organization had been firmly established, but its policy owed more to liberal thought than to the socialist ideas and militant trade unionism that had been responsible for its formation.

---

[54] Ibid., p. 2853.

II

A National Party and a National Policy

After the establishment of the Commonwealth on the first day of the new century it would be necessary, if one were to obtain the whole picture of the developing labour programme, to follow the activities of the party in both the federal and state spheres. Here, however, the greatest emphasis will be laid on labour policy as expressed in the platform and performance of the party in the Commonwealth parliament, where the issues being decided were of the greatest moment.

The Labour Party entered Commonwealth politics with a programme that had been decided upon at an interstate conference of four state parties early in 1900. The platform adopted was confined to four planks which were acceptable to the representatives of all states.[1] As in the states, federal labour policy was to be accumulated with political experience. It was to be an empirical policy, a policy of practical politics worked out in collaboration with liberals, in particular with Alfred Deakin. The Federal Labour Party was not a socialist party, although socialist ideas, and socialist pressures within the labour movement, played some part in deciding the direction in which its policy would evolve. In 1905 the interstate conference, on the motion of the New South Wales delegates, adopted as its objectives:

(a) The cultivation of an Australian sentiment based on the maintenance of racial purity and the development in Australia of an enlightened and self-reliant community;
(b) The securing of the full results of their industry to all producers by the collective ownership of monopolies and the extension of the industrial and economic functions of the State and the Municipality.[2]

Socialism was to find no place in the programme until sixteen years later, when developments in the labour movement and the political party tipped the balance in favour of its adoption as the party

[1] See L. F. Crisp, *The Australian Federal Labour Party, 1901-1951*, p. 25.
[2] Ibid., p. 271.

193

objective. In the meantime, for the leaders of the party and for the majority of the rank and file, socialism was simply a remote but possible future social order that would result from a process of slow but inevitable growth in which the extension of the industrial and economic functions of the state would be the mechanism of change. Andrew Fisher, second leader of the Federal Party, said, 'No party worthy of the name can deny that its objective is socialism, but no socialist with any parliamentary experience can hope to get anything for many years to come other than practical legislation of a socialist character'.[3] W. M. Hughes was expressing the same idea when he wrote in 1908, 'there is no such thing as voting for socialism. Socialism wants no voting for; it only wants room to grow and move'.[4] As far as possible the Labour Party remained silent on socialism but, when forced to comment, referred to it as being beyond the scope of practical politics.

With the establishment of the Commonwealth the Labour Party emerged as the party of intransigent Australian nationalism. As against other parties, Labour asserted the primacy of Australian interests, but never to the point where the elastic bonds of empire would break. On occasions Labour members were accused by their opponents of disloyalty to the empire, but in reality their policy was such that, on the one hand, it satisfied an electorate that was prepared to be disloyal if disloyalty meant putting Australian interests first and, on the other, contributed to the creation of the Commonwealth of Nations.

The Labour Party had an opportunity to express this intransigence in connection with the White Australia policy, the first important matter to be dealt with by the new parliament. As we have seen, the issue of White Australia had been resolved in practice before 1890 except in Queensland, where the importation of Pacific islanders continued during the nineties. This had been vigorously opposed by the labour movement and frowned on by the governments in all the other colonies but had been continued by the Queensland government, which was responsive to the demands of the sugar planters.

Thus, except for opposition in Queensland and a scattered opposition in the other states from employers' organizations,[5] there was general agreement on the need to prohibit the entry of Asians

[3] Cited L. Ross, 'From Lane to Lang'. *Australian Quarterly,* December 1934.
[4] W. M. Hughes, *The Case for Labour,* p. 92.
[5] E.g. *Daily Telegraph,* 20 September 1901. Report of Conference of Sydney Chamber of Commerce.

into Australia. J. C. Watson, first leader of the Federal Labour Party, argued that the prohibition was sanctioned by the need for racial preservation. He brought the discussion to the lowest level of racial intolerance when he employed the formula that was already at that time discredited. 'The question is', he said, 'whether we would desire that our sisters or our brothers should be married into any of these races to which we object.'[6] He pointed to the economic aspect, which he said concerned not only the workers but also small shopkeepers, who would be subject to competition from the 'inferior' races. In the north of Queensland pearl fishing would be monopolized by Malays, Japanese, Javanese and Filipinos. Then again he hastened to emphasize that the economic issue was subsidiary, the racial being the larger and more important. If this were so, then it followed that exclusion should extend not only to the working-class Asians but should include all classes because 'with the Oriental, as a rule, the more he is educated the worse man he is likely to be from our point of view. The more educated, the more cunning he becomes'. The speech reveals a careful consideration of the electorate: it was wide enough to appeal to anyone who was afraid of competition from cheap labour, or who was racially prejudiced, or both. The only member on either side of the House who argued for the adoption of the measure on purely economic grounds was H. B. Higgins. He professed a profound admiration for the ancient civilization and culture of the Chinese; he regarded the racial argument as disingenuous; and he said, 'I am willing to assent to this legislation upon the sole ground—if that were the sole ground—the ground of preventing the lowering of the standard of life'.[7] But for the Labour Party the White Australia policy had become a racial policy as well.

The adoption of the mechanics of the Bill provided another opportunity for Labour Party intransigence. The method of excluding intending immigrants under the Bill was by dictation test as suggested by the imperial government. The Labour Party moved an amendment for the direct exclusion of any 'aboriginal native of Asia or Africa'. The amendment was moved, according to the party, because they refused to be hypocritical and insisted on making an express statement of what they were doing. But it would seem that the more important reason was that they were making a display of intransigence for the benefit of the electors, safe in the knowledge that the Bill would pass in spite of their amendment. J. C. Watson said bluntly, that if it were rejected by the colonial office, it would clarify the position. 'The sooner we understand what our powers are,

[6] C. of A. *Parl. Deb.*, iv. 4633 ff. [7] Ibid., p. 4656.

and how far this autonomous government with which we are supposed to have been endowed is a reality . . . the better it will be for all.'[8] It was not an issue that would divide the empire, nor in fact did the amendment have any chance of passing; the Labour Party could, therefore, be as belligerently nationalist as it chose, with no other effect than of convincing the electorate that the Labour Party was the party of Australian nationalism. It was an earnest of what the whole emphasis of labour policy in imperial relations would be. They would assert national interests at all points and satisfy the labour movement that Australian interests were being served, but where they were in conflict with recognized imperial interests they would never carry their assertion to the point of demanding what would ultimately be unacceptable to the British government. They strengthened the hand of Deakin and the other liberal-imperialists in their dealings with the British government, and they satisfied the labour movement that Australian interests were safe in their hands.

The defence policy of the Labour Party was closely related to its policy on White Australia; involved in it was the concept of the white, democratic, Australian nation. Notably absent from it was any idea of the internationalism of the working class. As the policy developed, the characteristic of the labour nationalism of 1890—the identity of class and national interests—was transformed to the view that national interests were not opposed, but were complementary, to imperial interests, a transition made the easier by Britain's gradual recognition that Australia could not be treated as a colony but must necessarily be regarded as an emerging nation. Furthermore, as the new relationship became acceptable to Britain, the gap between the imperial-minded Australian and the Australian nationalist narrowed. By 1910 the utterances of Labour leaders were almost indistinguishable from the opinions of those whom, twenty years before, the founders of the Labour Party had attacked. This aspect of changing labour policy is most noticeably present in connection with the creation of the Australian naval forces. The Labour Party came to agree that the most suitable naval force for Australia would be a national force integrated with the Royal Navy, a point of view that was acceptable to a majority of people in Australia and also to the British government. However, the changes in defence policy between 1900 and 1910 must be examined in more detail.

At the beginning of the century the labour movement was inclined to oppose anything that smacked of militarism. The Australian

[8] Ibid., p. 4636.

movement shared that attitude with labour movements in all countries. The tradition of Eureka was still a force, and the employment of troops against the striking shearers in Queensland was a recent memory. Gatling guns and artillery had been deployed against striking miners in New South Wales. Militarism was seen as opposed to the cause of labour. Dislike of militarism was fundamental in the working-class opposition to the Boer War. The utterances of labour leaders are filled with admiration for the farmer patriots of the Transvaal. Even W. A. Holman, of all the labour leaders the one who opposed participation in the Boer War more on the grounds of theory than of sentiment, frequently couched his arguments in terms of opposition to militarism. Nevertheless, within a very few years the labour movement, with the exception of the left wing, had been won for a policy of compulsory military service.

Defence policy was treated from the beginning as a non-party matter. In the first parliament, W. M. Hughes announced himself in support of the principle that the first duty of every man was to defend his country. In answer to those in the labour movement who were pointing to the Boers who, although untrained, were proving a match for the best British troops, he argued that the situation was different. All the Boers were bushmen who could ride and shoot, but only a minority of Australians could do either. He advocated compulsory military service as the most democratic method, since it involved an equal sacrifice by all. He pointed to the Swiss system of compulsory service, and since Swiss democratic practices had long been admired by the labour movement, it was a telling argument. Australia, he believed, must be prepared to defend herself against the teeming millions of Asia, temporarily held back by a restrictive wall but waiting for the moment to break down the barrier by military means.

The Labour Party as a whole was not prepared to accept Hughes's position in 1901. Senator Pearce referred to the Defence Bill of 1901, which incorporated the principle of compulsory service without making provision for compulsory training, as

> one of the greatest dangers that ever confronted the people of Australia . . . Born as we are in the atmosphere of liberty and free government, we will not become a part of a force which strikes deeply at the root of free government as this Bill does . . . The Bill had its origin in the mind of the military commandants, but the string they played upon to dupe a credulous public was our White Australia policy.[9]

[9] Cited L. C. Jauncey, *The Story of Conscription in Australia*, p. 12.

If the Labour Party and the labour movement as a whole were to be convinced of the correctness of Hughes's viewpoint, it was obvious in 1901 that a great deal of effort would be needed. By 1908 Hughes had won, and compulsory military service was written into the programme of the party.

The cause of the change is to be found partly in the skilful advocacy of compulsory training by W. M. Hughes and other leading members of the party, partly in international conditions. The defeat of Russia by Japan had been watched with keen interest by those only too anxious to point the moral of Australia's danger. It was followed by a spate of 'yellow peril' propaganda. The *Bulletin* raised the cry that Australia was in danger, and the *Lone Hand* specialized in detailing the 'Asiatic Menace'. Newspapers printed lengthy correspondence arguing that 'White Australia' was in danger from the 'Yellow North'.[10] Despite the fact that no Asian country had ever shown any inclination to move in Australia's direction, nor indeed had the peoples of any Asian country shown any very strong desire to emigrate there, the press was able to create an atmosphere of fear of the unknown dangers that lay beyond the northern horizon. The apprehension expressed in an article, 'White, Yellow and Brown', was widely felt: 'against the two white peoples with important establishments in the Pacific, the United States and Australia, are arrayed the millions of brown men, ambitious, arrogant and poor'.[11] To the special danger to Australia from the north was added the possibility of war in Europe. Germany was already being seen as a danger to Australia, and her position in the Pacific made it all the more immediate.

In September 1905 a meeting in Sydney founded the Australian National Defence League, of which one of the vice-presidents was J. C. Watson and one of the joint secretaries W. M. Hughes.[12] Its purpose was to secure 'universal compulsory training (military or naval) of the boyhood and manhood of Australia for purposes of national defence, the military training to be on the lines of the British Royal Naval Reserve, modified to suit local circumstances'. J. C. Watson saw as the danger to Australia the pressure of the population of the old world and the awakening of the East. In these circumstances, he argued, the only way to prevent war was to prepare for it. He answered the argument that imperial forces could be depended upon by appealing to nationalist sentiment. Dependence on Britain was out of harmony with the Australian spirit of self-

---

[10] E.g. *Daily Telegraph*, 31 August, 14 October 1904.
[11] *Lone Hand*, 1 July 1911. [12] *Call*, 8 August 1906.

reliance, but on the other hand the integrity of the empire could only be secured by each unit being prepared to defend itself. W. M. Hughes attacked the opponents of compulsion, arguing not only that it was democratic but that democracy could not survive without it. Compulsory training was essentially democratic, he argued, because it called on everyone for the same sacrifice. Apparently to him it differed from conscription in that it did not foster militarism. It was superior to a permanent army because a permanent soldiery was interested in fomenting war, a citizen soldiery in preventing it. Above all, he said, there could be no danger in compulsory service in a country where the people had complete control of the government.[13]

In 1907 Alfred Deakin decided in favour of compulsory military service. The following year the Federal Labour Party adopted in its programme, 'a citizen defence force with compulsory military training and an Australian owned navy'.

In moving its adoption J. C. Watson indicated that Deakin's scheme was largely due to W. M. Hughes. The whole matter of defence was urgent, he said, because Australia was in danger from the Japanese, a clever and warlike people. And for good measure, he saw in the Chinese, who were awakening from a long sleep, a further danger. Peace could only be preserved by preparation for war, the sole democratic preparation being the system of compulsory service. Any other kind of army would mean that arms and military knowledge would remain the possession of the master class.

Seven members in a conference of thirty-one opposed the motion, but the opposition was rather half-hearted. Frank Anstey was opposed to militarism and afraid that compulsory service might operate against the workers. Mrs Dwyer of New South Wales was also shocked and 'bitterly regretted that anything legalising murder should emanate from the Labour Party'. King O'Malley opposed it on the grounds that any army would come under the control of 'gilt spurred roosters' and arrogant officers. W. A. Holman supported the motion reluctantly and only because he was afraid that Japan could not be trusted, 'until they had definite proof of her respect for international obligations'.[14] Thus there remained within the Labour Party some opposition to a policy that brought down on the party the anathema of the left-wing of the movement. Nevertheless the adoption of the policy by the party was a logical outcome of the basic political propositions accepted by its members. The fear of militarism had been overcome by the conviction that an army

[13] Ibid., 8 August 1907. [14] *Worker*, Brisbane, 18 July 1908.

of civilians could not be used against the working-class movement. In the very act of advocacy, too, the attitude towards militarism itself had changed. In answering those who opposed compulsory training, the advocates themselves called up the same emotions to which militarism appeals. When the defence Bill of 1909 was introduced the Labour Party claimed responsibility for it,[15] and W. M. Hughes treated parliament to an emotional declamation of the oath of a Swiss soldier, in which he reached great heights of militaristic ardour.[16]

In the establishment of the Australian navy the Labour Party also took a leading part. At the Colonial Conference of 1902, at which Australia was represented by Sir Edmund Barton and Sir John Forrest, the naval agreement of 1887 was amended by increasing the size of the squadron, increasing the amount payable by Australia for its upkeep, and providing for a branch of the Royal Naval Reserve in Australia. This was quite unsatisfactory to the Labour Party, whose national feeling demanded the formation of an Australian navy. In the first months of the first parliament W. M. Hughes had demanded the withdrawal from the agreement of 1887 and the establishment of an Australian navy of which the people might be proud.[17] In 1904 the first Labour government put forward the proposal, which was received with much ribald criticism by the Opposition, that Australia should set about forming a mosquito fleet for the defence of the coast line. The opposition to it scornfully argued that an Australian fleet would be unable to reach the levels of efficiency of the Royal Navy and furthermore that Australia was defended by the Royal Navy itself. But for Hughes and the Labour Party the important thing was the formation of an Australian national navy.

By 1907 the Labour Party was amending its attitude. It had become less insistent on a completely separate navy and was prepared to accept an Australian force that was part of the imperial force. At the Imperial Conference in 1907 the naval agreement of 1902 was terminated and Alfred Deakin announced the government's intention of establishing an Australian squadron. It would be closely associated with the Royal Navy and its standards would be those of the Royal Navy. In war-time it would be undoubtedly put under the command of the Admiralty, but it would remain as an Australian naval force. It would be an Australian force but an imperial force too, for as Deakin put it, 'every development of the naval force in Australia is a development of the naval forces of the

[15] C. of A., *Parl. Deb.*, lii. 4454. [16] Ibid., p. 4474. [17] Ibid., iii. 3293.

Empire'.[18] In 1900 the Labour Party would have seen a contradiction between the interests of Australia and the empire, but in 1907 they were accepting the view that there was no conflict between Australia gaining the greatest degree of freedom and doing it as a member nation of the empire. The nature of the political relations within the empire were changing—were approximating more to the Commonwealth of equal nations—and at the same time the Labour Party's attitude to empire was undergoing a concurrent change. The Labour Party fully accepted the government's plans for the Australian fleet unit as they developed. Indeed they claimed the policy as their own. The only major difference that appeared between the Labour Party and the government was whether the fleet should be built in Britain or Australia. The Labour Party favoured Australia but were so concerned to get the work under way that they modified their attitude and agreed to only part of the work being done in Australia. The Labour Party had pressed for Australian interests to be served, but by 1910 they saw no conflict between Australia and Britain. As he welcomed the arrival of the first ships of the Australian navy at Fremantle, Senator Pearce, the man who had opposed compulsory military service in 1900, let fall words that any imperialist would not have wished to disown. He said, 'the party to which he belonged was trying to realise the high ideals of humanity. There was no surer guarantee for working out those ideals than the Union Jack, the symbol of the British Empire. They had to look further afield than the mere defence of Australia, and be prepared to defend that flag and all it represented'.[19] Thus by 1910 the Labour Party no longer saw any contradiction between their professed nationalism and their new imperialism.

It has been seen that the distinctive type of socio-economic legislation of the first ten years of the Commonwealth was what became known as the New Protection. The Labour Party played an important part in having this legislation adopted, but it was not until 1908 that New Protection was written into party policy. Since the first Federal Labour Party contained approximately equal numbers of free-traders and protectionists it was decided to retain the unity of the party by 'sinking the fiscal issue' and advocating a referendum to decide fiscal policy. Nevertheless, labour increasingly supported legislation of a protectionist character, and gave as its reasons other elements of its policy. The Sugar Bounty Act was supported because it was necessary if sugar were to be grown and the White Australia

[18] Jebb, *The Imperial Conference*, pp. 475-6.
[19] *Daily Telegraph*, 28 November 1910.

policy preserved. The principle of the Australian Industries Preservation Act was supported because the protection of the specified industries was accompanied by a guarantee that the benefits of protection would be shared by the workers through the intervention of the Arbitration Court. The same measure was a legislative attack on monopoly. Nevertheless, the party conference of 1905 rejected the motion that 'all candidates be pledged to the New Protection, securing protection to the manufacturers through the Customs House and for the workers through Industrial Arbitration Acts'. The motion was rejected because it was maintained that it would split the party. The conference preferred that the parliamentary party should follow a policy of protection without its being fully recognized as such. The evasion was very similar to that made by the craft unionists before 1890 when they supported the encouragement of native industries without admitting that their policy was protection. Without directly supporting the motion, J. C. Watson made it quite clear at the conference that he was in favour of the New Protection. He said that the whole history of the labour movement in Australia had not been based on the attitude of 'crying for the moon' but of accepting what was practical and immediate. He considered that the success of the Labour Party had been brought about, not by following out theoretic ideas, but because they recognized that this or that measure advocated by them was something immediately tangible. In effect Watson maintained that free trade has a comprehensive political theory just as socialism has a theory, but the Labour Party must not identify itself with any theory—rather it must support individual reforms because they would be of immediate benefit to the workers. He ignored the fact that the ability of the party to support one measure and oppose another depended upon the existence of some criteria of judgment—criteria that in effect constituted a theory in the sense in which he was using the term.

From an examination of the total body of labour policy it is quite clear that the central fact accepted by the Labour Party leaders was that they should increase the extent of state intervention in industry. They were if necessary quite prepared to call this socialism if it were insisted that Labour was a socialist party. In reply to a taunt that the Bill was socialistic, J. C. Watson, when speaking on the Australian Industries Preservation Bill, did not demur. 'I contend,' he said, 'that it is socialistic to employ the resources and machinery of Government to protect from the rapacity of a few individuals those who are unable to protect themselves'.[20] The new

[20] C. of A., *Parl. Deb.*, xxxi. 457.

protective legislation had this effect, he believed, therefore it was gradually adopted unashamedly by the parliamentary party. This consistent support for measures of an increasingly preferential character produced the wry comment by Joseph Cook, that, 'there is not much free trade about the Labour Party now'.[21]

The contradictory position of the Labour Party without a fiscal policy but at the same time strongly supporting the New Protection might have continued, but for the decision of the High Court on the validity of the Excise Tariff Act. Mr Justice Higgins had found that the wages paid by H. V. McKay were not 'fair and reasonable' and consequently he could not benefit under the terms of the Act. McKay refused to pay the excise duty, and in the ensuing action a majority of the High Court found that the Act was invalid.[22] This decision seemed to jeopardize the entire system of Commonwealth arbitration to which the Labour Party gave full support, and since it did that the whole question of arbitration and the new protection was thrown into the melting pot.

From the establishment of the Commonwealth it was the set purpose of the Labour Party to legislate for an arbitration court whose jurisdiction would be as wide as possible. This arose from Labour's general attitude towards the federal system and the inclination towards a unitary state, and it was strengthened by the fact that many of the unions were already federated or amalgamated national unions and were in favour of a court that could determine conditions for the whole country. Furthermore, an effective Commonwealth court would result in the extension of such federations and amalgamations. The fact that Queensland had no satisfactory arbitration machinery and Victoria had wages boards made the Commonwealth court the more important. Then after 1907 the presence of H. B. Higgins on the bench of the Commonwealth court inclined labour to the opinion that its case would be more favourably heard there.

It was the importance attached to the Commonwealth court by the Labour Party that alone distinguished their attitude from that of Alfred Deakin. Deakin was ever conscious of the need to preserve the spirit of federalism, but the Labour Party was primarily concerned with making the Commonwealth court as powerful as possible. The Arbitration and Conciliation Bill introduced by Deakin in 1903 was in general perfectly acceptable to the Labour Party. It was similar to the New South Wales Act, except that it provided

[21] Ibid., p. 1106.
[22] R. v. Barger; Commonwealth v. McKay (1908), 6 C.L.R. 41.

for conciliation to be followed by arbitration only where the conciliation was unsuccessful. In introducing the Bill, Deakin referred to it as marking 'the beginning of a new phase of civilisation. It begins the establishment of the People's Peace, under which the conduct of industrial affairs in the future may be guided.'[23] He regarded it as a logical continuation of the process by which society had accepted the King's Peace. Just as the anarchical power of the feudal nobles had been subjected to the control of the central state, so the power of the employers and trade unionists was to be brought under the law. Such an extension of state power, he believed, could not be gainsaid by either workers or employers. The Labour Party fully accepted the idea of 'the new province for law and order', and W. M. Hughes, on behalf of the unions, gratuitously surrendered the right to strike, 'to the average unionist so priceless a heritage that he can hardly realise that anything can sufficiently compensate him for his loss'. All was sweetness and light as Sir Malcolm McEacharn, an employer, supported the principle of the Bill in the belief that the 'stand and deliver' type of unionism to which he had been accustomed in 1890 had been replaced by an attitude that allowed 'the employers to meet their men with pleasure and discuss matters in a conciliatory spirit'. Arbitration, he believed, was responsible for this change in attitude, and the changed attitude would ensure that arbitration would work.

The Labour Party's point of departure was on the question of the court's jurisdiction. In accordance with section 51(xxxv) of the Constitution, section 4 of the Bill defined an industrial dispute as one that extended beyond the limits of any one state, but it specifically excluded state public servants. It was Labour's policy to include public servants of both state and commonwealth governments within its jurisdiction. The point was important, as large numbers of workers were employed by state governments—for example, the railway workers—and of course it was labour policy to extend the function of the government as an employer. Labour insistence that public servants should not be excluded from the jurisdiction of the court caused the postponement of the Bill and the eventual defeat of the first Deakin administration. When the Bill, after a rough passage, finally became law in 1904 it was in accord with the labour viewpoint.

Labour's confidence in the Commonwealth court appeared to be justified by the award, very favourable to the Australian Workers'

---

[23] C. of A., *Parl. Deb.*, xv. 2864.

Union, made in 1906.[24] In the same year, however, in the Railway Servants Case, the High Court held that the section of the Arbitration Act which had purported to bring government employees under the jurisdiction of the court was invalid.[25] This was the first of a series of decisions which confirmed the labour opinion of the need to extend the powers of the Commonwealth parliament. Nevertheless, in the following year the Harvester judgment temporarily restored the workers' confidence in the court. The *Australian Worker* referred to it as 'a triumph of equity and marked the inclusion of the last phase of human life left outside the scope of the law'. The Brisbane *Worker* referred to it as a 'notable judgment'. The *Worker's* satisfaction seemed to be justified by the gloomy forebodings of the *Sydney Morning Herald* editorial writer, whose opinions were taken to be those of the most conservative of the employers. Whilst agreeing that it was impossible to dispute the justice of the principle laid down by the court, the *Herald* was pained by the inference that McKay had employed 'sweated' labour. It foresaw the ruination of many small employers, the crippling of some industries, and the diversion of capital from Australia.[26]

However, from the labour point of view the Harvester judgment was the apex of the Commonwealth court's activity. In two important decisions the High Court set aside judgments of the Arbitration Court. In the Broken Hill Case,[27] and more importantly the Bootmakers' Case,[28] the High Court whittled down the supposed powers of the Commonwealth court. Section 38(b) of the Arbitration and Conciliation Act 1904, which purported to authorize the court to declare any condition of employment included in an award to be a common rule for the industry, was found to be beyond the powers of the Commonwealth parliament. This meant that the court could not function as a legislative organ for the whole of industry, but was restricted to acting as arbitrator in particular disputes. Increasingly, labour had come to view the court as a quasi-legislative organ and increasingly identified itself with the policy of establishing regula-

[24] Australian Workers' Union v. Pastoralists' Federal Council of Australia (1907), 1 C.A.R. 62.
[25] Federated Amalgamated Railway & Tramway Service Association v. New South Wales Railway Traffic Employés Association (1906), 4 C.L.R. 488.
[26] *S.M.H.*, 11 November 1907.
[27] R. v. Commonwealth Court of Conciliation and Arbitration; *Ex parte* Broken Hill Pty. Co. Ltd. (1909), 8 C.L.R. 419.
[28] Australian Boot Trade Employés Federation v. Whybrow & Co. (1910), 10 C.L.R. 266; R. v. Commonwealth Court of Conciliation and Arbitration and Boot Trade Employés Federation; *Ex parte* Whybrow (1910), 11 C.L.R. 1; Australian Boot Trade Employés Federation v. Whybrow (1910), 1 C.L.R. 311.

tions for industry by means of arbitration decisions. Thus the decisions of the High Court cut directly across the line of this developing policy. The further decision of the court on the Excise Tariff Act was linked, in the mind of Labour Party members, with the restrictions placed on the powers of the court in its purely arbitration capacity.

The series of decisions of the High Court had two important effects: it made the question of constitutional amendment to extend the powers of the Commonwealth parliament an immediate issue; and it provided the impetus that resulted in the Labour Party overcoming its contradictory position on the fiscal issue and fully accepting the policy of support for the New Protection. New Protection became the most important plank of the fighting platform, and the general platform called for an amendment to the Constitution to ensure effective legislation for the New Protection and arbitration. In effect, the limits imposed on the powers of the Commonwealth parliament by the High Court's interpretation of the Constitution hardened the labour support for all types of legislation that were placed in jeopardy by the court's decisions. In particular this meant the complex of socio-economic legislation.

Thus the Labour Party arrived at a national policy by devious means. Much of it was borrowed directly from Alfred Deakin, but on the other hand one of the factors in fashioning Deakin's policy was his knowledge of the attitude of the labour movement. Such a mutual dependence could not have been possible had the labour policy been peculiarly working class. It was possible only because the labour programme became increasingly acceptable to the middle class and, indeed, to sections of the employers.

The liberal cast of labour policy is sharply revealed in its attitude to the land. Labour did not produce an independent policy on the land, but merely adopted unequivocally policies that had long been supported by liberals and radicals. This is not to suggest that the question was treated lightly; in fact the reverse is true. In the several states, elections were fought between 1900 and 1910 on the land question; in 1909 the Labour Party's land-tax proposals were the issue on which the government was defeated; and land policy was a prime issue in the election of 1910. In 1910, the first Labour government with a clear majority was returned, pledged to carry through its land taxation proposals. What were these proposals?

In the Commonwealth sphere there was to be a progressive land-tax levied on the unimproved capital value which would bring in revenue and would also, it was hoped, assist in the breakup of the great estates. The Bill provided for a tax of 1-1/30,000d. on the first taxable £1 (the first £5,000 of land value was exempt), and thereafter the rate increased by 1/30,000d. for every additional £1 up to £75,000, at which point the tax on an additional £1 was 6d. On the excess of value over £75,000 a flat rate of 6d. in the £1 applied. In his speech on the Bill, Andrew Fisher made it quite clear that the aim was to break up the great estates. Just how this would be brought about had been explained by Mr Watt of Victoria in his speech introducing the Victorian Land Tax Bill of 1909—a speech of which Andrew Fisher approved and which expressed the labour point of view more clearly than did that of the labour leader. He said,

> this Bill seeks to impose a progressive tax upon unimproved land values, first of all with the object of promoting conditions favourable to more extensive agricultural settlement, and secondly, with the object of raising additional revenue . . . In seeking to place in this Bill . . . such conditions upon the owners of land as will induce them to put it to a higher productive use, or sell it to those who will use it to better advantage, the government are animated by the conviction that a man who holds land out of use, or in comparative idleness, while others are searching for acres to cultivate, is opposed to the progressive development of the state.[29]

The effect of the Commonwealth measure on the relatively small property owner was insignificant—£24 per annum on property worth £10,000. But for property valued at £80,000 it was above £1,000 a year.

In the states, meanwhile, governments had also been imposing land taxes and adopting measures to assist the small-scale settlers to take up farms. Without entering into the details of the means adopted to assist small-scale settlement, it can be said that they were along the same lines as had been worked out in the nineties. The only distinctive aspect of labour policy here was that the Labour Party favoured the permanent lease of Crown lands to settlers rather than the outright sale of the freehold. In New South Wales this resulted in a sharp difference between the Labour Party and Joseph Carruthers in 1904, but it did not prevent the party from reversing its position when in power in 1912. Then, even the distinctive element of refusing to sell Crown lands was dropped, and the labour policy was virtually the same as that of many liberals.

Thus, in relation to the land, the Labour Party took up the struggle for basically the same objectives as the earlier radicals. The methods of achieving the objective were somewhat different. The ideas of George influenced the policy of progressive taxation, and

[29] Cited, J. M. Garland, *Economic Aspects of Australian Land Taxation*, p. 30.

the idea of nationalization influenced the Labour Party in opposing the sale of Crown lands. But by 1912 the second of these had been jettisoned and the first was seen to be having only limited success.

The cause of the movement away from a distinctive labour position is quite clear. The party lacked any comprehensive guiding theory, and as it developed an existence increasingly independent of the unions from which it had sprung, its leaders adopted purely opportunist policies. They stated quite clearly that if they were to win a majority in parliament they required the electoral support of people other than trade-unionists, and it was these marginal votes that tended to decide the limits of labour policy. Thus the tendency was for labour policy to be no more and no less than a complex of radical-democratic and nationalist aims that were acceptable to the majority of the Australian people.

With the increasing moderation in labour policy, however, there appeared that conflict between sections of the trade-union movement and the Labour Party that has been characteristic of Australian politics ever since. The conflict resulted from the dissatisfaction of many unionists with policies that seemed to them not sufficiently in their interests, and the dissatisfaction was given some direction by the small left-wing socialist organizations whose influence increased as the Labour Party became decreasingly a specifically working-class party. Let us look briefly at the left-wing organizations and their influence on the trade unions.

As we have seen, small groups of socialists had existed in all the colonies from the middle of the eighties. They were the means by which contemporary socialist thought reached the Labour movement and before 1890 played some part in the establishment of the Labour Party. In New South Wales after the formation of the Labour Party the Australian Socialist League continued its existence as an affiliate of the new party. Its leaders saw the organization as a means of influencing the Labour Party towards socialism. By 1898, however, with three of its previous leaders, W. A. Holman, W. M. Hughes and G. S. Beeby in parliament, the Socialist League became alienated from the Labour Party, to whose policy it declared itself opposed. The Easter conference of the league in 1898 decided to stand candidates in the forthcoming elections. Although none actually stood, the league made it the occasion of announcing their complete break with the Labour Party. They declared that the Labour Party had ceased serving the special interests of the workers and had become the 'tail of Reid's free traders'.[30] They argued that

[30] *People and the Collectivist*, 30 July 1898.

'palliatives' were for true socialists but a stepping-stone to the reconstruction of the whole social fabric, and they considered that the Labour Party had lost this perspective. In 1901, the league sponsored six senate candidates who stood as the Socialist Labour Party in opposition to the Labour Party. In their manifestos and election propaganda the Socialist Labour Party adopted a doctrinaire socialist position.

They described the workers as wage slaves. Under capitalism, the government was necessarily an instrument of capitalist class rule. Only under a system of collective ownership of the land and the instruments of production could a government be really democratic. The people would be convinced of the necessity for a co-operative commonwealth by the 'industrial and political organisation of the workers—mental and manual; distribution of socialist literature and lectures on socialism and social and political and industrial questions'.[31] The aim of the propaganda would be to secure the election of socialists to the federal and state parliaments and municipal councils, to introduce socialism by parliamentary means. All immediate demands were dropped in the belief that the advocacy of 'palliatives' diverted the minds of the workers from the socialist objective. The purity of the party was to be secured by a pledge that members would not belong to or support any other political organization or party. The Labour Party was labelled the 'fakir' or 'bogus' Labour Party, and the Socialist Labour Party proclaimed itself the only true political instrument of the workers.

The Socialist Labour Party considered that it was a Marxist party. Its motto was 'workers of the world unite', and the lists of suggested reading for members included the *Communist Manifesto, Socialism Utopian and Scientific, The Origin of the Family* and Marx's *Capital*. The organization had an important effect in encouraging the study of Marxism in Australia; on the other hand, the pedantic theoretic nature of the organization militated against its winning any great following amongst the workers. It is probable that the 3,109 votes cast for one of its senate candidates in 1901 represented its influence amongst the people at that time,[32] and it is probable that it did not greatly increase.

In Victoria a somewhat different development took place. Up to 1903 socialist organization was not so highly developed as in Sydney. Various socialist and anarchist groups met in Melbourne, and some short-lived attempts were made to link them up with the Australian

[31] *Constitution of the Australian Socialist League*, 1901.
[32] *People*, 27 April 1901.

Socialist League. In 1892 H. H. Champion, who had been a leader of the British Social Democratic Federation, attempted to form such a federation in Australia. He appears to have had little success. There was, indeed, little continuity in the attempts to form left-wing organizations in Victoria until 1903, when the arrival of Tom Mann in Melbourne acted as a stimulus. He began a course of lectures on social problems, the lectures being organized by a Social Questions Committee that in 1905 became the Victorian Socialist Party. Largely owing to Mann's influence and a policy of co-operation with the Labour Party, it became the most important socialist group in Australia, having a membership in 1907 of nearly two thousand.[33]

In 1903 Tom Mann was an international socialist who placed great emphasis on the value of strong trade unions, which he regarded as the means of winning concessions for the workers and also as schools in the class struggle. He differed from the Australian Socialist League in his estimation of the Labour Party. He considered that the Labour Party, although not socialist, would go much further in the direction of socialism if it had the support of a socialist electorate.[34] Consequently he believed that the correct function of the socialist party should be to act as a means of propaganda to influence the Labour Party and the workers generally. That a majority of the Labour Party did not accept the idea of class warfare or the economic interpretation of history he regarded as inevitable and as constituting a challenge to the socialists to convince them of the correctness of international revolutionary socialism. He considered that the Labour Party was not a real socialist party only because its members had not been exposed to socialist theory; 'not to allow for and properly appreciate this fact,' he wrote, 'would mean that we should soon become doctrinaire, exclusive, pedantic, and narrow and therefore should soon become comparatively useless and perhaps even mischievous'.[35]

The first annual report of the Victorian Socialist Party outlined the theoretical position that had been propagated in numerous meetings. It posited that the evolutionary development of capitalism is towards collectivism or socialism, but the actual transformation of capitalist into socialist society would be such a fundamental change that it would constitute a revolution. The evolutionary development would be the result of the antagonism between the working and capitalist classes and would be resolved by the workers organizing

[33] *The International Socialist Review*, 13 April 1907.
[34] T. Mann, *The Labour Movement in Both Hemispheres*, p. 7.
[35] T. Mann, *Memoirs*, p. 202.

politically and industrially to capture political power and get rid of the class state. The report did not specify how political power would be won, but it is apparent that the Victorian socialists were thinking in terms of constitutional methods. The attitude of the Socialist Party towards the Labour Party meant that a number of Labour members were influenced by its views, and since it did not take up the same dogmatic position as the Socialist Labour Party in Sydney, it had more influence amongst the workers.

Nevertheless by 1907 the attitude of the leaders of the Victorian Socialist Party had changed. They were preparing to break completely with the Labour Party and to attempt to unite the left-wing forces. In that year a unity conference was called on the initiative of a socialist group in Broken Hill—a group that had been strongly influenced by the Victorian Socialist Party. The conference met in Melbourne with representatives of the Socialist Labour Party of Sydney, the International Socialist Club of Sydney, the Social Democratic Federation which had recently been revived in Sydney by H. H. Champion, the Broken Hill Socialist Propaganda Group, the Social Democratic Vanguard of Brisbane, the Social Democratic Association of Kalgoorlie, and the Victorian Socialist Party.[36] The conference decided to form a Socialist Federation of Australia of which the components were the groups represented at the conference. The Socialist Labour Party, whose motion that the other bodies should amalgamate with it was rejected, withdrew from the conference and became a bitter opponent of the federation. However, the opposition appears to have lain not in any basic political disagreement but in personal antagonisms and rivalries between the leaders of the two organizations. In 1910 the federation, without altering its loose federal structure, changed its name to the Australian Socialist Party.

The formation of the Socialist Federation was accompanied by an important change in policy. The close relationship that had existed between the Victorian Socialist Party and the Labour Party was terminated by the decision that no member of the new Socialist Federation would seek election as a member of the 'Australian Labour Party or any other non-socialist party'.[37] Tom Mann had given up hope of the Labour Party becoming a socialist party. In 1908 he insisted that the labour members 'behaved in no way superior to capitalist members', and that the Labour Party was no longer a workers' party but was the party of the middle class. It opposed monopolies, for example, to curry favour with the small

[36] *The Flame*, July 1907.   [37] Ibid.

business people and not to prosecute the Socialist policy of nationalization.[38] The new tendency in the Socialist Federation was to place all faith in industrial unionism, the federation adopting the 1905 preamble of the Industrial Workers of the World, whose doctrine was already being taught by I.W.W. clubs formed in Sydney, Melbourne and Adelaide.

Up to 1907 the socialists had placed their faith in political action, but now it appeared to them that their faith had been misplaced. The Labour Party had deserted the cause of the workers, and the socialist parties appeared to be having little influence on the votes or opinions of the workers. In reaction against politicalism of all kinds the socialists turned to the doctrine of industrial unionism. The I.W.W. preamble was a bold declaration of the class war. 'The working class and the employing class have nothing in common. There can be no peace as long as hunger and want are found among millions of working people, and the few who make up the employing class have all the good things of life.'[39] Although not repudiating political action so completely as did the Chicago preamble of 1908, the 1905 preamble declared in favour of industrial unionism as the method of uniting the workers for the class struggle. In advocating industrial unionism the preamble attacked craft unions as instruments of the capitalist class because they divided the workers and misled them into believing that employers and employees had some interests in common. In 1908 the second conference of the Socialist Federation revised the attitude of the previous year by indicating that in their view industrial unionism was a logical development from trade unionism, rather than its enemy.[40]

The theoretical position reached by the Socialist Federation, which had become the Australian Socialist Party, is revealed in a statement of principles made in 1910. The objective was the common ownership of the means of production, to be secured by propaganda and industrial unionism. 'Palliatives' were opposed because they obscured the workers' historical objectives of emancipation from wage slavery and because they proved to be of little immediate benefit to the workers anyway. Furthermore, any basic struggle would have the incidental effect of causing the capitalist class to grant concessions as sops to the workers. That would be incidental to the main struggle and consequent on it.

The outlook of the Australian Socialist Party was both a cause and

[38] Ibid., December 1907.
[39] As adopted by the Socialist Federation. *The Flame*, 8 August 1908.
[40] *The Flame*, 8 July 1908.

a result of new attitudes amongst many trade unionists who were rejecting the policy of 'leave it to the Labour Party'. In particular, many workers were becoming dissatisfied with arbitration. The left-wing socialists had opposed arbitration from the beginning. To them the submission of a trade-union case to a judge and two assessors representing capital and labour meant in fact a submission to two representatives of capitalist interests, one of whom was nominally a worker, but who, like the Labour Party, was labour only in name. They held that any breach in the right to strike was taking away the workers' most important weapon, therefore labour support for arbitration was an act of treachery.[41] Theirs was a small voice in 1900 but by 1908, in the light of arbitration's failure to work as had been expected, there were many more workers prepared to agree with the left-wing socialists. In February 1908 the Melbourne Trades Hall Council found it necessary to give a considered reply to the resolution, 'that in view of the fact that arbitration courts and wages boards have failed to give the protection to the workers that they so much desired, the Trades Hall Council be requested to consider the advisability of organising on the lines of the I.W.W.'.[42] In the same year a resolution was put to the Trades Union Congress by the Newcastle Labour Council urging the adoption of the I.W.W. constitution and preamble. The changing attitude is reflected in the incidence of strikes. Although there are no statistics for the years up to 1908, it is certain that there were few strikes in the first years after 1901. George Black maintains that there were only two strikes lasting more than three days between 1901 and 1904.[43] In 1908, however, there were 223 strikes; in 1909, 151; and in 1910, 126. These included the major strikes at Broken Hill and Newcastle.

Thus as the Labour Party's policy matured there was already developing a vocal and militant opposition within the labour movement. This opposition has remained, and tensions between the party and sections of the industrial movement, varying in intensity, continue to characterize Labour politics. In fact, Labour policy is the resultant of many forces. Of these the two most important are the realities of which politicians are conscious and those that unionists experience.

---

[41] *The People and the Collectivist*, 14 July 1900.
[42] *Australian Worker*, February 1908.
[43] 'Arbitration's Chequered Career', p. 2.

Bibliography

I BOOKS

Bailey, K. H., 'Self Government in Australia 1860-1900', *Cambridge History of the British Empire*, vol. vii.
Beer, M., *A History of British Socialism*. 2 vols. London, Allen & Unwin, 1948.
Bellamy, E., *Looking Backward*. London, Redman, 1948 (first published 1887).
Black, G., *A History of the N.S.W. Political Labor Party*. Sydney, Jones, n.d.
—— *The Labor Party in New South Wales: A history from its formation in 1891 until 1904*. Sydney, Worker Print, n.d.
—— *Why I am a Republican*. Sydney, 1891.
Bodelsen, C. A., *Studies in Mid-Victorian Imperialism*. Copenhagen, Gyldendalske Boghandel, 1924.
Bowering, J. (ed.), *The Works of Jeremy Bentham*. 11 vols. Edinburgh, Tait, 1843.
Brereton, J. Le Gay (ed.), *Henry Lawson by his Mates*. Sydney, Angus & Robertson, 1931.
Butlin, N. G., *Private Capital Formation in Australia, Estimates 1861-1900*. Canberra, Australian National University, 1955. Social Science Monograph no. 5.
Carboni, Raffaello, *The Eureka Stockade* . . . introd. by H. V. Evatt. Mosman [N.S.W.], Sunnybrook Press, 1942.
Churchill, W. L. D., *Lord Randolph Churchill*. 2 vols. London, Macmillan, 1906.
Clark, C. M. H. (ed.), *Select Documents in Australian History 1851-1900*. Sydney, Angus & Robertson, 1955.
Clark, V. S., *The Labour Movement in Australasia: A study in social-democracy*. New York, Holt, 1906.
Coghlan, T. A., *Labour and Industry in Australia*. 4 vols. London, O.U.P., 1918.
Crisp, L. F., *The Australian Federal Labour Party, 1901-1951*. London, Longmans, Green, 1955.
Currey, C. H., *The Irish at Eureka*. Sydney, Angus & Robertson, 1954.
Dewey, J., *The Living Thoughts of Thomas Jefferson: Presented by J. Dewey*. London, Cassell, 1941.
Dicey, A. V., *Lectures on the Relation Between Law and Public Opinion in England during the Nineteenth Century*. London, Macmillan, 1948.

Dilke, C., *Greater Britain*. 2 vols. London, Macmillan, 1868.
Engels, F., *Herr Eugen Duhring's Revolution in Science*. London, Martin Lawrence, n.d.
Evatt, H. V., *Australian Labor Leader*. Sydney, Angus & Robertson, 1940.
Fitzpatrick, B. C., *The British Empire in Australia: An economic history, 1834-1939*. Melbourne, M.U.P., 1941.
—— *A Short History of the Australian Labor Movement*. Melbourne, Rawson's, 1944.
Furphy, J., *Rigby's Romance*. Sydney, Angus & Robertson, 1946.
—— *Such is Life: Being certain extracts from the diary of Tom Collins*. Sydney, Angus & Robertson, 1948.
Garland, J. M., *Economic Aspects of Australian Land Taxation*. Melbourne, M.U.P., 1934.
Gilchrist, A. D. (ed.), *John Dunmore Lang: An assembling of contemporary documents*. 2 vols. Compiled by the editor, 1951.
Grahame, S., *Where Socialism Failed*. London, J. Murray, 1912.
Greenwood, G., *The Future of Australian Federalism*. Melbourne, M.U.P., 1946.
Hancock, W. K., *Australia*. London, Benn, 1930.
Historical Studies of Australia and New Zealand. Eureka Centenary Supplement. Melbourne, 1954.
Hobhouse, L. T., *Liberalism*. London, O.U.P., 1944.
Hovell, M., *The Chartist Movement*. Manchester, Manchester U.P., 1918.
Howell, G., *The Conflicts of Capital and Labour*. London, Macmillan, 1890.
Hughes, W. M., *The Case for Labour*. Sydney, Worker Trustees, 1910.
Jauncey, L. C., *The Story of Conscription in Australia*. London, Allen & Unwin, 1935.
Jebb, R., *The Imperial Conference*. London, Longmans, Green, 1911.
Jefferys, J. B. (ed.), *Labour's Formative Years 1849-1879*. London, Lawrence & Wishart, 1948.
Land and Labour in Victoria by an Old Colonist. Melbourne, Wilson, McKinnon & Fairfax, 1856.
Lane, E. H., *Dawn to Dusk*. Brisbane, Brooks, 1939.
Lane-Poole, S. (ed.), *Thirty Years of Colonial Government: A selection of despatches and letters of Sir George Bowen*. London, Longmans, Green, 1889.
Lang, J. D., *Freedom and Independence for the Golden Lands of Australia*. Sydney, Cunninghame, 1857.
—— *An Historical and Statistical Account of New South Wales*. London, Sampson Low, 1875.
La Nauze, J. A., *Political Economy in Australia: Historical studies*. Melbourne, M.U.P., 1948.

Mackay, G., *The History of Bendigo*. Bendigo, Mackay & Co., 1891.
McGregor, D. H., *Economic Thought and Policy*. London, O.U.P., 1949.
Mann, T., *The Labour Movement in Both Hemispheres*. Melbourne, Miller Printing Co., 1903.
—— *Memoirs*. London, Labour Publishing Co., 1923.
Martin, E. A., *The Life and Speeches of Daniel Henry Deniehy*. Melbourne, Robertson, 1884.
Merivale, H., *Lectures on Colonisation and Colonies*. London, O.U.P., 1928.
Morris, E. E., *A Memoir of George Higinbotham*. London, Macmillan, 1895.
Morris, M. (ed.), *From Cobbett to the Chartists*. London, Lawrence & Wishart, 1948.
Murdoch, W., *Alfred Deakin: A sketch*. London, Constable, 1923.
Namier, L., *Basic Factors in Nineteenth Century European History*. London, Athlone Press, 1953.
Nelson, W., *Foster Frazer's Fallacies and Other Australian Essays*. Sydney, Gordon & Gotch, 1910.
Norton, J. (ed.), *The History of Capital and Labour*. Sydney, Oceanic, 1888.
Parrington, V. L., *Main Currents in American Thought*. 3 vols. New York, Harcourt Brace, 1927.
Pratt, A., *David Syme: The father of protection in Australia*. London, Ward Lock, 1908.
Reeves, W. P., *State Experiments in Australia and New Zealand*. 2 vols. London, Grant Richards, 1902.
Roberts, S. H., *Contacts between the Orient and Australia*, in Ross, I. C. (ed.), *Australia and the Far East: Diplomatic and trade relations*. Sydney, Angus & Robertson, 1935.
—— *History of Australian Land Settlement 1788-1920*. Melbourne, Macmillan in association with M.U.P., 1924.
Roydhouse, T. R., and Taperell, H. J., *The Labour Party in N.S.W.* Sydney, Edwards Dunlop, 1892.
Rusden, G. W., *History of Australia*. 2 vols. London, Chapman and Hull, 1884.
Shann, E. O. G., *An Economic History of Australia*. Cambridge, C.U.P., 1948.
Shaw, G. B., *The Fabian Society: The early history*. Fabian Tract no. 41. London, 1892.
Spence, W. G., *Australia's Awakening*. Sydney, Worker Trustees, 1909.
—— *History of the A.W.U.* Sydney, Worker Print, 1911.
Sutcliffe, J. T., *A History of Trade Unionism in Australia*. Melbourne, Macmillan, 1921.
Taylor, W. F., *The Economic Novel in America*. University of North Carolina, 1942.

Trevelyan, G. M., *Life of John Bright*. London, Constable, 1913.
Turner, H. G., *A History of the Colony of Victoria*. London, Longmans, Green, 1904.
Wakefield, E. G., *A View of the Art of Colonisation*. Oxford, Clarendon Press, 1914.
Ward, J. M., *Earl Grey and the Australian Colonies 1846-1857*. Melbourne, M.U.P., 1958.
Ward, Russel, *The Australian Legend*. Melbourne, O.U.P., 1958.
Webb, S. & B., *Industrial Democracy*. Edinburgh, The authors, 1913.
Willard, M., *History of the White Australia Policy*. Melbourne, M.U.P., 1923.
Williams, R. G. S., *Australian White Slaves*. Sydney, Summons Bloxham, 1911.
Withers, W. B., *The History of Ballarat*. Ballarat, Niven, 1887.

II JOURNAL ARTICLES

Adams, F., 'The Labour Movements in Australia', *Fortnightly Review*, lvi, 1891.
Arndt, H. W., and Butlin, N. G., 'National Output, Income and Expenditure of New South Wales, 1891', *Economic Record*, xxiv, 1950.
Champion, H. H., 'The Crushing Defeat of Trade Unionism in Australia', *Nineteenth Century*, xxix, 1891.
Churchward, L. G., 'The American Influence on the Australian Labour Movement', *Hist. Studies*, v, 19.
Clark, D. P., 'The Colonial Office and the Constitutional Crisis in Victoria 1865-8', *Hist. Studies*, v, 18.
Currey, C. H., 'The Legislative Council of N.S.W.', *Royal Australian Historical Society Journal*, xxix.
Fry, E. C., 'Outwork in the Eighties', *University Studies in History and Economics*, ii.
Kent, B., 'Agitations on the Victorian Goldfields, 1851-4', *Hist. Studies*, vi, 23.
Mills, J. E., 'The Composition of the Victorian Parliament 1856-81', *Hist. Studies*, ii, 5.
Picard, F., 'Henry George and the Labour Split of 1891', *Hist. Studies*, vi, 21.
Ross, L., 'From Lane to Lang', *The Australian Quarterly*, December 1934.
Serle, G., 'The Victorian Legislative Council 1856-1950', *Hist. Studies*, vi, 22.

III NEWSPAPERS AND PERIODICALS

Age, Melbourne, 1860-90.
Argus, Melbourne, 1850-1910.
Australian Radical, Sydney, 1888-90.

Australian Star, Sydney, 1887-1910.
Australian Workman, Sydney, 1891-7.
Boomerang, Brisbane, 1887-92.
Boomerang, Melbourne, 1894.
Call, Sydney, 1906-9.
Commonweal, Melbourne, 1891-3.
Daily Telegraph, Sydney, 1883-1910.
Dawn, Sydney, 1888-1905.
Empire, Sydney, 1850-75.
Flame, Broken Hill, 1906-9.
Hummer, Wagga Wagga, 1892-3.
International Socialist Review for Australasia, 1907-10.
Lone Hand, Sydney, 1907-10.
New Australia, Sydney, 1892-4.
New Order, Sydney, 1894.
People, Sydney, 1900-10.
People's Advocate, Sydney, 1848-56.
People and the Collectivist, Newcastle, 1898-1900.
Radical, Sydney, 1887-8.
Republican, Sydney, 1887-8.
Ross's Monthly, Sydney, 1915-23.
Shearers' Record, Melbourne, 1888-91.
Shearers' and General Labourers' Record, Melbourne, 1891-3.
Sydney Morning Herald, 1850-1910.
Worker, Brisbane, 1890-1910.
Worker, Sydney, 1893-1910.

IV GOVERNMENT DOCUMENTS

Commonwealth Arbitration Reports, vols. i-viii.
Commonwealth Law Reports: Cases determined by the High Court of Australia, vols. i-ix.
Coghlan, T.A., *The Seven Colonies of Australasia*. Sydney, Government Printer, 1893.
—— *Wealth and Progress of N.S.W., 1886*. Sydney, Government Printer, 1887.
—— *Wealth and Progress of N.S.W., 1887-8*. Sydney, Government Printer, 1889.
—— *Wealth and Progress of N.S.W., 1892*. Sydney, Government Printer, 1893.
Commonwealth of Australia, *Parliamentary Debates*, vols. i-lx.
Great Britain, *Hansard*, 3rd series, vol. cx.
Hayter, H. H., *Victorian Year Book*. Melbourne, Government Printer, 1893.
New South Wales, *Votes and Proceedings of the Legislative Assembly*, 1857-1900.

New South Wales, *Votes and Proceedings of the Legislative Council,* 1850-6.
New South Wales, *Parliamentary Debates,* 1st series, vols. i-cviii; 2nd series, vols. i-xxxix.
Queensland, *Parliamentary Debates,* vols. xlv-cvii.
Queensland, *Votes and Proceedings of the Legislative Assembly,* 1878-1910.
Report of Royal Commission on Strikes. Sydney, Government Printer, 1891.
Victoria, *Parliamentary Debates,* vols. i-cxxvi.
—— *Votes and Proceedings of the Legislative Assembly,* 1856-1900.
—— *Votes and Proceedings of the Legislative Council,* 1851-6.
Victorian Hansard, vols. i-xi. Melbourne, Wilson and Wilkinson, 1856-65 (*see also* Victoria, *Parliamentary Debates*).

V OFFICIAL DOCUMENTS

Australian Socialist League. *Constitution,* Sydney, 1901.
Intercolonial Conferences:
  First Intercolonial Trades Union Congress, *Report of Proceedings.* Sydney, Samuel Edward Lees, 1879.
  Second Intercolonial Trades Union Congress, *Official Report.* Melbourne, Walker May, 1884.
  Third Intercolonial Trades Union Congress, *Official Report.* Sydney, Boston, 1885.
  Fourth Intercolonial Trades Union Congress, *Official Report.* Adelaide, Burden & Bonython, 1886.
  Fifth Intercolonial Trades Union Congress, *Official Report.* Brisbane, Warwick & Sapsford, 1888.
  Sixth Intercolonial Trades and Labour Union Congress, *Official Report.* Hobart, Tasmanian News, 1889.
  Seventh Intercolonial Trades and Labour Union Congress of Australasia, *Official Report.* Ballarat, Anderson, 1891.
N.S.W. Labour Defence Committee, *Report and Balance Sheet.* Sydney, Higgs & Townsend, 1890.
N.S.W. Land League, *Manifesto.* Sydney, 1858.
Pastoralists' Federal Council of Australia, *Official Statement of the Facts and History of the Shearing Difficulty in Australia: Compiled for presentation to the Royal Commission on Labour* (England). Sydney, The Council, 1891.
Political Labour League, *Manifesto.* Sydney, 1897.
Victorian Convention, *Resolutions, Proceedings and Documents.* Melbourne, Walsh, 1857.

VI MANUSCRIPTS

Baker, D. W. A., 'The Origins of the Robertson Land Acts.' M.A. thesis. Melbourne University Library.

BIBLIOGRAPHY

Black, G., 'Arbitration's Chequered Career.' Typescript. Mitchell Library, Sydney.
Crowley, F. K., 'Aspects of the Constitutional Conflict between the two Houses of the Victorian Legislature 1864-68.' M.A. thesis. Melbourne University Library.
Fry, E. C., 'The Condition of the Urban Wage Earning Class in Australia in the 1880's.' 2 vols. Ph.D. thesis. Australian National University Library.
Ingham, S. M., 'Some Aspects of Victorian Liberalism, 1880-1900.' M.A. thesis. Melbourne University Library.
Labour Council of N.S.W., Minutes.
    Executive Committee, January 1880-August 1890; January 1893-July 1894. General Meetings, May 1871-September 1876; March 1880-July 1894. Parliamentary Committee, 1884-94. Mitchell Library, Sydney.
Martin, A. W., 'Political Groupings in New South Wales, 1872-89.' Ph.D. thesis. Australian National University Library.
Melbourne Trades Hall Committee and Trades Hall Council, Minutes 1877-94. In possession of Trades Hall Council, Melbourne.
O'Connor, (Mrs), 'History of the Suffrage Movement.' Typescript. Mitchell Library.
Parnaby, J. E., 'The Economic and Political Development of Victoria 1877-81.' Ph.D. thesis. Melbourne University Library.
Philipp, J., 'Trade Union Organisation in N.S.W. and Victoria.' M.A. thesis. Melbourne University Library.
Scott, Rose, Papers. Mitchell Library, Sydney.
Sydney Lodge Operative Stonemasons Society, Minutes 1873-84. In possession of Operative Stonemasons Union, Trades Hall, Sydney.
Ward, R. B., 'The Ethos and Influence of the Australian Pastoral Worker.' Ph.D. thesis. Australian National University Library.

Index

Age, 60, 91, 92
Amalgamated Miners' Association, 78, 102-3
Amalgamated Shearers' Union, 102-4
Amalgamated Society of Engineers, 73, 74
Anderton, J. E., 125
Anstey, F., 199
Applegarth, R., 77
Arbitration, see Industrial arbitration
Aristocracy, creation of Australian, 6-7, 17-19, 33
Asian labour, 8
Asians, exclusion of, 116-17, 162-4, 194-6
Australian Industries Preservation Act, 1906 (Com.), 166
Australian Labour Federation, 104, 106-8, 124, 144-7
Australian Socialist League, 124-6, 208
Australian Socialist Party, 212

Ballarat, miners' agitation at, 26-30
Ballarat Reform League, 24, 27, 28-9
Barkly, H. (Sir), 66n.
Beeby, G. S., 208
Bellamy, E., 105-6, 121-3
Bendigo, miners' agitation at, 25
Bentham, J., 87
Bentley, J., 27
Berry, G. (Sir), 41, 63-6, 84
Black, G., 28, 29
Black, J., 42
Black, N., 64
Boer War, 197
Bounties Act, 1907 (Com.), 167
Bowen, G. (Sir), 63, 66
Boyd, B., 5
Broken Hill Socialist Propaganda Group, 211
Buckingham, Duke of, 57
Buller, C., 3
Burt, T., 79, 82
Bush workers, influence of, 7-8, 18, 99, 102, 112-14

Cameron, A., 81-3
Canterbury, Lord, 66n.
Capitalism, 34
Carboni, Raffaello, 22-3, 24, 26, 30
Cardwell, E., 56

Carruthers, J., 185, 191, 207
Chamber of Manufactures (Melbourne), 90, 92
Champion, H. H., 210
Chartism, 8, 9, 13-16, 24, 30, 71, 73
Chinese labour, 78, 158
Collins, Tom, see Furphy, J.
Colonial conferences, 117, 200
Compulsory military training, 197-9
Conspiracy and Protection of Property Act (G.B.), 79
Constitution Acts: (1842), 2, 4; (1850), 2; (Enabling Act) (1855), 3, 19-20
Constitutional Association, 8
Constitutional crisis in Victoria (1866-70), 53-61; (1877-81), 62-6, 84
Convict labour, 8
Cook, J. (Sir), 139, 203
Co-operative Communities Land Settlement Bill (Qld), 149
Co-operative Land Settlement Act 1893 (Qld), 160, 190
Co-operatives, mining, 22
Cotton, F., 136
Cowper Ministry (N.S.W.), 42
Criminal Law Amendment Act (G.B.), 79
Crown Lands Alienation Act, 1861 (N.S.W.), 43
Crown Lands Bill, 1857 (Vic.), 38-41
Crown Lands Occupation Act, 1861 (N.S.W.), 43-4
Crown Lands, Royal Commission on, 36-7
Cummins, S., 24
Curley, J., 97, 185
Customs Tariff Acts, 1906 (Com.), 165-6

Darling, C. (Sir), 55-7, 59, 61, 63, 66n., 69
Darling, R. (Sir), 11
Davidson, M., 118
Deakin, A., 117, 165, 193, 199, 200, 203, 206
Defence, 164-5, 196-201
Democracy: agitation for, 20-32; and federation, 181-3; and private property, 6; and radicalism, 1, 6, 8-9, 12-13, 19; dangers of, 18-19, 60, 64, 66; political, 12, 50, 176-7; see also Franchise

223

224 INDEX

Deniehy, D., 17, 19
Dibbs, G. R. (Sir), 135, 137, 184
Dicey, A. V., 86-7
Don, C. J., 69, 75
Douglas, B., 69

Egalitarianism, 7, 33, 37, 42
Eight Hours Bills, 1869, 1871, 1873 (Vic.), 75
Eight-hour day, 71-6, 78
Eight Hours League, 71-2, 80
Employers' Liability Act (1897), 159
Eureka stockade, 21, 24, 26, 29-31
Excise Tariff Acts (Com.): (1902), 165, (1906), 165, 166, 167; High Court decision on, 203

Factories and Shops Act, 1896 (N.S.W.), 158-9
Factories and Shops Act, 1896 (Vic.), 158
Factories and Shops Act, 1896 (Qld.), 159
Factory Acts, 1873 (Vic.), 88-9; (1896), 156
Farrell, J., 121
Fawkner, J. P., 36, 38, 42
Federation of Commonwealth, 180-3
Fisher, A., 194, 207
Fitzroy, C. (Sir), 11
Forlonge, W., 35, 37
Franchise: female, 177-80; male, 15, (N.S.W.), 32, 42-3; (Vic.), 31-2, 33, 39, 40, 41, 52; miners', 20, 23-4, 28, 31; plural, 176; property, (N.S.W.), 2, 8-9, 19, (Vic.), 7, 20, 32, 64-6, universal, 12
Freedom of contract, 110, 130
Free selection, 39, 41-7, 59; see also Land legislation
Free Selectors' Association, 83
Free trade, 60, 95; see also Protection
Furphy, J., 113-4

George, H., 40, 105, 119-21
Gipps, G. (Sir), 5, 11
Glassey, T., 147, 149
Gold, effect on society, 67, 70
Goldfields, agitation on, 20-32, 68; see also Ballarat; Bendigo
Goldfields, Royal Commission on, 30
Gold-miners, 8-10, 15-18, 20, 22, 78; licence fees, 21, 24-6, 30-1
Grant, J. M., 59
Gray, W., 41, 69
Grey, G. (Sir), 176
Griffith, S. (Sir), 123, 162

Hall, G. J., 147
Hancock, W. K. (Sir), 114-15
Harpur, C., 17
Harvester judgment, 168, 205
Higgins, H. B., 168, 182-3, 195, 203
High Court of Australia, 167-8, 205, 206
Higinbotham, G., 52, 53, 58, 61-2, 69, 112, 117
Holman, W. A., 170-1, 186-7, 197, 208
Hoolan, J. P., 147-8
Hotham, C. (Sir), 27, 28-9, 31
Houghton, J. T., 138, 186
Hughes, W. M., 170-1, 187, 191, 192, 194, 197-9, 204, 208
Humffray, J. B., 28, 29, 30

Imperial Conference (1907), 200
Imperial federation, 117
Imperialism, 111-12, 115
Imperial navy scheme, 117-18
Independence: colonial, 10-11, 51, 57-9, 61; see also Republicanism; Self-government; economic, 15-16, 22-38
Industrial arbitration, 155-7, 167, 183-4, 186-9, 203-6
Industrial Workers of the World, 189, 212-13
Intercolonial Trade Union Congresses, 93-6, 98, 132-3
International Socialist Club, 211

Kennedy, T., 30

Labour Defence Committee, 132-4
Labour Electoral Leagues, 135-9 passim
Labour Settlements Act 1893 (N.S.W.), 190
Lalor, P., 28, 29, 32
Land alienation, 33-7, 44-5, 47-8
Land Convention (Vic.), 39-41, 42
Land Laws, Morris-Ranken committee of inquiry into, 44
Land League (N.S.W.), 42
Land legislation, 33-43, 60; N.S.W., (Robertson Land Act, 1861), 42, 46, 47, 67; Qld, 48-9; Vic., (Duffy Land Act, 1862), 47, 59, (Grant Land Act, 1865), 47, 59, (Grant Land Act, 1869), 48, (Labour Party policy), 190-2, (Nicholson Land Act, 1860), 41, 47, 59
Land nationalization leagues, 121
Land reform, 15-16, 22, 26, 32, 33-6, 46-7, 49, 57, 59, 61, 65, 67, 83
Labour Settlements Act, 1893 (N.S.W.), 160-1

INDEX 225

Land tax: Labour Party policy, 206-8; N.S.W., 191, 207; Vic., 64, 207
Lane, W., 105-6, 123-4, 126, 145-6, 160, 172-5, 178
Lang, J. D., 9-13, 42, 112
La Trobe, C., 27, 35
Lawson, H., 113, 118
Lawson, Louisa, 179
Liberalism, 3-4, 10, 143-4
Linacre, A., 72
London Trades Council, 73
Lowe, R., 8, 20, 42

McCulloch, J. (Sir), 53-5
McDermott, H., 8
Macdonald, A., 79, 82
McEacharn, M. (Sir), 204
McGowen, J. S. T., 97, 136-7, 189
McGregor, D. H., 87
McIlwraith, T. (Sir), 149
McKay, H. V., 168, 203
McNamara, W. H., 125
Mann, T., 210-11
Manufacturers Encouragement Act, 1908 (Com.), 167
Martin, J., 9
Masters and Servants Act (N.S.W.), 135
Melbourne Trades Hall, see Trades Hall, Melbourne
Middle class, political attitudes, 5, 8-9, 12-13, 16-17, 38, 51-2, 66-7, 84
Migration, 15, 40, 76-8, 83
Militarism: Labour attitude to, 196-201 *passim*
Mines Regulation Act, 1898 (Qld), 159
Molesworth, W. (Sir), 3
Morris-Ranken committee on Land Laws, 44
Mutual Protection Association, 8
Murphy, W. E., 84

Nationalization, 171-2
Nationalism, 7, 10, 18-19, 51, 60-1, 112-15, 194-6
National Reform and Protection League (Vic.), 84
National Union of Miners (G.B.), 79
Navy, 200-1
New Australia, 172-5
Newcastle, Duke of, 3, 36
New Guinea, 115
New Hebrides, 115
New Protection, 165-7, 201-2
Nicholson, W., 41
Nordau, M., 118
Norton, J., 98

O'Brien, B., 13
Occupations of the people, 100-1

O'Connor, F., 14
O'Malley, King, 199
Owen, R., 13, 14

Pakington, J. (Sir), 1, 3, 20
Parkes, H. (Sir), 8, 19, 67, 115, 135, 155, 177
Pastoralists' Federal Council, 131-2
Peace Preservation Bill (Qld), 149
Pearce, G. (Sir), 197, 201
Pensions, old age, 161-2
People's Parliamentary Associations, 145
Powers, C., 149
Progressive Political League (Vic.), 142-4
Protection: N.S.W., 78; Vic., 54-5, 57-61, 64, 77-8, 83-4; see also Free trade
Protection League (Vic.), 84
Property interests, defence of, 6-7, 41, 53-4, 62, 64-6

Queensland Labourers' Union, 103
Queensland Shearers' Union, 103-4

Radicalism, British, 13
Raffaello, Carboni, see Carboni
Reeves, W. P., 156
Reform League (Newcastle), 83
Regulation of Mines and Machinery Act, 1877 (Vic.), 78
Reid, G. H. (Sir), 137, 156, 177, 189, 191
Republicanism, 10, 22, 28; see also Independence, colonial
Republican League, 118-19
Republican Union, 118
Responsible government, agitation for, 2, 4-5, 16-18, 67-8; see also Self-government
Revolutionary spirit on goldfields, 28
Robertson, J. (Sir), 8, 42, 44
Rogers, F. (Sir), 53, 55, 62
Royal Commission on the Goldfields, 30-1
Royal Commission on Strikes, see Strikes
Royal Commission on the Tenure of the Wastelands of the Crown, 36-7
Russell, J. (Lord), 1
Ryan, T. J., 147

Scobie, J., 26-7
Scott, Rose, 177-8
Self-government, colonial, 1-4, 11; see also Independence, colonial
Service, J., 65
Sharp, W. A., 136, 138

226　INDEX

Shearers' Accommodation Act, 1901 (Qld), 159-60
Short Hours League, 75
Single Tax League, 136
Smith, T., 72
Social Democratic Association of Kalgoorlie, 211
Social Democratic Federation, 211
Social Democratic Federation (England), 124
Social Democratic Vanguard, 211
Socialism, 171-2, 202; *see also* Australian Socialist League; Australian Socialist Party; Bellamy, E.; Industrial Workers of the World; Lane, W., and New Australia; Socialist Labour Party
Socialist Federation of Australia, 211
Socialist Labour Party, 209
Spence, W. G., 96-7, 102-3, 124, 127, 132, 187-8
Squatters: political attitudes, 4, 6-7, 9, 13, 16, 22, 35, 49, 50-2, 67; tenure, 4-5, 16, 34-7, 39-42, 44-6, 48-9, 59; *see also* Land legislation
Steamship Owners' Association, 131
Stephens, J., 72
Stephens, J. R., 13
Strikes, 89, 90, 109, 129-35, 138, 145, 155
Suffrage, *see* Franchise
Sugar Bounty Act, 1903 (Com.), 166, 167
Sutton, H. M. (Sir), 57
Sweating, 91
Syme, D., 60

Tariff League (Vic.), 60
Taylor, A. G., 135
Trades and Labour Council: Queensland, 93, 124; Sydney, 81, 83, 92-3, 128-9, 135, 138
Trades Hall (Melbourne), 69, 72-3, 80-1, 84
Trades Hall Council, 89-90, 92, 129, 139-42

Trade Union Act, 1871 (G.B.), 79
Trade Union Act, 1881 (N.S.W.), 82
Trade Union Congress (G.B.), 73-4
Trade Union Funds Protection Bill, 1876 (N.S.W.), 82
Trade Unions: amalgamation of, 78; and chartism, 15; and political action, 69-70, 73-5, 79-80, 82-4; formation of, 8, 70, 89; legislation concerning, 79-80, 82-3; of skilled workers, 73-4, 78; relations with Labour Party, 142-8
Trenwith, W. A., 91, 185, 187

Unemployment, 76-8, 138-40
United Labour Party of Victoria, 144

Vern, F., 29
Victoria: constitutional crises (1866-70), 53-61; (1877-81), 62-6, 84; separation from N.S.W., 2
Victorian Socialist Party, 210-11

Wages Boards, 156-7
Wakefield, E. G., 3, 11, 33
Wallace, A. R., 120-1
Watson, J. C., 194-6, 198, 199, 202
Webb, S. and B., 93
Wentworth, W. C., 2, 5-6, 8-9, 17-20, 42
White Australia, *see* Asians, exclusion of
Women's Christian Temperance Movement, 177
Workers' Political Associations, 145
Workers' Political Organizations, 145
Working class: and chartism, 13; and land reform, 38, 42; and political action, 5, 16-17, 52, 66-7, 70, 74, 82-4; and protection, 77-8; and radicalism, 8-9, 13, 52; and 'self-improvement', 71, 73
Working Men's Defence Association, 83
Workrooms and Factories Law Amendment Bill, 1885 (Vic.), 92